MW01294566

Advance Praise

"*Absolute Pleasure* delivers exactly that! Knowing that so many fellow lonely young outsiders were guided to the light over at the Frankenstein place and found where they truly belonged reaffirms my lifelong passion and fandom for all things *Rocky Horror*. I smiled so much while reading this that my face began to ache."

—PEACHES CHRIST, filmmaker and cult leader

"*The Rocky Horror Picture Show* rocked my world as a teenager in the '70s, and the light it showed me over at the Frankenstein place was where I first learned I could remove the cause, and enjoy the symptom, of being trans. The essays in this expansive anthology are so many lighters, held aloft, that illuminate the enduring influence of this film."

—SUSAN STRYKER, author of *When Monsters Speak*

"As someone with a Tim Curry tattoo on my arm, *Absolute Pleasure* sent glorious shock waves of recognition through my body with each and every soul-baring essay. I felt validated, fascinated, and 'touch-a touch-a' touched by every joyous, bittersweet, libidinous, liberating, mascara-smeared confession from fellow Transylvanians."

—DARREN STEIN, director of *Jawbreaker*

"Virgins and veterans alike will find something to contemplate in this wide-ranging collection, which is not afraid to interrogate a beloved classic while also celebrating its profound impact on weirdos and misfits across generations. As one of those weirdos, I'm so glad it exists."

—JESS ZIMMERMAN, author of *Women and Other Monsters: Building a New Mythology*

"A collection as colorful, subversive, and comforting as the film it celebrates, *Absolute Pleasure* immortalizes in print *The Rocky Horror Picture Show*'s still-unrivaled capacity for building queer connection and community in ways both wistful and wicked."

—JOE VALLESE, editor of *It Came from the Closet: Queer Reflections on Horror*

ABSOLUTE PLEASURE

QUEER PERSPECTIVES ON ROCKY HORROR

EDITED BY MARGOT ATWELL
FOREWORD BY CARMEN MARIA MACHADO

THE FEMINIST PRESS
AT THE CITY UNIVERSITY OF NEW YORK
NEW YORK CITY

Published in 2025 by the Feminist Press
at the City University of New York
The Graduate Center
365 Fifth Avenue, Suite 6200
New York, NY 10016

feministpress.org

First Feminist Press edition 2025

 This book is made possible by the New York State Council on
the Arts with the support of the Office of the Governor and the
New York State Legislature.

First printing September 2025

Cover design by Ro Salarian
Text design by Drew Stevens

Library of Congress Cataloging-in-Publication Data
Names: Atwell, Margot editor | Machado, Carmen Maria writer of foreword
Title: Absolute pleasure : queer perspectives on Rocky Horror / edited by
   Margot Atwell ; foreword by Carmen Maria Machado.
Description: New York City : The Feminist Press at the City University of
   New York, 2025.
Identifiers: LCCN 2025018681 (print) | LCCN 2025018682 (ebook) | ISBN
   9781558613508 paperback | ISBN 9781558613515 ebook
Subjects: LCSH: Rocky Horror picture show (Motion picture) | Sexual
   minorities in motion pictures | Sexual minority culture | Cult
   films—Social aspects | LCGFT: Film criticism | Essays
Classification: LCC PN1997.R57547 A37 2025 (print) | LCC PN1997.R57547
   (ebook) | DDC 791.4/372—dc23/eng/20250506
LC record available at https://lccn.loc.gov/2025018681
LC ebook record available at https://lccn.loc.gov/2025018682

PRINTED IN THE UNITED STATES OF AMERICA

Contents

To you,
if you want to belong here.

Welcome home.

Content Note

The Rocky Horror Picture Show contains potentially objectionable content including violence, murder, incidents of rape or very unclear consent, racist and ableist tropes, cannibalism, and more. The essays in this book engage with those subjects and also include personal stories and cultural analysis on subjects including transphobia and homophobia, AIDS, dysphoria, mental health issues, grief, death, and loss. Several of the writers in this book have chosen to include specific content notes with their pieces.

Please take care of yourself, and know that the essays in this book might not be right for all readers at all times.

Foreword

Carmen Maria Machado

WHEN I WAS a kid, there was a theater near the Lehigh Valley Mall that had midnight showings of *The Rocky Horror Picture Show* every weekend. My mother spent years hustling me past its lurid poster. I loved the lips. I just didn't know what they meant.

Then, one Saturday night, we went to a late showing of a romantic comedy and came out just as the *Rocky Horror* audience was streaming in. As I watched the theatrical parade of freaks and weirdos that compelled me in ways I didn't understand, I asked my mother what was happening. Who were these people? She grabbed my hand and hauled me through the crowd and out into the parking lot. "It's not for children," she said. Her favorite refrain. The same reason I didn't know what a dress had to do with the president. Years later, when I went for the first time of many times to my university's annual performance of *Rocky Horror*, I told this story to the person who was lacing up my corset. The freaks and weirdos were here, and I loved us.

In 2003, it was announced that the theater—at that point home to one of the last and longest runs in the movie's history—was closing and scheduled to be demolished. The final showing was legendary. People arrived in a hearse and carried a casket inside. Hundreds filled the theater. After it was over, participants ripped seats out of the floor and shredded the screen. "What started as a night in which people talked of the sense of community they shared through a campy Halloween movie," a lightly scandalized local reporter wrote, "ended as a morning in which the police were called."

One of the more disconcerting moments of my professional life came during an event at the Brooklyn Museum in the fall of 2022, when I sat on a stage with writer and critic Sarah Fonseca fielding questions about our respective essays in *It Came from the Closet: Queer Reflections on Horror*, which had just been published. My essay on *Jennifer's Body* (2009) extensively discussed one of my least favorite types of criticism du jour: the thought-terminating accusation of "queerbaiting." The subject seemed to invigorate the audience; the Q&A covered little else. In the middle of it all, someone raised their hand and told me about a conversation they'd recently encountered which accused *Rocky Horror* of queerbaiting. What, they asked, did I think of that?

I sat there for what felt like a long time, trying to find an answer that felt suitably appropriate for a public forum. Everything that came into my brain felt uncharitable or full of despair. Is this where we have landed? Young people shoving the rich legacy of queer art out of the way in pursuit of some imaginary perfect text? I answered the question eventually, though I can hardly remember what I said. But here—on the first pages of a book that examines *Rocky Horror*'s legacy in all its queer, defiant, transgressive, flawed, chaotic glory—I know what it should have been: Imperfect texts are all we have, and they are not above criticism but they will always have something to teach us.

Plus: Costumes? Theatrics? Community? Camp? Halloween? The police get called? Y'all, that's the gayest fucking thing I've ever heard.

—Carmen Maria Machado
Iowa City, IA
April 22, 2025

Introduction

Margot Atwell

ROCKY HORROR BEGAN as a musical first staged in London in June 1973. It was originally planned to run for one month in the sixty-three-seat Royal Court Theatre Upstairs, a small space for experimental new work. The music, lyrics, and book were written by out-of-work actor Richard O'Brien, whom the film's fans will recognize as Riff Raff, and directed and produced by Jim Sharman. *The Rocky Horror Show*, as its first iteration was called, was surprisingly popular and received good reviews: "It achieves the rare feat of being witty and erotic at the same time."[1] Tim Curry, who originated the role of Dr. Frank-N-Furter, was described as giving "a garishly Bowiesque performance as the ambisextrous doctor."[2] Nobody, not even O'Brien, expected very much from the show; in 2013, he told *The Guardian,* "I didn't think it would be a hit. I thought we'd have our three weeks of fun on the Royal Court's upstairs stage then move on."[3] But instead, *The Rocky Horror Show* was so popular that in 1974, it debuted in Los Angeles, Sydney, Copenhagen, and Madrid, and, having outgrown its original home, moved to larger theaters in London and ran until 1980.

After American film and record producer Lou Adler saw the show in London, he snapped up the American and film rights for *Rocky Horror*, executive producing the film with a budget of around $1.2 million.[4] Richard O'Brien recounts, "The only imperative from 20th Century Fox was that we include some

1

American actors. That's why Barry Bostwick and Susan Sarandon play Brad and Janet—they were actually an item during
filming, too. And then the whole thing nearly got canned when
there was a change of head at Fox."[5]

The film, titled *The Rocky Horror Picture Show*, was released
in 1975, on August 14 in the UK and September 26 in the
US. "The movie bombed. It was pulled from the eight theaters
it was playing and its Halloween opening in New York was
cancelled."[6] Legendary film critic Roger Ebert called it "a
horror-rock-transvestite-camp-omnisexual-musical parody"
and insisted that it "would be more fun, I suspect, if it weren't
a picture show. It belongs on a stage, with the performers and
audience joining in a collective send-up."[7]

"'It was doomed from the start,' said Tim Deegan, who
worked with Mr. Adler and Fox in what seemed a vain effort
to find an audience."[8] Noting the success of *Pink Flamingos*
in late-night time slots, he convinced the folks at the Waverly
Theater in New York City to launch a midnight showing on
April Fool's Day, 1976. The manager there, Denise Borden, also
saw something in the film. "Denise would play the record album
of the *RHPS* sound track before the showing of the film to warm
up the audience, and a party atmosphere was generated as a
result. The audiences naturally began to respond, by booing
the villain and cheering the heroes. . . . This spawned a whole
group of regulars who weekly reserved the same seats in the
first row of the balcony."[9] These regulars started dressing up
as *Rocky Horror* characters and began the now-iconic tradition
of callbacks: funny and irreverent audience responses to key
lines and moments in the film. Sal Piro, cofounder and president of The Rocky Horror Picture Show Fan Club, recounted
that "a few of the regulars began to lip-sync the record that
is played before the movie in front of the audience. This was
spontaneous and it developed into a mini floor show before
the movie. Audience response was tremendous."[10] The regulars at the Waverly Theater created more and more elaborate
ways of engaging with the film, creating a regular series of

callbacks, adding prop gags like some fans holding newspapers over their heads during the storm scene while others used squirt guns to make it rain, and throwing toast. "The use of lines and props spread rapidly from theater to theater across the country. Hearsay, newspaper and magazine articles, and the fact that New York City *Rocky* fans visited theaters playing the show in other parts of the US are the reasons for this phenomenon."[11] The film has been shown in theaters in limited release ever since, apparently the longest theatrical release in film history.[12]

In October 2022, I attended a launch event for *It Came from the Closet,* an anthology of essays by queer and trans writers on horror films that were formative for them. The sold-out four-hundred-person auditorium at the Brooklyn Museum practically vibrated with excitement, even before high-femme dyke drag artist Miss Malice took the stage and performed a riveting number as a sexy vampire. Following that, anthology contributors Carmen Maria Machado and Sarah Fonseca read their essays from the book, then Miss Malice moderated a conversation between them.

In the Q&A session afterward, a person who seemed to be in their late twenties or early thirties asked, "What do you say to people who say that old media like *The Rocky Horror Picture Show* is problematic, queerbaiting, and no longer relevant?" A buzz went through the crowd as Carmen Maria Machado leaned toward her mic and said, "Tell 'em to say it to my face."

I laughed, but I had already been turning that question over in my head since I'd realized several months before that the film, which had been so important to my understanding of myself and my identity, and queerness in general, was approaching its fiftieth anniversary.

Walking out of the auditorium into the cool October night with a colleague in his twenties, I thought about how dramatically different the queer and trans representation was in the books, films, and media he had grown up with than it had been in the world I'd grown up in just over a decade earlier. I told him about how much my friends and I had all loved *Rocky Horror* as teenagers, and mused, "I wonder if *Rocky Horror* is actually as good as I remember it being, or if we just loved it because it was one of the only places where we could see possible versions of ourselves or visions of our futures?"

Film was an extremely influential artistic and entertainment medium in the United States in the twentieth century, and the powerful Hollywood film industry substantially shaped the myths and stories Americans have told about ourselves and others. This was partly due to the state and availability of technology which today we might think of as dated, but which was cutting-edge a hundred years ago. In 1930, 65 percent of Americans attended the cinema weekly,[13] while only around 40 percent of households owned a radio, and television was not commercially available yet—the majority of American households did not have a television until the '50s.[14] This meant that film was one of the primary ways that Americans consumed stories in the mid-nineteenth century.

In the 1920s and '30s, following numerous Hollywood scandals including a prominent actor being charged with manslaughter in the death of an actress, the US film industry faced increasing pressure from the government and the Catholic Church to clean up its act.[15] In 1934, William Hays, the chairman of the Motion Picture Producers and Distributors of America, created the Production Code, a set of rules governing what could and could not appear in films, commonly known as the Hays Code. It was voluntarily adopted and enforced rather than risking more stringent regulation from the government or condemnation and boycotts from the Catholic Church. "The Hays Code forbade the use of profanity, obscenity, and racial slurs and included detailed instructions outlining how certain topics should be shown onscreen, especially proscribing graphic violence, criminality, substance use, promiscuity, miscegenation, and homosexuality."[16] Films that included any of these things could not be distributed through mainstream film-industry channels.

The three main principles of the code: "1. No picture shall be produced that will lower the moral standards of those who see it. Hence the sympathy of the audience should never be thrown to the side of crime, wrongdoing, evil or sin. 2. Correct standards of life, subject only to the requirements of drama and entertainment, shall be presented. 3. Law, natural or human, shall not be ridiculed, nor shall sympathy be created for its violation."[17]

Because of these strict prohibitions, overt homosexuality could no longer be shown in films. "For all its efforts, the production code didn't erase homosexuals from screens, it just made them harder to find."[18] For example, films made use of stock character archetypes like the sissy, a flamboyant man who read as homosexual if you knew what you were looking at. In later decades, the code was interpreted more loosely, giving rise to the gay villain: a film character who is explicitly queer but must be punished for it to set everything right in the moral universe before the credits roll. The ubiquity of the queer film villain over decades of the Hays Code's enforcement, along with iconic queer-coded Disney villains such as Ursula, Jafar, and Scar, has given rise to a strong identification with villains among many queer people.

The Hays Code was in effect from 1934 until 1968, and was repealed just seven years before *The Rocky Horror Picture Show* was released. And it's noteworthy to me that *Rocky Horror* itself plays by some of the code's rules, killing off the characters who are explicitly queer.

The late 1960s into the 1970s was a period of greater visibility and acceptance of queer and gender-nonconforming people in the United States, with the 1969 Stonewall Riots creating a watershed moment for these communities. The 1967 Sexual Offences Act decriminalized homosexual sex between consenting men age twenty-one and over in England and Wales, though Scotland and Northern Ireland didn't follow suit until 1980 and 1982, respectively. *The Rocky Horror Picture Show* was made in a moment of increasing visibility and decreasing stigma for queer people in the US and UK. However, things were still far from perfect for queer people in the 1970s, and the preceding decades of invisibility and repression had definitely taken their toll.

Rocky Horror was already established in the queer alternative canon by the time I was born, and it had been around for a generation by the time I discovered it as a teenager. The film has been shown in theaters consistently since its release in 1975, creating real-world physical portals to the strange, genderfucky world of Transylvania, where queers and outcasts here on planet Earth could find each other and build community, or just spend a safe evening in a darkened room, watching a really weird film surrounded by friendly faces. *Rocky Horror* became for me a secret handshake, a sign that someone else was queer, or at least exactly the right kind of weirdo.

Returning to 2022: I was curious whether, in a world so radically changed from my childhood, *Rocky Horror* would still resonate with people. In a cultural landscape with complicated portrayals of queer and trans people and characters in every type of media and entertainment, at a level that was unimaginable to me even a decade prior, do younger generations still need *Rocky Horror*? With all its flaws, does the film still offer something to queers and weirdos today? These questions stuck with me, and I began to work on this book as a way to answer them, talking to queer, trans, and gender-nonconforming people across geography and generations, trying to understand more about how we think about representation and stories, gender and sexuality, language and its evolution, sex and love and consent, harm and murder (and cannibalism?!) and also, so importantly, community and family and music and joy.

Reading the essays in this book, by writers whose experiences span the full fifty-year history of the film, it's clear that the songs and characters of the film still offer something of value.

Different elements of the film resonate with different people, or sometimes even at different points within one person's life, and the writers have wildly different interpretations of characters, scenes, and songs. Writers' opinions especially diverge around Dr. Frank-N-Furter and the correct interpretation of the Doctor's gender and sexuality.

There are also some strands of agreement among writers, such as frustration with biased, racist, and harmful callbacks, which are still yelled in some theaters even today, and admiration of Eddie, sometimes as a butch-coded dreamboat.

But it is clear from these essays that the film *is* still resonating with new watchers, even in the last few years. How incredible that a single film, the iconic colorful camp disaster *The Rocky Horror Picture Show*, can continue to speak to and nourish audiences around the world for half a century.

I understand why. Being raised in a world that tells you that who you are on the deepest, most fundamental level is wrong, it's hard to learn to trust that maybe, just maybe, that isn't true or fair.

And once you start questioning how society got it so wrong about you, it's hard not to keep questioning everything else it tells you, about yourself and everyone else. And conservative people, people in power, want more than anything else for nobody to question a world that is organized for their substantial, overwhelming privilege and benefit. As the Transylvanians say: "It's just a jump to the left . . ." (But as we know, "it's the pelvic thrust that *really* drives them insane.")

In a devastating example of time warp, since I began to shape this book in the summer of 2022, the pendulum of progress has been aggressively yanked back in the US, the UK, and elsewhere in the world, with transgender and queer people among the favorite targets of those in power. In the US, hundreds of bills have been proposed or passed regulating and harming trans and queer people; books by and about trans and queer people have been banned from shelves in schools and libraries;

and even fairly mainstream media outlets such as *NPR*, *The New Yorker*, and *The New York Times* have written about Americans electing a fascist government, which will be taking over just days after I am writing this, months before this book will be released for you to read.

Fascists hate transness and queerness, and proved it tragically a generation before *Rocky Horror* was released. The pink triangle on Frank-N-Furter's lab coat is a reference to the symbol that queer people were forced to wear by the Nazis, who rounded them up, forced thousands of them into concentration camps, and murdered them as part of the Holocaust in the 1930s. What was already history by the time *Rocky Horror* was made has returned to blood-curdling relevance with some of the dark threats of Project 2025.

I don't know what the future holds, but I do know that queers and weirdos and perverts and dissidents and radicals and, in Ursula K. Le Guin's prescient words, "realists of a larger reality" will need ways to joyfully connect with each other, more than we ever have before.

So perhaps there is still a need for *The Rocky Horror Picture Show,* as a secret handshake and a place to gather. Fortunately, there's a light glowing at the Frankenstein place, a beacon and an invitation for all of us, if we want it.

—Margot Atwell
Brooklyn, NY
January 8, 2025

Notes

1. Michael Billington, "Rocky Horror Show Opens in London–Archive, 23 June 1973," *The Guardian*, June 23, 2020, https://www.theguardian.com/culture/2020/jun/23/rocky-horror-show-opens-in-london-archive-1973.
2. Billington, "Rocky Horror Show Opens in London."
3. Kate Abbot, "How We Made: The Rocky Horror Picture Show," *The Guardian*, March 4, 2013, https://www.theguardian.com/stage/2013/mar/04/how-we-made-rocky-horror.
4. "The Rocky Horror Picture Show," IMDb, accessed March 24, 2025, https://www.imdb.com/title/tt0073629/.
5. Abbot, "How We Made: The Rocky Horror Picture Show."
6. Tony Sokol, "The Rocky Horror Picture Show And Its Lasting Legacy," Den of Geek, August 14, 2019, https://www.denofgeek.com/movies/the-rocky-horror-picture-show-and-its-lasting-legacy/.
7. Roger Ebert, review of *The Rocky Horror Picture Show*, dir. Jim Sharman, *Chicago Sun-Times*, August 18, 1976, https://www.rogerebert.com/reviews/the-rocky-horror-picture-show-1976.
8. Marc Spitz, "'Rocky Horror' Is Doing the Time Warp, Forever," *New York Times*, October 2, 2015, https://www.nytimes.com/2015/10/04/movies/rocky-horror-is-doing-the-time-warp-forever.html.
9. Sal Piro, "It Was Great When It All Began," The Rocky Horror Picture Show Official Fan Site, accessed March 24, 2025, https://www.rockyhorror.com/history/howapbegan.php.
10. Piro, "It Was Great When It All Began."
11. Piro, "It Was Great When It All Began."
12. Saskia O'Donoghue, "Culture Re-View: The Longest-Running Theatrical Release in Film History Launches," *Euronews*, August 14, 2023, https://www.euronews.com/culture/2023/08/14/culture-re-view-the-longest-running-theatrical-release-in-film-history-launches.
13. Michelle C. Pautz, "The Decline in Average Weekly Cinema Attendance, 1930–2000," *Issues in Political Economy* 11 (2002), https://ecommons.udayton.edu/cgi/viewcontent.cgi?article=1023&context=pol_fac_pub.
14. "History and the Census: Philo Farnsworth and the Invention of Television," United States Census Bureau,

September 1, 2023, https://www.census.gov/about/history/stories/monthly/2023/september-2023.html.

15. Bob Mondello, "Remembering Hollywood's Hays Code, 40 Years On," *NPR*, August 8, 2008, https://www.npr.org/2008/08/08/93301189/remembering-hollywoods-hays-code-40-years-on.

16. *Britannica*, "Hays Code," by Jordana Rosenfeld, accessed December 20, 2024, https://www.britannica.com/art/Hays-Code.

17. Motion Picture Association of America, "The Motion Picture Production Code of 1930 (Hays Code)," accessed December 20, 2024, https://josephsmithfoundation.org/docs/the-motion-picture-production-code-of-1930-hays-code/

18. *The Celluloid Closet*, directed by Rob Epstein and Jeffrey Friedman (Warner Brothers, 1995), 16:45.

There's a Light:
The Queer Chaos and Magic of
The Rocky Horror Picture Show

Jane Claire Bradley

"ON THE OPENING CHORD on the opening night of the original stage version at the Royal Court," *The Rocky Horror Picture Show* director Jim Sharman once said to *The New York Times*, "an electrical storm broke out over London, and that lightning has been chasing it ever since."[1]

Over half a century later—including countless performances, screenings, books, theses, and adaptations—obsessives the world over are still grappling with the legacy of that once-in-a-lifetime, lightning-in-a-bottle magic captured by O'Brien, Sharman, and company those fifty fateful years ago.

That debut 1973 stage performance may have been its first unleashing into the world, the catalyst that set an unprecedentedly momentous and unpredictable thunderstorm into motion. But even before then, we could say the clouds were already churning, that the downpours were already starting: In 1967, sex between men in England and Wales had finally been decriminalized, followed by the Stonewall Riots in 1969 and the UK's first Pride march in 1972. But homosexuality was still listed as a psychiatric disorder in the Diagnostic and Statistical Manual of Mental Disorders, and explicit queer representation in mass media was still a distant dream. And then along came *The Rocky Horror Picture Show*. Lightning struck, not just once, but over and over and over again, electrifying millions of hearts one by one, a high-voltage thunderbolt of recognition and obsession.

Every viewer struck by those thunderbolts can retell the story of their first time. Everyone has an anecdote, rendered in hyper-vivid detail, about how it happened for them. Patricia Quinn's lips, Richard O'Brien's voice. That iconic onscreen lipsticked mouth, hanging in black oblivion. As Michael Blyth, then-programmer for queer film festival BFI Flare, recognized on *The Evolution of Horror* podcast: "You know if you're going to love that film within a minute. If you respond to that opening sequence, you're going to have the fucking time of your life."[2] For those destined to become transfixed, infatuated, and obsessed, those first few seconds of "Science Fiction / Double Feature" are usually enough to do it.

Formative moments change us. Time becomes elastic. A memory becomes imprinted, every aspect freeze-framed and seared deep into our brains and souls. Here's mine: I was at my nan's ramshackle rural Welsh cottage for the weekend, in her chintzy but bohemian living room: lamplight, red leather button-back settee cobwebbed with cracks at the arms, a glossy dark-wood TV cabinet with doors that latched to hide the screen, an antique wooden globe that opened in half to reveal a secret cache of wine and whiskey bottles. In a blue haze of cig smoke, the grown-ups balanced tumblers of booze on their knees while my siblings and I sat cross-legged on the carpet, competing with Nan's arthritic red setter and her two snooty ragdoll cats for the space closest to the fire. Allowed to stay up past our bedtimes for a very special occasion: a first VHS viewing of *The Rocky Horror Picture Show*.

In retrospect, we were definitely too young, even if the adults in the room put their hands over our eyes during Frank-N-Furter's silhouetted bedroom scenes with Brad and Janet and the infamous swimming pool orgy during the film's grand finale. But even with my age still in single digits, this wasn't my first exposure to fringe culture. My dad was a biker and a rocker, had been in motorcycle gangs and punk bands, our weekends with him soundtracked by ear-splitting renditions of anthems by the Sex Pistols and Motorhead. He had taken my siblings and me on various ill-fated and ill-advised road trips through apocalyptic weather in the sidecar of his motorbike. During the '80s and '90s in the UK, bikers had a degree of dubious notoriety: regularly denounced by the tabloids and other mass media as being antisocial criminals, violent scumballs, predators, and everything in between, to be avoided wherever possible by anyone not part of the scene. So it was a shorthand I recognized, when one motorbike after another howled past Brad and Janet's car during that torrential downpour, and when, as the couple huddled under that dripping newspaper at the castle's doorway, an ominously timed bolt of lightning revealed the row of bikes lined up outside. It was code for deviance, danger, and menace: *Here be outsiders, escape while you still can, you're a long way from home.* But for my siblings and me, bikes outside anywhere meant loud music and leather jackets and probably some fun to be had while the adults were otherwise occupied and we went dangerously unsupervised. I was a long way from finding my own queer subculture and family, but I had no fear of otherness. And I was even further away from putting language to it, but I already knew that those typecast by society as freaks and weirdos often took a perverse pleasure and joy in that categorization, reveling in being seen as deviant outsiders while forging their own communities, rituals, and rites of passage. To me, bikers didn't mean danger. They meant family, freedom, belonging, and home.

Although the Transylvanians cavorting inside Frank's castle once Janet and Brad are finally, reluctantly, ushered inside didn't look like any bikers I'd ever seen, I'd been primed by those earlier glimpses of their motorcycles to feel an affinity with them, an instinct confirmed by their immediate descent into the "Time Warp," a song that had by then penetrated pop culture enough that I already knew the all the lyrics and dance moves. All this to say: At this point, we're only twenty minutes into the movie, and I'm already *obsessed.*

And then . . .

You know where I'm going with this, don't you?

Our first glimpse of Dr. Frank-N-Furter's tapping rhinestoned heels as he descends in the elevator to join the party. Excess. Glamour. Punk rock, but with glitter. Something inside me exploded. I fell in instant love. This was my first experience encountering an explicitly, defiantly, unashamedly queer character, and it was like coming home. By the midway point of Frank-N-Furter's first number, in which he removes his cape with a dramatic flourish that reveals his fishnet stockings, sparkly corset, and bulging lace underwear, my brain was blown into smithereens.

Frank-N-Furter is a joyfully ambiguous character who defies classification: The mad scientist may be a classic B-movie archetype, but I don't know of any others with tattoos, pearl necklaces, and the gay pride pink triangle stitched onto their lab coats. In the movie, straitlaced Brad and Janet are our cardigan-clad, white-underweared, virginal stand-ins for heteronormativity, and Frank-N-Furter gleefully shows them a path away from the expected, vanilla, mainstream world and toward one which celebrates disinhibition and deviance. They go from dreaming it to being it, to tasting blood and wanting more, more, more. As the couple crawls in the rubble during the film's closing credits, it's as creatures forever changed by crossing paths with Frank.

While not without his problematic elements—Frank-N-Furter is a murderer and cannibal, with a dubious-at-best understanding of consent—this was nevertheless my first time seeing a character who took so much brazen joy in being as radically transgressive, sexual, and shocking as possible. And it was *world altering.*

Even as a kid, I knew enough to recognize the fetishistic elements of things like stockings, gloves, lingerie, and heels: I knew these things were signifiers of sex and obscenity, things that were supposed to stay behind closed doors, not be celebrated with family singalongs, fancy-dress theme parties, or jubilant wedding-dance-floor renditions of the "Time Warp." And yet, there we were, embracing Frank as our violent, murderous, and manipulative lingerie-clad antihero. *The Rocky Horror Picture Show* takes absolute pleasure in blurring and breaking down boundaries, in format, genre, and audience as well as around thematic content like sex, sexuality, and gender. "*The Rocky Horror Picture Show* challenged movie musicals. It challenged movies, in general. It defied the concept of acceptable cinema. It celebrated corruption and debauchery like few films before it."[3]

This deliberate, mischievous, defiant ambiguity applies to Frank too. From my first viewing, I could see he was in some ways the film's villain, but I was still obsessed with his charisma, his power, his *style*. And part of that came from that very ambiguity, from not knowing his gender, sexuality, or even his species. (I mean, he makes some claims to identity in "Sweet Transvestite," but it's not until much later that the viewer finds out that the Transylvania referenced in the song actually refers to another galaxy somewhere in distant outer space.) Being sexually confused by Frank-N-Furter has become a queer rite of passage, and I was no exception. And it was Frank-N-Furter who taught me how so much of queer glamour, queer charisma, and queer power gets its potency and impact from precisely this ambiguity: from ripping up the rule book of social convention, following desire, and embracing the strange, unknown, and extreme. In an era when so many queer people experienced shame and confusion about their identities and desires, Frank-N-Furter was a much-needed model of unapologetically rejecting shame and societal expectation and instead finding joy, family, community, and meaning in his celebratory approach to his self-expression and lifestyle.

This has been echoed by others who found what they needed in Frank, such as queer and trans writer Alice Collins. A film producer and horror fanatic, Collins explains: "The first depiction of a trans person I ever saw was Frank. I never thought they were freaky or weird. They looked like fun, and I enjoyed that they didn't care what anyone else thought and how they were unabashedly themselves. I thought it was so cool and wanted to be like that: giving zero cares as to what anyone thought of me. It gave me strength to grow a thicker skin and try more things out of the ordinary; I looked up to Frank. For the longest time before seeing the movie, I'd always wished I could switch between gender at will and it was really cool to see someone who could at least on the surface do so before my eyes."[4]

It's been acknowledged many times over that "*The Rocky Horror Picture Show* has defined what we mean by a 'cult' movie, though few can ever hope to match its phenomenal level of ritualized worship."[5] And while the movie certainly eventually evolved a worldwide devoted congregation of fanatics, with established devotional rites, those words *ritualized worship* lead me to reflect further on Frank as leader and figurehead of the "unconventional conventionalists" who assemble at the castle for the Annual Transylvanian Convention. To the gathered Transylvanians, Frank's closer acolytes, and Brad and Janet, Frank models an unapologetic, unashamed, brazenly sexual and queer way of being, and he is revered and feared for it by those around him. It leads those in his orbit to start experimenting with their own desires for power and pleasure: Riff Raff terrorizes Rocky with lit candles, causing him to break free of his chains and escape, setting all sorts of later pandemonium in motion. After being seduced by Frank, Janet has her tryst with Rocky, claiming her desire to be thrilled, chilled, and fulfilled and become a creature of the night, while Columbia and Magenta watch with glee. Although Frank, an intimidating figure, is initially treated with reverence and devotion, claiming his rightful throne during "Sweet Transvestite" with the others arrayed around him, he also incites their rebellion. He sets the other characters on a journey of experimentation, expansion, and ultimately defiance. And we could argue that this is a necessary function of Frank: It's a hell of a responsibility being the loudest, most glamorous, and almost literally balls-out seductive, sexy, and psychotic leader of any circle or subculture. But in embodying this role, Frank gives those around him a permission slip toward their own arcs of discovery: They rebel against expectations (even if those expectations are from Frank himself) and claim their own power and desires. And just as those arcs and shifts are portrayed in the movie itself, those same trajectories are echoed in the ways millions of queer people have instantly formed such enduring relationships with Frank and the movie more generally. In *Rocky Horror*, we saw something we needed and had been hungering for, and we took its invitation as a permission slip and catalyst for our own evolutions.

In an oft-quoted definition of fantasy, Rosemary Jackson explains that "fantasy characteristically attempts to compensate for a lack resulting from cultural constraints; *it is a literature of desire, which seeks that which is experienced as absence and loss*"[6] (emphasis mine). *This* is the core magic and power of *The Rocky Horror Picture Show*: that it depicted unapologetically weird, queer characters experiencing joy, pleasure, desire, belonging, family, and community—things which at the time, and even now, weren't always immediately or easily available to queer people—and in doing so created the very conditions for those people to find each other. In contrast to the absence and loss that were (and can still be) such painful parts of the queer experience, the movie used camp, theatrics, and rock 'n' roll to craft an unabashedly original, odd, and joyful alternative vision. And in doing so, it mapped out a path toward those very things—queer community, family, meaning, and belonging—for entire generations to come.

The Rocky Horror Picture Show was filmed in just six weeks at Oakley Court, now a luxury hotel but at the time a derelict ruin. A popular filming location for Hammer Horror films, it had no bathrooms and no heating, leading to Susan Sarandon getting pneumonia on set, and—according to some possibly apocryphal stories—also directly leading to the frenzied passion in the swimming pool scenes, because the actors were told that the more enthusiastic they were when the cameras were rolling, the sooner they'd be allowed out of the unheated pool. The first movie-making experience for most people on set, Jim Sharman

recalls that "it was so low-budget I think it was always considered an oddity by the studio; they would never have imagined it
as a potential blockbuster, more like a sleeper, which it turned
out to be. It was the low budget that restricted, yet also liberated
us . . . It was considered so cheap and quirky that, mercifully,
we were left to our own devices to make the film we wanted
to make."[7]

Queer creatives often struggle to access institutional or other
forms of financial support, and we're no strangers to making
bizarre, brilliant, radical things happen on minimal budgets.
The tight purse strings involved in the production of *The Rocky
Horror Picture Show* play a key part in its uniqueness and
charm. Costume designer Sue Blane, for instance, only had
a total budget of around a thousand pounds to get the entire
cast outfitted, and, well, they do say necessity is the mother of
invention, don't they? This limitation necessitated significant
creativity and imagination, and Blane's use of torn fishnets,
hair dye, and glitter, among other aesthetic choices, have been
credited with having a clear influence on the fashions of emerging British punk subculture in the mid- to late '70s.

This is another fundamental part of why *The Rocky Horror
Picture Show* was so influential for me: It taught me the necessity of imagination, audacity, and *trust*. I've watched the film
infinite times since that first fateful thunderbolt night, and I
still get the same fizziness in my bloodstream, that same power
surge of affection, excitement, and electricity. This shamelessly
strange film, made in only a few weeks in a freezing, spooky
ruin, was a true before-and-after split that changed queer
culture beyond recognition, and did it with absolute joy, irrev-
erence, and a soundtrack of total bangers. "I've often described
it as a big home movie," Jim Sharman has said. "In that sense,
it captures a moment in time in a way that has proved curiously
timeless. Technically, there's plenty that could be better, but
then it wouldn't be what it is."[8]

Even the first few times I watched the film at such a formative age, long before I could recognize or articulate this, I'd

already been connected to other culture that was directly and indirectly shaped by *Rocky Horror*. Did I know, then, that I was going back to source material that had already been transmitted down into our cultural DNA, that the films and music I'd go on to love as a teen and an adult could all trace their roots back there? Not consciously. I'm probably being over-romantic, but I like to think part of my fascinated reaction had to do with a felt sense of heritage and lineage: It was a broadcast coming through loud and clear, like the one from that RKO tower.

And all of that makes me question whether the film's creators, cast, and crew knew just what they were unleashing, as they battled storms, icy temperatures, and shoestring budgets to bring this bizarre thing to life. I'd like to think that somewhere in all of the chaos of production and the criticism that followed, there was a defiant kernel of *trust*. Trust that their unconventional conventionalists would hear the transmission coming from that beacon, and that we would answer that summons as soon as we were able. "The mainstream audience only saw the surface, and they turned away," Sharman recognized. "But the late-night audience picked up on what was under that surface—and it spoke to them." We were summoned, struck by lightning and electrified, and—first one by one, then in our thousands and ultimately millions—came crawling across the planet's face, ready to do the Time Warp again.

Notes

1. Mark Spitz, "'Rocky Horror' Is Doing the Time Warp, Forever," *New York Times*, October 2, 2015, https://www.nytimes.com/2015/10/04/movies/rocky-horror-is-doing-the-time-warp-forever.html.
2. Mike Muncer, host, *The Evolution of Horror*, podcast, season 7, episode 9, "The Rocky Horror Picture Show" with Michael Blythe, August 5, 2021.
3. Doug Jamieson, "The Enduring Legacy of The Rocky Horror Picture Show," *Filmotomy*, July 16, 2018, https://filmotomy.com/the-enduring-legacy-of-the-rocky-horror-picture-show/.
4. Alice Collins, "How I Learned to Stop Worrying and Love 'The Rocky Horror Picture Show' Again [Trapped By Gender]," *Bloody Disgusting*, June 5, 2020, https://bloody-disgusting.com/editorials/3587316/learned-stop-worrying-love-rocky-horror-picture-show-trapped-gender/.
5. Larushka Ivan-Zadeh, "The Rocky Horror Picture Show: The Film That's Saved Lives," *BBC Culture*, June 19, 2020, https://www.bbc.com/culture/article/20200618-the-rocky-horror-picture-show-the-film-thats-saved-lives.
6. Rosemary Jackson, Fantasy: *The Literature of Subversion* (Routledge, 1981).
7. Jim Sharman, interview by the RHPS Official Fan Club, The Rocky Horror Picture Show Official Fan Site, August 5, 2008, https://www.rockyhorror.com/history/interviews_jimsharman.php.
8. Sharman, interview by the RHPS Official Fan Club.

Going Home:
Found Family and
The Rocky Horror Picture Show

Margot Atwell

CW: homophobia, murder, HIV/AIDS

I GREW UP in the '80s and '90s in a quiet, leafy, overwhelmingly white and affluent suburb, where I walked the two blocks to my grade school every day, and after school played wiffle ball and hide-and-seek with the other kids in my neighborhood.

My parents and extended family were all religious—Catholic on my mom's side and Episcopal/Presbyterian on my dad's. I sang in the church choir for years, donning robes and a halo in the Christmas pageant and performing in the annual children's play based on Bible stories. These tended to center a faithful man imperiled, like Jonah and the whale or Daniel in the lion's den.

My father traveled for work almost constantly and worked long hours in the city even when he wasn't traveling, so my mother, two brothers, and I spent a lot of time just the four of us. She often told us stories while she was driving, to school, sports practices, the library. When I remember my mother telling me something as a kid, I always picture us in the car, an old Ford Taurus station wagon.

My mom occasionally told a story about *The Rocky Horror Picture Show*. My parents had met when they lived in San Francisco in the late 1970s. When they were on a date one night, a teenager had asked her and my father for $1.37 so she could see *Rocky Horror* at the nearby theater. My mom described *Rocky Horror* to us as a weird film that was screened at midnight, where audience members brought squirt guns to make it rain in the theater, threw rice, and shouted responses to the screen. That story was fascinating to me for reasons that I couldn't identify at the time, but it struck me as out of character for my parents. Then again, so did their having lived in San Francisco in the 1970s and early 1980s. It hinted at a past that was somewhat fractured from who they seemed to be in the present as I was growing up.

My mom sometimes told us stories about the early days of the AIDS crisis and its impacts on her gay male friends and colleagues at the phone company where she had worked in San Francisco. The way she tells it, everyone's gay lover kept getting diagnosed with cancer, until it seemed impossible that so many young gay lovers could have cancer. She described the fear, the desperation, the way unscrupulous people took advantage of that fear to sell gay men egregiously expensive cocktails of medications that were just over-the-counter vitamins, and they bought them and took them anyway, because what else could they do?

I later learned that the first cases of the illness that would turn out to be AIDS were reported in 1981, kicking off a pandemic and crisis for queer and trans people around the world. By the end of 1983, the year I was born, the US had over 4,700 reported cases of AIDS, and more than 2,000 people had died.[1] The US government was slow to take the epidemic seriously and take action to mitigate it, which many people chalk up to the fact that it was seen (erroneously) as a disease only affecting queer people.

The month I was born, Jerry Falwell, a hyper-conservative Baptist pastor, televangelist, and cofounder of Moral Majority, who had the ear of President Ronald Reagan, debated gay reverend Troy Perry on television on CBC. Falwell declared that "93 percent of all Americans believe that homosexuality is not an acceptable alternate lifestyle," that AIDS was "caused by homosexual promiscuity," and demanded that "the homosexual bathhouses, which everyone knows are just for the most dirty, vulgar, filthy, bloody occurrences, anal intercourse, and worse" should be shut down because, he asserted, that was where AIDS was being transmitted. He also advocated strongly for conversion therapy for gay people.[2]

President Reagan, who had taken office in January 1981, did not even publicly acknowledge AIDS until September 1985.[3] By 1994, AIDS had become the highest cause of death for Americans ages twenty-five to forty-four.[4]

It's hard to describe how different the world was before the internet was widely used and accessible. It's really not possible anymore to be sheltered the way I was when I was growing up. To learn about people and ideas outside of what you could find in your neighborhood and school, the only options were mass media such as films, radio, and television—including shows as dubiously informative as *Jerry Springer* and *The Jenny Jones Show*—or physical media such as books, magazines, and newspapers. And in the mass media culture of the '80s and early '90s, queer representation was vanishingly rare and mostly bad.

Until I was a teenager, I didn't even *really* know what "gay" meant. The messages I remember from the news and information sources I ambiently absorbed as a child were that gay men were promiscuous and sinful, should be pitied or hated, were punished by contracting AIDS, and died alone after being rejected by their families of origin. RuPaul's debut album, *Supermodel of the World*, made waves the summer I turned ten, and he was widely considered an incomprehensible freak by the adults in my sphere, if he was considered at all.

I didn't know any gay people or lesbians—not a neighbor or a friend of the family or an aunt living with her "roommate" for a couple decades. I had no reference point beyond the media, church, family, and people in my town. "Lesbian," if it was mentioned at all, meant fat, hairy, mannish, tragically unstylish, desperate, perhaps predatory . . . nothing a person would aspire to, and nothing explicitly about sex either. As if women turned to lesbianism as consolation when they couldn't get a man.

There was also a family story, told rarely in a hushed whisper, about a distant cousin who had been the victim of a brutal gay bashing and "was never the same." I never met him, since he died before I was born.

Beginning in third grade, when I transferred to a tiny, fancy conservative private school a few towns over, I was often bullied by classmates for my nerdiness, awkwardness, intelligence, small size, and more. People just looked at me—my round glasses huge and owlish on my tiny freckled face, brown hair chopped short in a pixie cut, wearing a plaid flannel with my dad's old army pants falling off my hips—and thought to themselves, "There's something about that I just don't like." And they did not keep those thoughts to themselves. My classmates knew I was gay before I did.

As a child, I had a ceaseless inner monologue, but rarely opened my mouth to share my thoughts with others. I felt a deep and pervasive sense of discomfort and wrongness, as if who I was on a fundamental level was shameful and unacceptable, and if anyone discovered who I really was, they wouldn't love me—they wouldn't even want to know me. I immersed myself in books, walking down the hallways at school insulated by the fantastical fog of fictional worlds.

In the '90s, "gay" was the favorite slur for teenagers. When I was in high school, the best that queer people were told we could aspire to receive from others was "tolerance" (no diversity, equity, or inclusion). Once I learned what a lesbian was, I had a strong suspicion that I was one, but I didn't share that thought with anyone else for a long time.

I first encountered *The Rocky Horror Picture Show* at CTY, a summer program for "gifted and talented youth" run by Johns Hopkins University, where kids ages twelve to sixteen would take college-level courses in three weeks over the summer. So, summer school for kids so nerdy we *chose* extra school. At my regular school, kids worked hard to get good grades but didn't really care much about what we were learning. It was considered strange and off-putting that I did, that I read for fun, that I wrote stories during my lunch breaks.

For the first time in my life, I encountered other kids like me: kids who read for fun, kids who were endlessly curious and unapologetically nerdy. Intelligence and a love of learning were valued and respected by my peers, rather than being mocked or prized only in the context of climbing the steps on the respectable ladder toward college.

One night at dinner, I sat down at a table where a skinny boy was reading a thick mass-market paperback with a spaceship on the cover. When I asked him what it was about, he kind of flinched when he said it was *Star Wars*, but his face unlocked when I responded, "Oh cool, I love *Star Wars*," and he lit up as he began to describe the extended universe of *Star Wars* novels to me.

Some kids wore bathrobes on Thursdays for reasons I was assured related to *The Hitchhiker's Guide to the Galaxy*, a book I had never read but which made the number forty-two extremely important among my new friends.

I was taken seriously as a writer, workshopped and critiqued among other kids who loved to write as much as I did. In my classes, I was introduced to Lorrie Moore and the wild concept of writing a short story in second person, and Angela Carter, whose voice in a story like "The Erl-King" changed what it felt possible to achieve with writing.

I met other kids I related to, lots of them. My new friends and I bonded quickly over our shared interests, and I tentatively started sharing my real self with them. I finally felt like the person I was in my heart wasn't doomed to being solitary and lonely, or else permanently locked into pretending to be different or more or less than I was.

Each Friday at CTY there was a dance, which felt like a totally different experience from the middle school dances I'd attended, where I hung out on the sidelines with another friend or two, or tried to dance, burning with mortification at the idea that people might be looking at me, judging me, and sometimes confirmed in my suspicions by a cutting remark or stares and laughter from more popular kids. But at CTY, I felt like I could let out my held breath, relax my shoulders, and be as much of myself as I knew how to be at age twelve. I danced and jumped around awkwardly to pop songs with other kids who were doing the same, grinning at each other all night.

I noticed that some of the older kids got more excited about some songs, like "It's the End of the World as We Know It," and "Forever Young," and a weird upbeat rock song I'd never heard before called "Time Warp," which had instructions for a dance embedded in its lyrics. I peered around at the other kids to make sure I was doing it right. During the chorus, when "it's the pelvic thrust" was sung, the older kids would yell "group sex, group sex, group sex, group sex" while thrusting their hips wildly. Sex of any kind wasn't on my radar yet—I had my very first kiss that summer, a chaste peck with a boy who broke up with me two days later—but I giggled as I thrusted along with everyone else.

Every dance ended with "American Pie," when all the kids formed circles, throwing our arms around each other's shoulders and swaying together. I learned that these songs were "canon," an important part of the CTY experience, a legacy that was passed down from year to year.

The friendships I made at CTY became my lifeline during the school year. We kept in touch by paper letters and occasional strictly rationed, expensive long-distance phone calls, then later by email and AOL instant messenger. Talking to those friends helped me cope with the intense pressure of trying to survive the punishing conformity of my conservative, all-girls private school. I lived for the few weeks each summer when I felt I could be my real self, surrounded by people whose friendship felt deep and true, the kind of love that felt more like family than friendship.

Somehow, all the religion I had grown up steeped in didn't really stick, and I had a crisis of faith when I was fourteen that has never resolved. Once I understood how brutally unjust the world was, I could never reconcile that with the comforting image of an omnipotent and loving God I had been raised with. An atheist friend clued me in that I could get out of attending tedious hypocritical church services by volunteering to teach Sunday school and babysit in the church nursery. I happily offered to do community service and began to spend Sunday mornings taking care of toddlers instead of listening to sermons.

In 1997, Ellen DeGeneres came out as a lesbian in a *Time Magazine* cover story before the character on her eponymous show came out to a live audience of forty-two million people, of whom I was not one, but it was such a major cultural moment that I heard about it anyway. Showrunner Dava Savel described that the angry letters and death threats received afterward were part of the backlash they expected. And though she, Ellen, and the other writers received an Emmy award for their work on the episode, Savel and the other writers were fired after the end of that season, and the show was canceled after ratings tanked in its fifth and final season.[5] People in my town rolled their eyes and scoffed about Ellen DeGeneres after that. The message was clear.

Later that year, the summer I turned fifteen, my CTY friends and I switched to a different college campus which also hosted the program. The new site had more interesting advanced courses, skewed a bit older, and felt a little cooler, according to a friend whose older brother had been to multiple sites. I was excited to take fiction and poetry writing classes and eagerly agreed.

My first day there, I saw butch girls for the first time in my life. In the coming weeks, I often saw two of them together, a highly visible and cool romantic couple of "Nevermores"—teens in their final year of the program, essentially high school seniors. They wore Doc Martens and lay on the lawn in front of the brick building where we took classes, one with short, tousled hair resting her head on the other one's stomach, or standing in line in the cafeteria, the short-haired one slipping one finger through the belt loop of her girlfriend's cargo pants, cocky smile on her face, pulling her in for a deep kiss.

Their friend was a tough and beautiful girl with her long, wild, honey-blond hair always hanging loose. When I saw her wearing a hand-dyed thrifted slip dress with combat boots, chunky silver rings on most of her fingers, her eyes lined messily with black eyeliner, her lips looking just-bitten red—my first experience of queer femme style—I burned with a feeling of desire I'd never had before, but which I now understand was deep recognition and envy.

This felt like a place where self-expression and experimentation around gender, sexuality, and more were celebrated and not just "tolerated." A gay boy with long hair introduced himself with the name of a tree, which he later told me he had chosen himself. I made out with someone who told me he wasn't a boy or a girl and chirped with pleasure when I tousled his dark hair. He said he was thinking about changing his pronouns to xe/xir/xirs, and I practiced saying the unfamiliar words in my dorm room later.

One day the first week, a bunch of the older kids dressed up in drag, the boys wearing dresses and stuffing borrowed bras with socks, one of the butch girls wearing a mustache penciled on with eyeliner. I had never seen someone in drag outside of a play or Monty Python sketch before. It felt exciting and transgressive, and sexy in a way I found a little confusing.

Later that week, I finally saw *The Rocky Horror Picture Show*, lying on the scratchy carpet of a rec room, surrounded with other teenagers giggling and yelling and playing with each other's hair, a couple people making out in the corner. Watching *Rocky Horror* for the first time felt like being Dorothy landing in

Oz, stepping out of a home rendered in black and white into a Technicolor wonderland. *Rocky Horror* wasn't gay, it was queer. It was weird and horrifying and violent and sexy and fun, full of campy winks and nods, and the total opposite of everything that heterosexual, cisgender, monogamous, patriarchal society demanded and enforced.

At the first dance that summer, when the familiar guitar riff that opens "Time Warp" began, people screamed and ran to the center of the floor. At the previous site, we had sung along and gone through the motions of the dance, but here, it was something different entirely. A few of the queer kids took turns lip-syncing to the characters' verses and vamping for each other. When the chorus hit, we all danced and sang the "Time Warp," stepping and thrusting and becoming Transylvanians together. Pelvic-thrusting and yelling "group sex!" surrounded by a circle of other queer kids felt extremely different than it had just a year before. It was sexy and frenetic and mind-altering to be part of something so weird and joyous. At the end of the song, as it was winding down, instruments slowing and warping, all the dancers slowly wound themselves down to the floor and collapsed in heaps, giggling and panting from the three minutes of intense exertion. I lay there with them, boneless and relaxed, gasping for breath and feeling incredible euphoria.

My sense of the world and its possibilities for me reorganized themselves that summer, a seismic shift. I understood innately that I couldn't share these new revelations with my family, or let them see these budding new parts of me.

Just over a year after Ellen came out, in October 1998, a twenty-one-year-old college student, Matthew Shepard, was viciously attacked, beaten, and tied to a fence where he was left to die near where he lived in Laramie, Wyoming.[6] The brutality of the attack was devastating to me and to many other young queer people, though I still only knew a few others at that time. Media coverage of his murder and the subsequent trial of the two murderers focused intensely on the fact that Matthew Shepard was gay, and whether that was a motivation or an excuse for the unconscionable crimes. Mostly, people acted like his murder was a shame but sort of understandable.

The brutal homophobic torture and murder of Matthew Shepard, and the way regular people in my world responded to the news, right as I began to understand myself as queer, was heartrending proof that *we* were *not okay*, and we could not expect safety, or even sympathy.

I felt further and further from the people around me, and forced myself to keep up the façade that I was a good straight kid with absolutely no sinful or perverted thoughts or desires. It felt easier and safer to let my parents believe in the version of me that fit with their expectations and aspirations.

The summer I turned sixteen, my Nevermore year at CTY, I kissed a beautiful soft-butch girl—my first time kissing a girl. It felt profoundly different, soft and comfortable and exciting, and I had wanted it so badly. I wanted to do it again immediately, but she laughed and ran off.

Later that week, she borrowed my combat boots to perform "Out Tonight" from *RENT* for the talent show. My heart squeezed in an unfamiliar way when I saw her onstage, her short hair teased messy, dancing sexily in a short black skirt and fishnets, and *wearing my boots*.

After the six weeks of camp that summer, I could never return to CTY: I was too old. I felt like Wendy Darling, trapped away from Neverland and forced to grow up in a world where magic is real but nobody else believes in it, a world that doesn't make sense. My brilliant, fun, creative, queer, loving, curious, weird CTY friends had become my family, and we clung to each other all the tighter after we couldn't go back. I started looking forward desperately to the escape hatch of college, imagining a place where I hoped I could find other people like me.

A deep rift opened between my biological family and me. I have a clear memory of a dinner where a relative confidently declared, in a voice resonant with Old Testament authority, "Homosexuality is an abomination." My heart started racing and I burned with shame and anger, a well of bottomless grief opening inside me. I stared at my plate to try to avoid letting anyone see how I felt as the rest of the conversation faded to static around me. I was sixteen and already understood myself to be "one of those." That night, I filed this information away, understanding it to mean that I was "an abomination" in their eyes and could not let my family know this about myself unless I was ready to potentially be cast out and lose them.

I fought with my parents until they finally let me leave the straightjacket of the ritzy private school I had been attending and hating for nearly a decade, and transferred to the much, much bigger local public school a few months into my junior year. It was more than five times the size of the private school, so it was easier to escape the scrutiny and punishing judgment of my peers. I found a group of people who reminded me of my CTY family, a group of outcast freaks, queers, and goth "vampires" who dressed in all black, with long trench coats and pleather dusters, heavy silver jewelry and black eyeliner on everyone regardless of gender. The size of the group and the whiff of danger implied by the dramatic garb meant that we were left alone by other students . . . more or less.

My spooky friends insulated me from any real social consequences for getting involved in the school's Gay-Straight Alliance, which I joined right away—the word "straight" in the name doing a lot of work providing closeted queer kids like me with plausible deniability. My parents did not even seem suspicious when my high school presented me with an award for my incredible work as the club's "straight" president my senior year.

A few of my new friends were putting on a production of *Rocky Horror* at the local teen center. Seeing the chaotic queer genderfuckery in person, in my hometown, opened another crack in the restrictive walls of my small world. *Rocky Horror* became for me both a passport to a world where it was okay to be as weird and queer and shiny and extra as I wanted to be, and a secret handshake; a quick coy reference would tell me that someone was queer, or at least my type of weirdo.

After my senior year, I headed to Smith College, which had such a reputation for queerness that my father soberly warned me about the lesbians the summer before I left for school. Apparently, my stint in the Gay-Straight Alliance hadn't tipped him off. I worked hard to keep my face blank as I nodded and thanked him for the advice.

Away from the gaze of my family and conservative hometown, I grew more open and confident. I started a new literary magazine with two friends from my first-semester poetry class. One of them, Tammis, was in her fifties and lived in a gorgeous house right off campus. She seemed to have lived a dozen lives before getting to Smith. She suggested we name our magazine *Labrys* after the double-headed battle axe legendarily used by Amazonian warriors, which some lesbians in the 1970s had claimed as their symbol. I loved the word, the image, and the sense it gave me of a long, proud queer history.

One Halloween, my friends and I attended a shadow cast performance of *Rocky Horror*. We sipped from a flask in the back row, shouting and messing up the callbacks, full of rowdy queer joy and love. Afterward, I skipped across the darkened campus, pavement damp and shining under the streetlights from recent rain, shivering in my fishnets and surrounded by the brilliant queer weirdos who had become my family. I felt peace, possibility, and hope for a future that looked something like this.

After college, I moved to New York City, the birthplace of the *Rocky Horror* shadow cast, a place where I could be as queer and weird as I wanted. I started working in book publishing and joined a roller derby league—the fishnets, exaggerated draggy makeup, and general queerness of the campy, chaotic underground sport felt like home to me.

Over time, I have become someone I couldn't even have dreamed of as a kid growing up in conservative, straight, white-bread suburbs, in a country that thought people like me were sinful, diseased, and should die, or at least be converted to something else. I don't even try to look straight: I haven't seen my natural hair color in two decades, and I dress in outfits that wouldn't stand out at all in the Frankenstein place.

In June 2015, five months into my first real long-term relationship with a beautiful, brilliant woman, a Supreme Court decision made same-sex marriage legal across the whole United States while I was in San Francisco for work. Watching the San Francisco Pride parade the day after the decision, I cried. When I called her, she and her sisters and mother were watching the Pride parade in New York. For a moment, it felt like the world got a little bit bigger and brighter for people like us.

I came out to my parents and other relatives in my thirties, and they got to know the woman I love and eventually married. They celebrated our wedding with us at The Strand bookstore in New York. Seeing my parents embrace her as a daughter is something I never imagined, as a terrified teenager just beginning to understand herself, might one day be possible.

For queer people, our families of origin so rarely share our queer identities, and it can be hard to feel fully at home with people whose experiences of the world are so different from ours. I believe that finding and building our own families will always be part of the queer experience. But I have been so heartened to see more families embracing and supporting their queer and trans kids over the past several decades. It has transformed what feels possible for a kid or teen discovering they are not quite like everyone else.

Today, I live in a two-family townhouse in Brooklyn with my wife, her sister and her sister's husband, and a few rascally dogs. We share meals and daily intimacies, and have become foundational supports for each other in times of illness and despair, as well as celebration and great joy. Last Halloween, the four of us went to a live performance of *Rocky Horror* featuring some of our favorite drag performers at the House of Yes in Bushwick. My wife made an incredible Eddie—who has always seemed kinda dyke-coded to me—and I posed with her in front of the theater in my Columbia costume. At the end of the show, Janet reached out to me where I was sitting in the second row and pulled me onstage to dance with the cast for the final "Time Warp." For a moment, everything felt shiny and perfect and gay.

I found, and built, a family around whom I can be my true self. Nothing in the world I grew up in showed that this life I have created could ever be an option for me. I have so often felt like I've been stumbling forward without a map. And while queer representation in every facet of media and culture has increased and improved in ways that were unimaginable to me even a decade ago, I am still so very grateful for the lifeline of *Rocky Horror*, extended through space and time to show me that in this world, there is queerness and joy, and that, someplace, one day, I might be able to have both together.

Notes

1. Joseph Bennington-Castro, "How AIDS Remained an Unspoken—But Deadly—Epidemic for Years," *History,* June 1, 2020, https://www.history.com/news/aids-epidemic-ronald-reagan.
2. Jerry Falwell and Troy Perry, "Jerry Falwell and Troy Perry debate the morality of AIDS in 1983," aired July 6, 1983, on *CBC*, https://www.cbc.ca/player/play/video/1.3332889.
3. Jack King, "The Drama That Raged Against Reagan's America," *BBC*, October 19, 2020, https://www.bbc.com/culture/article/20201019-the-drama-that-raged-against-reagans-america.
4. Lisa Cisneros, "40 Years of AIDS: A Timeline of the Epidemic," USCF News, June 4, 2021, https://www.ucsf.edu/news/2021/06/420686/40-years-aids-timeline-epidemic.
5. Scottie Andrew, "'Ellen' Came Out as Gay Nearly 30 Years Ago. TV Hasn't Been the Same," *CNN*, October 7, 2024, https://www.cnn.com/2024/10/06/entertainment/ellen-degeneres-coming-out-sitcom-cec/index.html.
6. "Our Story," Matthew Shepard Foundation, accessed December 1, 2024, https://www.matthewshepard.org/about-us/our-story/.

Tinted

Rosie Long Decter

THE RUMOR WAS that our principal thought she was saying yes to *Little Shop of Horrors*. Looking back, it seems likely that she didn't know what she was agreeing to when she signed off on a high school production of *The Rocky Horror Show*.

My high school was casually violent, conservative in an absent-minded way. It was easy to ignore as long as you could slip into the mold and stiffen.

Perched at the top of a sloped driveway, looking out onto a leafy neighborhood in Toronto's west end, the school had a grandiose air. Our auditorium held a famous Group of Seven mural, and our school cheer bore a passing resemblance to the Yale fight song.

We had a few gay teachers and a student group for queer kids, SASS—Students Against Sexual Stereotyping. One year during Pride week, the school raised a rainbow flag outside the front doors, but it was ultimately torn down.

In 2010, the year our young, ambitious drama teacher decided to stage a teenage *Rocky Horror*, I was fifteen. I had a sense, by that time, that my desires were accumulating in particular ways. I knew I had been intensely, even unhealthily attached to my middle school best friend, and also that I liked thinking about boobs. I didn't talk about it. *Glee* was doing its best to change the hearts of every homophobe in North America, but "gay" was still an insult, and high school still a hazard.

When I found out we were putting on *Rocky Horror*, I was crestfallen. I had seen bits and pieces of the film as a kid. I was afraid of it. It felt garish and strange and vaguely threatening. A door to a world gone wrong.

My friend Anthony was also unsure. Anthony was a saxophone player. We met in band class and bonded over a shared love of musicals. His mother had been a singer and his father a jazz aficionado, and they came to every school concert. They were divorced, but the kind of divorced couple where you think, *they must have really been something together*. Kids in our grade teased Anthony and called him gay. He insisted he wasn't. In our freshman year, he had told our friends he had a crush on me.

We both auditioned. I performed—what else—"Defying Gravity" from *Wicked*. When the drama teacher asked if I was auditioning for any part in particular, I said no. None of the characters spoke to me.

Anthony and I were cast in the chorus. The ensemble was mostly juniors and seniors, with a few of us sophomores and two freshmen. I watched the movie in full before rehearsals started in January, and though I could now follow the plot, the emotion still didn't translate. Rather than draw me into its otherworldly thrills, *Rocky Horror* left me feeling alienated, on the outside of Dr. Frank-N-Furter's mansion looking in.

Around the time rehearsals started, I had my first kiss. A boy I was friends with invited me over, and when we were lying on the couch in his basement he said, *Hey, I think we should secretly date*. He had already struck out with my best friend, so I was next in line. Then he pointed to his lips and I kissed him.

When we made out for the first time, it was very wet, like pushing together two overripe avocados, and I thought *oh, I'm never doing that again*.

Putting on a show requires deconstructing it. You learn the songs and scenes out of order, slotting them all into place in your head. Then during tech week, you run through it in order, hoping to stitch it together into a natural progression shortly before you have to sell it all to the audience. That process can make it hard to understand the arc of a piece, the way it's meant to build and unfold.

Pulling apart *Rocky Horror*, though, gave me a slow mode of entry. One by one, the songs and scenes worked their way into my nervous system. Individually, they seemed less inscrutable than when taken all together as one jarring fever dream.

It helped that the music was a gold mine of full-throttle theatrics, dripping in excess. When we learned the backing vocals for songs like "Hot Patootie" and "Make You a Man," their rock and roll dramatics started to cohere for me, slotting into my brain next to Freddie Mercury, Tina Turner, and Green Day. Anthony and I learned to love *Rocky* as we practiced each note, memorized each step, posing onstage in Frank's make-believe mansion.

I also started to see my peers differently. Alyssa, a blond keener who usually annoyed me at choir practice, now seemed intimidating as she adopted Riff Raff's vocal tics. Sam, a popular party girl I wouldn't have expected to go near a drama class, became a sultry, beguiling Magenta.

Doe-eyed Sophie seemed to transform just as much as her character, embodying Janet's hero's journey from sheltered prude to proud slut. It was mesmerizing listening to her shape her clear falsetto into lusty gasps on "Touch-a Touch-a Touch-a Touch Me" without pause or misgiving. She tapped into something that I thought we were meant to keep quiet.

And then there was Clara, a senior I had never seen before, our Frank. She had dark curls and a hint of rasp in her voice, and she stepped into Frank's seductive confidence with natural ease, completely at home in his lab. Where Tim Curry played Frank as an enormous, larger-than-life presence, Clara played him coolly, matter-of-fact, as if we should be so lucky to share his stage.

When we blocked "Sweet Transvestite," our teachers encouraged the chorus members to fawn over Frank, servants to his whim. I remember looking up at Clara, following her as she led us around the stage, and hoping her eyes would land on me, just for a moment.

My boyfriend and I did make out again. I started to like the sensation of pressing against someone, leaning into friction, feeling tension rising. I wrote little songs about him. I bought him a teddy bear on Valentine's Day and he made me a mix CD. I liked when he sucked on my neck.

He kept wanting more, and I got very good at saying no. It wasn't that I didn't want to explore, but I couldn't wrap my head around sharing that part of my body with someone yet. Those pieces of myself still felt taboo. So much could go wrong. The more he asked, the less I wanted to try. He told me it was causing him physical pain. He told me he loved me, and I said *thank you*.

His best friend suggested I start masturbating. His logic was that if I knew how it felt, I might be more likely to want it from someone else. Giving in, I started touching myself. It didn't make me want to have sex, but it did make me want to keep masturbating.

He broke up with me shortly after.

I fell behind in my classes and became a bore to my friends. I spent more and more of my time on Tumblr. But I could still turn it on for *Rocky*, sinking my self-pity into the show's histrionics.

As opening night approached, I became a full *Rocky* convert. I worked up the courage to pitch myself for a solo in the opening number and was cast as one of four Usherettes who stalked the aisles, transporting audience members into the B-movie mood. If some aspects of the show still eluded me—what was Meat Loaf's deal, exactly?—I felt like I understood the trajectory of a descent into something seedy and unfamiliar, the discovery of pleasure and danger.

"Rose Tint My World," the nine-minute set piece in the third act, which builds to *Rocky*'s climax, became my favorite part of the show. At that point in the narrative, heroes Brad and Janet, alongside Frank's acolytes, Columbia and Rocky, have been trapped and turned to stone. Frank unfreezes them to perform, in corsets and feather boas, an impromptu cabaret.

Columbia is unfrozen first. "It was great when it all began," she sings, describing Frank's nasty habit of throwing over lovers for the latest shiny thing. Rocky and Brad follow, narrating newfound sexual drives that enthrall and terrify them. "Take this dream away," Brad begs.

For Columbia, Rocky, and Brad, the rose that tints their world is a stupor, something they feel powerless against. For Janet, though, it's euphoria.

"I feel released / bad times deceased / my confidence has increased," she sings. In Frank's mansion, Janet discovers a hunger that moves her to break from the past. Rose colors every-thing, making her world anew.

Then Frank takes the spotlight. Over twinkling piano, he sings about a moment of queer recognition: "Whatever happened to Fay Wray / that delicate satin-draped frame?" he asks. "As it clung to her thigh / how I started to cry / 'cause I wanted to be dressed just the same." In the movie, as Frank sings, the RKO movie studio logo is projected behind him, positioning him as a classic Hollywood starlet like Wray herself, enacting his dream.

Frank embraces this longing, turning it into an instruction. "Give yourself over / to absolute pleasure," he intones. "Don't dream it, be it."

The other cabaret performers join in, repeating the phrase. "Don't dream it, be it" becomes a communal refrain, something that collectively might come to life.

When we performed "Rose Tint My World," the directors had us line up in front of the stage. They told us to act like we were indulging in absolute pleasure during Frank's solo. Initially, as we rehearsed, I faked it, taking steps like a kid in her mom's heels. But soon I found myself slipping into the feeling. I stretched out my arms seductively, ran my hands down my stockings, surrounded by friends doing the same, all of us pretending like we knew what lust meant, or starting to find out.

Whoever we were during school hours, as we performed "Rose," we became a chorus of freaks. Fantasy and reality blurred, and it didn't particularly matter whether it was a dream or not. To mime desire was to live it.

We got our costumes before the dress rehearsal. The leads were faithful to the movie: Sophie in Janet's pristine white bra, Clara in Frank's black lingerie, our curly-headed Rocky in tiny gold shorts.

The chorus members wore brightly colored tutus and black leather vests. Anthony was the only boy in the ensemble and he wore the skirt well. I liked the tutu but I loved the vest. In our lipstick and leather, we both looked changed, me and Anthony. Like and unlike ourselves.

The actual performances of our two-night run went by like a bender, all adrenaline and collapse. I heard afterward that the principal was shocked by the show—so was my dad—but nothing came of it, no statement or reprimand. We were a brief charge of alterity into a school that thrived on sameness, a wrinkle easily smoothed.

The next year, Anthony and I started a glee club together. Some of our *Rocky Horror* friends joined. In our final year of high school, Anthony came out to me. I was grateful for his trust, an intimacy built by singing other people's songs together, developing our own cultural shorthand. We had elbowed out some breathing room in that school and filled it with extravagant noise.

Around graduation, I came out too. My yearbook quote was "Don't dream it, be it." It took another four years until I started dating girls, and more still until I felt confident about sex, like I could speak what I wanted into the world.

Dreaming it and being it are not really sequential acts. Becoming is a circuitous endeavor.

"Don't dream it, be it" is the motto of a spectacular antihero, a hedonist and scientist and purveyor of beautiful things. Frank suffers from delusions of grandeur—and dreams those delusions into being.

Of course, things end badly for Frank. His dream is snuffed out by Magenta and Riff Raff, who declare Frank's indulgence a liability. The party is over, absolute pleasure too dangerous to permit. But Brad and, especially, Janet, are forever changed by what happened in the mansion. Where once she wanted a ring and flowers, now Janet needs more.

Through audience surrogates Brad and Janet, *Rocky Horror* works to seduce viewers into otherness, via the rose-tinted pleasures of excess. If our high school production felt radical to me at the time, I realize now that teens have been performing *Rocky Horror* for decades, acting it out at midnight screenings, seeking it out at repertory theaters and drag shows, teaching it to each other at parties.

Rocky's queer style is referential, steeped in early rock and roll and Hollywood Golden Age nostalgia. Frank recognizes his gender nonconformity watching old movies and faded stars; younger generations recognize their queerness watching Frank. An aesthetic repertoire is passed on, like a recipe or a theory.

If I wasn't yet ready to date girls, *Rocky Horror* gave me a window into what my dreams could become.

Like learning to kiss or singing in a choir, performing in *Rocky* introduced me to new kinds of feeling. I never saw clearly again.

Asexuality in Transylvania

Genevieve Hammang

IT'S MY JUNIOR YEAR in college when I find myself standing onstage at Santa Cruz Cinema in a line of virgins. *Rocky Horror Picture Show* virgins, to be precise. We are facing a crowd of drunk, laughing college students and graduates. This is a less traditional place, so our virgin *V*'s are scrawled in red lipstick in many different places: on a cheek, an arm, a leg. Mine is cradled in the shallow V-neck of my dress. Though my skirt is knee-length and my tights are opaque, I feel as exposed as the gentleman next to me wearing only booty shorts.

I wish I knew someone in the audience.

Since we're in "quirky" Santa Cruz, it's also themed: Pokémon. I had no ideas for a costume, but I have seen at least one man wearing a luxurious fake fur vest, a gold thong, and nothing else.

Our Dr. Frank-N-Furter for the evening is the emcee. Light glances off the sparkles on her corset as she announces the game at hand: Each of these *Rocky Horror* virgins, who have never seen a live shadow cast of the movie, must compete to become the Virgin Sacrifice. Who wins? Whoever makes the most convincing Pokémon orgasm noise.

Fuck me.

Dr. Frank-N-Furter goes down the line of virgin competitors, assigning each of us a Pokémon to mimic. As she gives me mine,

Clefairy, my mind goes blank. I've never excelled at improv. What does this Pokémon even look like? I had a poster of the original 150 Pokémon on my wall for ten years but now, under pressure, I can't remember a single one.

Out of time. Even though we've only had a few seconds to think, Dr. Frank-N-Furter is already going down the line again, asking for our best orgasms. But nobody else is trying to tailor their noise to their Pokémon. They're just enthusiastically moaning away.

When it's my turn, I grab my hair with one hand, hitch up the front of my skirt with the other, and howl "CLEFAIRY" in my best orgiastic voice. Then I let my knees give way and fall flat on my back like I'm an '80s rock star wailing on a guitar.

The crowd goes wild.

That night, even I wouldn't have guessed I was asexual.

I've always loved romance.

I devoured every shade of the genre through middle and high school. My stomach fluttered over tender confessions and stumbled outright over sex scenes.

I dreamed of my very own prince. Or at least a hot senior to make out with.

Neither ever came.

It was easy enough to dismiss at the time. I had crushes, but there was never the right moment to act on them. First, I was too awkward to try. Then I was too busy with schoolwork and college applications.

As the years went on, the reasons changed: I intimidated people. I had too much reading to finish. I was too in love with my classes to focus on people. Every time I met up with friends from high school, they'd ask about my love life and I'd wave off their questions with a smile. I was comfortable in my singleness.

But from time to time, I still wondered.

I end up tying with one of my neighbors for the title of Virgin Sacrifice. This complicates the game.

For anyone who's never seen a shadow cast of *The Rocky Horror Picture Show*, let me explain. During the show, a live cast acts out every scene while the film is playing. Every actor wears a full costume and everyone in the audience is invited to do the same if they wish. Audience members shout responses to the film's lines and lyrics as they play onscreen. Props are distributed for more physical jokes, like viewers putting a newspaper over their heads during the rain scene or throwing toast. It feels like watching a favorite movie with a group of friends, but your group fills up an entire theater.

The Virgin Sacrifice comes into play about halfway into the movie, during the scene in which the sensuous Dr. Frank-N-Furter separates and seduces both of the movie's virginal protagonists. Onstage in the theater, the Virgin Sacrifice performs a sexual act. In Santa Cruz, this is not literal—at most, it involves partial nudity and sticky food.

Normally, the Virgin Sacrifice does this with Dr. Frank-N-Furter. Tonight, I'll be doing it with the other winner.

Onstage.

In front of a packed theater.

Maybe it's a good thing I don't know anyone in the audience.

I knew what the word "asexual" meant by the time I graduated college, but it wasn't until several months later that the term really caught my attention. Living at home and without a job, I felt more lost by the day. Tumblr became a refuge and an education for me. Discussions of race, gender, and sexual identity piled up in my feed. I read each with interest and growing humility, but never really connected with them.

Until I saw the words "turned on by sex in stories but not with other people." I froze—and then scrolled past the post.

I still regret not exploring that further. But this term, this new definition of a familiar word, stuck with me.

It soon became an anchor. Words are heavy, especially those of identity, but this one felt right. By December, I'd come to terms with the idea, even if only to myself.

When the seduction scene starts to play onscreen, my co-winning Virgin Sacrifice and I are summoned. Before walking onstage, the actress playing Dr. Frank-N-Furter briefly explains the plan. My cowinner will take off his shirt and she will cover his chest in chocolate syrup and have him hold a chocolate kiss between his teeth. From there, it's up to me to lick all the syrup off and grab the kiss—without using my hands.

Simple enough. Even if a woman has to do all the work.

As we walk onto the stage and Dr. Frank-N-Furter starts prepping my cowinner, I consider what I'm about to do. Acting has always been fun for me. I never took theater because I felt it was A Little Much, but I'd read aloud as Romeo in my English class for our entire unit on Shakespeare and I'd enjoyed the skits in French class. Without a doubt, the best part was *always* the audience's reaction. What could I do to get a rise out of this group?

I'm wearing a thin white shift and tights under my dress tonight. So when Dr. Frank-N-Furter finishes her prep and steps back, I make a show out of stripping off the dress. The crowd cheers and hoots their drunken delight.

Then I get to work.

I didn't come out to anyone until two years after college. I don't know why. At the start, it felt too new, too fragile. I didn't want to defend it. Even later, once I was more comfortable, I couldn't think of a way to bring it up. It was a big deal, but I didn't want to steamroll over every conversation by announcing, "Hey, I'm asexual!" I wanted it to feel natural.

When I came out to my sister just before Christmas, I'm not sure it felt "natural." But it did feel right. And that ended up being more important. She listened and asked a few questions. She thanked me for telling her. She told me she loved me. And that was that.

A few months later, she sent me a letter and a package for my birthday. In the letter, she said that she'd tried to find books or stories about being asexual, but hadn't liked any of them. So she told me I should make my own. In the package was a blank sketchbook and markers.

I've cried a lot over my sister in the years since, but that was one of the few times that I was also smiling.

I start at his navel. I drop to my knees, and the crowd behind me roars with laughter. I had expected to be more nervous at the prospect of *licking* someone, but their cheers propel me onward.

I scoop up the bottom of the chocolate happy trail with the confidence of someone much, much drunker. I need to finish this before the seduction scene onscreen is over, but I do my best to draw it out. I lick up his belly in rough zigzags. When I reach his chest, I pay special attention to the sensitive skin around his nipples.

By this point, the movie and the crowd are so loud that I can't see or hear my cowinner's reaction. He stands stock-still with his arms out the entire time. As far as I can tell, he isn't turned on by this display. But isn't that the point? I'm putting the "play" back in display.

I haven't gotten all the chocolate off his chest, but by now I've reached his neck. So I pull back and straighten to my full height. I'm just a little taller than him.

I hover a few centimeters from his lips. I gently grab the tip of the chocolate with my teeth and pull out. The prize is mine and the crowd screams.

It's the closest to a kiss I've ever come.

Then it's done. We both give a bow, I grab my dress, and I float back to my seat. My tights are ripped at the knees and it's two-a.m. cold when the show finally lets out.

But several strangers stop to say hello and tell me how much they liked my performance. I smile the whole way home.

It's been a long time since the night I dropped to my knees in front of an audience full of strangers, longer than I've identified as asexual. I wrote this essay years ago, and when I pulled it out again for the *Absolute Pleasure* anthology, I expected that

I'd need to update it substantially. I was such a different person then.

But reading it, I found that perhaps I wasn't so different after all: My first time at *The Rocky Horror Picture Show* shadow cast remains a good case study of my complicated relationship with sex. It just needs a little recontextualization.

I went to many more *Rocky Horror* showings at Santa Cruz Cinema to support friends in the cast. The screenings were always a blast, an assault on the senses. At the time, I had only the faintest inklings of being some degree of bi- or pansexual, let alone asexual, but it was my first exposure to being part of the queer community, and it was lovely. Though I'm no longer in touch with some of those friends, the memories are still warm and bright and loud.

Ironically, I'm not very performative in my queerness. I dislike being sunburnt and wading through crowds at Pride, and even before COVID-19, I avoided big groups of people. For all that I'm a ham, I keep my public and private lives separate, and my queerness has always been a private thing. The people who know me know.

Then again, maybe I've just never really felt like I was a part of the queer community. I've never experienced face-to-face dismissal of my asexuality, but mostly that's because I don't talk about it. I know many asexual people much braver than me who have taken that risk and been disappointed. Staying quiet about my own identity has protected me from that pain, but at the cost of alienation.

Things have changed a lot since that night onstage. For me, for everyone. And not all for the good. I understand myself so much better now. But I look at the attacks on queer communities, the hateful transphobic shit people spew online and offline, and the bans on queer books across the United States, and I worry. I worry a lot about the future of the queer community, about kids who are just learning the language to better understand themselves. I see echoes of hateful movements from decades before. I wish I'd had access to some of the stories so many people are trying to blot out.

So maybe it's worth it be a little less private about this part of my life. Here goes:

I love porn and romance, but I've never been turned on by another person. I've had crushes, but I've never wanted to sleep with any of them. And I love, love, love performing sexuality, but for me, that's all it is. It's play. It's performance. I'll always crack dirty jokes, get butterflies in my stomach over a touching or steamy passage in a romance novel, and channel Mae West when I go to karaoke. But that's all I'm interested in.

When I think about *The Rocky Horror Picture Show*, I think about that night onstage and how tied up it is in the way I perceive my sexuality and my identity. I think about what it means for so many other members of the queer community, both loud and silent.

I'm asexual. That means a lot of things for a lot of different people. For me, being asexual doesn't mean being uninterested in sex. It just means my libido is a little less active than my taste for drama.

Time Slip:
Rewinding *Rocky Horror*

Mel King

I.

The summer before seventh grade, I came out as gay to my parents and one friend because I had a crush on the girl who sat in front of me in chorus. I was twelve and was the only queer person I knew. It was the year 2000, and I had few models for my future, aside from *Buffy*, Ellen, maybe *Will & Grace*. Around a year before I came out, Matthew Shepard, a white boy in Wyoming, had been beaten and left to die on a fence. When I came out to my mother, she said she was afraid my life would be hard. Later, she'd tell me she couldn't bring herself to ask: If it could happen to Matthew Shepard, could it happen to you? What I couldn't yet articulate was that I would risk everything for a chance to figure out who I might be.

After I told my father, he made me a mixtape: Indigo Girls' self-titled album on one side, *Brave & Crazy* by Melissa Etheridge on the other. He may not always communicate with words, but he finds a way to make his feelings clear. It was from him that I learned how to be a fan. Any actor, musician, or author would be lucky to have my father as a fan because once he decides he likes someone's oeuvre, he's all in. He kept buying Sinéad O'Connor's records after the Pope photo rip. He has read every book published by the other Stephen King, plus all the books he recommended. He's read, listened to, watched, and drunk everything Bob Dylan has put his name on. He doesn't mind when someone he loves gets weird; he is committed to their artistic journey. My father learned about Tim Curry in the mid-'70s when friends from my parents' theater group returned from London raving about *The Rocky Horror Show*. He bought the soundtrack and every other record and movie featuring Tim Curry. I grew up knowing the name because he featured prominently in one of my favorite childhood movies, *FernGully: The Last Rainforest*, as the terrifying evil smoke monster Hexxus. He was also in the movie version of Stephen King's *IT*, which I saw too young and which prompted my early—and persistent—fear of clowns. My parents paid no attention to parental guidance warnings; for them, good art was worth sharing at any age.

When my father suggested watching *The Rocky Horror Picture Show*, I balked. But his lifelong love of horror and genuine desire to get my brother and me interested in things he liked moved my fear to curiosity. My brother liked screening cult classics like *Pinhead* and *Rocky Horror* for his friends. He let me hang out with them because I was quiet, thoughtful, and easy to be around. I wasn't really watching the movies anyway; I was too busy nursing big, swooning crushes on several of his friends. The night he screened *The Rocky Horror Picture Show*, I wanted to woo and impress the pretty older sister of a girl in my grade.

My father kept most of his memorabilia in the basement family room. He knelt beside the VHS rack and pulled out a thick black book, fraying at the binding. The cover depicted a giant set of red lips, the lower lip bitten seductively by the front two teeth. Below the lips, *THE ROCKY HORROR PICTURE SHOW* appeared in a bloody font that felt familiar. When I was six or seven, I overheard my father singing "The End of the World" by Skeeter Davis, and I fell in love with the mournful melody. After that, he made me a tape of songs from his early '50s childhood about teenage tragedies, car crashes, and suicides. He had lettered the title "Teenage Death Songs" along the edge of the paper cassette tape insert so it looked like it was bleeding, just like this. Something stirred in me, like a new neural connection forming to try to understand what he wanted me to know. Dad popped the tape into the VCR, and we sat down to watch.

What did I think the first time I saw *Rocky Horror*? I realized this was a very different musical than I had ever seen. I felt confused by the camp and the glam. And yet, something about the sexual nature and the over-the-top performance felt dangerous and thrilling to my preteen self.

Throughout the film, my dad responded to some of the dialogue with pithy little lines.

"Dad, are you just making all that up?" I asked him after a few scenes.

"Not at all! It's such a cult classic that fans started writing all of these callbacks, and they spread. They're even in the book." He flipped through his big book of *Rocky Horror* and directed my attention to the callback section. What was this world my father was introducing me to?

I felt familiar stirrings low in my core at the sight of Susan Sarandon, wet in the rain or in her ripped slip. I recognized her immediately, already beloved to me from her role in *The Witches of Eastwick*. There was a decidedly queer sensibility to this spectacle I was watching, with different couples pairing off and switching up. Frank's eyes on Rocky's body. Even Eddie on the motorcycle felt like a butch icon. What I couldn't figure out, though, as I laughed and tried to do the Time Warp for the very first time, was whether or not queer people were the butt of the joke. I had heard the word "transvestite" and even "transsexual" on shows like Maury, Jerry Springer, and Sally Jessie Raphael, but it was always derogatory, making a spectacle of the people in the hot seat. I knew the acronym LGBT, but I'd never understood the "T." Hearing this music, watching Dr. Frank-N-Furter in fishnets and a corset, was this reclamation of the term? Was this gender play for the rock-and-roll fun of it? Or were the queer and trans aliens simply an easy target for a B-horror movie? Did my dad want me to see it and feel seen?

Though there is a beloved family photo of me as a toddler in a pink feather boa, at twelve, I wanted to be less visible. I was more comfortable receding into the shadows than standing in the light.

II.

Sometime after the *Buffy* musical episode "Once More, With Feeling" aired in 2001, I searched the internet for videos of Amber Benson singing. Amber Benson played the shy Tara, Willow's girlfriend. After a long-running crush on Clea DuVall, I was elated to learn I could crush anew. A fuzzy clip came up from VH1's *Rocky Horror 25: Anniversary Special.* In the video, the actress Elissa Donovan catches the audience up on where we are in the movie. "After disposing of Eddie, Frank turned his attention to Rocky, and then to Janet, and then to Brad. Janet, meanwhile, formed a special 'bond' with Rocky, as is about to be told to us by Amber Benson." Then the clip cuts to the scene from the film with Magenta and Columbia filing their nails and watching the monitors. "Tell us about it, Janet." Suddenly, Amber Benson is onstage in a bra and torn slip skirt, flanked by two gargoyles, with a screen playing the scene from the movie behind her. By the time she hit the chorus, she was singing well and going for it, but I was barely listening. I was watching Amber Benson dancing in a bra and was on fire. To have my queer icon singing "Touch-a Touch-a Touch-a Touch Me" made the desirous stirrings during my first viewing of the film seem negligible.

Sometimes, I imagined that I could will away my desires. Most of my friends in eighth grade had people to crush on whom they could kiss if the sparks aligned. I didn't yet know anyone who would risk dating me, but my celebrity crushes gave me a dim flicker of hope.

III.

On a frigid night in 2002, my father drove us both to the Albany Civic Theater for a live production of *Rocky Horror*. He had explained that shadow casts often acted out key scenes in front of the movie, but this was an actual musical production. I'm sure I wore my six-star rainbow shirt or my Pride seat-belt belt (staples for baby queers everywhere). I hoped there would be other queer people in the audience, that they would see me and know that I was one of them. But even if I didn't see any other visibly queer people, I believed that anyone choosing to spend time watching *Rocky Horror* would at least be comfortable with my presence.

I loved the electricity in the air and how everyone in the audience seemed to know what to do and say at different parts. I loved that my dad knew the show well enough to join in. I didn't know it well, so it felt like I was hovering outside the group, a feeling that thrummed below the surface for me most days. I couldn't help but wonder what it might feel like to be in this audience if I were there with another queer person. Watching the performance, I imagined where I might fit into that strange world. Who would I be? With my love of pompadours, leather jackets, and motorcycles, I thought Meat Loaf as Eddie might come closest, but even then, before I had considered my gender, I worried someone else might read me as girlish and think I'd be Columbia.

After the show, our car got stuck on the ice in the parking lot, and we had to call Triple-A. While waiting in the cold, our breath hanging in the air, we hummed the songs and debriefed the show. My dad liked how they staged Rocky's Frankenstein's-monster-like birth; Frankenstein remains his favorite monster. Though I couldn't have said it at the time, for as much as I adored the show, what I liked best was that my father saw an opportunity to connect with his queer kid and took it. Back then, I yearned to hear him say aloud that he was intentionally trying to bond; there's a sweetness in the understatement that I can see only in hindsight. In sharing this strange world of artistic weirdos, he offered an alternative path I might never have seen.

IV.

I didn't understand the word "transgender" until fall of 2003, a word given to me like a gift from my friend Paddy. I met Paddy at the open mic she hosted in downtown Albany. Twelve years my senior, she saw in me a queer kid in desperate need of guidance and, with my mother's permission, started driving me home. For weeks, Paddy had been slowly introducing me to new concepts like chest binding and packing. Paddy would mention that she used a strap-on, or that she shopped for clothes in the men's department. Nothing explicit, just one person sharing information with another. Sitting in her car in my driveway that night, it felt like we were crossing a threshold.

Paddy cleared her throat. "Listen, Mel. I'm TG, and I think you are, too."

I knew she was telling me something big, but I couldn't scramble those letters into meaning. "What's TG?"

"It's short for 'transgender.' It means I was born a girl, but that's not really who I am. Does that make sense?"

I could feel a slight tremble in my hands. I nodded, but I didn't know. I knew I liked girls, but I had never heard anyone say anything like what Paddy had told me. We had talked about how "gay" and "lesbian" weren't words that described us, that something felt missing. Paddy once said, "I can think of nothing girlier than two girls together." I felt a twinge of recognition, but I didn't know why.

She handed me a battered copy of *Stone Butch Blues* by Leslie Feinberg (Z"L) and my whole world cracked open.

Once I found the language, I felt myself alight, like a single word had the power of an incantation. I could speak myself into being again and again. My early practice of saying "TG. Transgender. I'm transgender," in front of the bathroom mirror would serve me well later when I would have to hold firm in my knowledge of myself. In the beginning, it felt exhilarating enough to have a word.

There was something about the "gender" in "transgender" that felt profoundly apt. "Transvestite" was too much about gender expression, and "transsexual" felt both clinical and fetishized. The word "transsexual," always said with the sibilant *s* and in red lips like the opening to *Rocky Horror,* terrified me. But I had not understood that I had a gender until I suddenly understood that mine might be more complicated. I felt uncomfortable all the time in my gendered body. I came out knowing I liked women, but a label like "lesbian" didn't entirely fit. I thought I'd grow up to be Shawn Hunter from *Boy Meets World,* and I knew I would grow up to be a boy. For as long as I could remember, I had told myself that if it didn't happen by my sixteenth birthday, it wouldn't ever happen. I turned sixteen that year.

There's a moment in *Stone Butch Blues* where Jess says, "I don't like being a neither," and hir girlfriend says, "there are other ways to be than either-or." At sixteen, I felt like a "neither," like I didn't belong where everyone around me thought I did. I felt like I was drowning; that book was a life raft.

V.

The following summer, my girlfriend did a precollege program at Harvard. We had one year left before she'd be off to college for real. I visited her in Cambridge a few times that summer. My mother drove me for my first visit, but hated the drivers and the poorly marked one-way loops of the city so much that she bought me a bus ticket to Worcester so she could pick me up there on the trip home. After my mother swore off Boston, I rode with my friend Alex. Five or so of us would pack into his zippy red Pontiac Sunfire and head east, trading off who got to sit shotgun. The rest of them would bunk on the dorm floor, but I got to stay in the top bunk bed with my girlfriend. It all felt so grown-up. I loved my weekends in Boston because we had no one to stop us from doing what we wanted. It felt like a taste of the freedom to come in life beyond high school.

The Lowe's Theater showed a shadow-cast screening of *Rocky Horror* every Saturday. We went every time I visited, which meant I became practiced in the ways of the live performance. I was never denoted a virgin, though, because I had already seen a live performance—with my dad. I watched my friends who had never seen it live before get called up onstage to pop a balloon on a chair or mime sexual acts.

What I loved about going to those shows was that it was a way for queers and queer-adjacent weirdos to come together in not-so-secret. I still wasn't sure that queer people weren't the butt of the joke, but at least there were more of us around. There was something about hiding in plain sight, being trans in a room full of people singing about transsexuals and transvestites, that made me feel invisible and unseen on one hand and like an undercover agent on the other. When the audience and cast sang about the transsexuals from Transylvania, they weren't singing about me. I was never going to be a fishnet-and-corset trans person, the campy queen at the end of *Rocky Horror*. Whatever my masculinity might look like in the future, I was a different kind of trans. Maybe Dr. Frank-N-Furter could make a man in seven days, but the feat seemed impossible to me.

I wrote this about my gender at sixteen: "Through the fog of what lies before me, certain things are clear: I am a person who is not comfortable with my name anymore. I am at odds with gender pronouns. I face almost insurmountable difficulty at the ubiquitous gender checkboxes on identification papers. There is no box for me. I am a gender outlaw." The more I learned about being trans, the more I felt terrified of my uncertain future. And yet, I knew I would choose that fear and unknown over forcing myself to fit into someone else's idea of who I should be. If I got lucky, I might find a crew of trans alien weirdos who would see me as one of their own. *Rocky Horror* was full of gender outlaws, and even if nobody but me felt like that in the theater that summer, it gave everyone permission to fuck around with gender for a night.

VI.

My younger self demanded so much from *Rocky Horror*. I wanted it to show me to myself. I wanted it to have been dreamed into being by queer and trans people. Mostly, I wanted more expansive representations of gender on film when I needed them most. Something that didn't present transsexual as one image. Who knows what could have cracked open for me sooner if I could have seen trans masculinity on the silver screen? There is a line between gender fucking for rock and roll and gender fucking for real. For some of us, gender fucking is a matter of life and death, actual survival. And yet, for the kid I was, *Rocky Horror* offered a window into pleasure with a queer sensibility, something I had never seen before. It offered a release valve, maybe even a few deep moments of feeling less alone in the world.

At thirty-six, twenty years after I first came out as trans, I'm fully here for a transsexual alien seduction crew—the gender fuckery, the sexiness, and the decadence. The gift of *Rocky Horror* is that it has both deepened and lightened for me with time. I need less from it now, which means that I can enjoy the pleasure and play more. I don't need to see myself mirrored back because I've learned how to build a body, a masculinity, a queerness, and a community that feels like my own. I can also delight in the ways that a film can play with gender and sexuality and offer permission to the audience to do so as well. In the current political firestorm taking direct aim at trans people, we are in desperate need of more gender freedom. Anywhere that people can loosen the reins of the gender binary creates a little more liberation for us all. Until we can all be our most liberated, gender-full or gender-free selves, I take some comfort in knowing there might be a planet out there that might feel to this aging trans man like going home.

Midnight Picture Show

Heather O. Petrocelli

MIDNIGHT IS THE queer hour, the sacred time when LGBTQIA+
people have carved out space for authentic self-expression and
collective connection. Under cover of darkness, away from the
scrutinizing gaze of normative society, queer communities
have long gathered with chosen family in underground clubs,
secret bars, and private homes to express our true selves. These
nocturnal sanctuaries are places of liberation where gender
can be fluid and sexuality can be free. The significance of
midnight to the queer community is powerfully demonstrated
in *The Rocky Horror Picture Show,* a parody sci-fi horror film
that was initially a box-office disaster but achieved cult status
through participatory screenings, which are both undeniably
queer and inextricably tethered to midnight. Brad and Janet,
the presumed heterosexual couple whose journey the movie
follows, seek out and receive help they did not know they needed
or wanted, experiencing a queer sexual awakening thanks to
the character who functions as a gateway to queerness: Dr.
Frank-N-Furter, whom present-day audiences might see as
both pansexual and genderqueer. The queer community's cult
adoption of *Rocky Horror* through midnight screenings, shadow
casts, and audience participation created a self-perpetuating
cycle, as successive generations of queers took the queerness on
the screen and amplified it by playing it out in real time in front
of the screen. This queer response to the film became as much

a part of the experience of the film as the film itself, especially as the shared response became a source of queer belonging and connection. Within *The Rocky Horror Picture Show*, midnight is a significant time for the characters—a liminal space that is significant to queer culture outside of the movie, becoming, then, a spark for an interconnected relationship between queer people and the cult film.

The audience first meets "normal kids" Brad Majors and Janet Weiss in the bright light of day as they attend a "normal" (cisgender, heterosexual) wedding. But it's not simply daylight. The film starts with a shot of the church steeple with a clock that reads 11:57 a.m. Exactly three minutes later, at noon, Brad starts to sing the song "Dammit Janet" during which he awkwardly proposes to Janet, singing, "I want to make you my wife." The film intentionally uses twelve o'clock to establish that midday is a time when normativity rules and cisheteronormativity forces individuals to follow its predictable, conventional trajectory (birth-marriage-procreation-death). After getting a flat tire later that night, Brad and Janet stumble through a rainstorm "in the velvet darkness of the blackest night," following a beacon toward a strange castle. Janet sings, "There's a guiding star, no matter what or who you are." This message of universal welcome and the film's change to a nocturnal setting immediately signal acceptance to queer people, who have long found and made community in and beyond the midnight hour. The film's story arc soars after Brad and Janet enter the castle and the coffin-shaped, skeleton-filled clock strikes midnight. This signals to a queer audience that we have entered a time and place where it is safe to "come out." Midnight opens up a world of possibility where one can cast aside self- or socially imposed limitations. The song that kicks off at midnight in the film, the iconic "Time Warp," invites Brad and Janet to slip into a mind-bending, clock-defying alternative reality: "With a bit of a mind flip / You're into the time slip / And nothing can ever be the same." Midnight invites queers to transcend the bounds of societal norms and connect with who we are. It ushers in queerness through the phantoms, desires, and longing that are usually hidden, yet flourish in the shadows. Midnight is when queer worlds of possibility exist. Midnight, then, is a liminal and transitional borderland between the past and the future, the self and the other. The essence of midnight brims with queer potential, so it's no coincidence that Brad and Janet's journey of liberation begins at midnight.

The portrayal of midnight revelry in *Rocky Horror* directly represents how queers historically have found and made communities at night. There is a long history of straight society terrorizing and policing queer communities through the persecution and criminalization of visible queer life, including nonnormative sexuality and gender expression. For example, authorities in the US and the UK have persecuted people (both cis and trans) for wearing clothes of a gender that are deemed not to match their perceived binary sex. Queer men throughout history have risked violence, entrapment, or life-ruining exposure if they engage the wrong man for physical intimacy. These aren't only problems from the past: In the United States, in reaction to increased visibility and acceptance of queer people in the 1990s and early 2000s, bigots with power are increasingly proposing and passing anti-LGBTQ+ legislation, policies, and practices with the aim of erasing queer people—especially trans people—from public life or even existence. Because of these historic and current persecutions, queers have long sought out the dark, meeting up in places from bars to bathhouses, parks to house parties, to find freedom away from the gaze of cisgender heterosexual society. Gathering in dark, undesirable, transitory, or hidden places has been necessary for queer people to find some semblance of safety. To express ourselves in relative safety, queer people still turn to the underground venues where queer culture has been able to flourish in the dark—finding ourselves and one another in those bars, parks, clubs, saunas, and private parties. Queer people have been and continue to be more vulnerable to persecution, harassment, and violence in the harsh light of day.

In addition to bars and clubs, the cinema offers another important space for queer connection. In darkened theaters, we queers have found ourselves and each other. Moviegoing is like church for many of us, a place where the projection of lights and shadows on the big screen—a reanimated past haunting the present—creates a collective experience, a sense of solidarity, and offers queer people a liminal space to (re)configure a queer past, present, and future that normative society otherwise denies us. I am not the only queer for whom film is more than a passion—it is part of who I am and how I relate to and connect with the world around me, in part because of what the cinema experience has given me. When queers gather in a movie theater, something special happens, especially when the experience is hidden from the gaze of normative society. Queer people (and even some straight people who feel like they fall outside the bounds of normativity in ways other than sexuality or gender) have found and made community among the darkness of midnight movie screenings, as exemplified by the adoption of *The Rocky Horror Picture Show* in 1976 by the queer community in Greenwich Village, then New York City's gay neighborhood. By the time I was old enough to see *Rocky Horror* as a genderqueer teen dyke in the late 1980s, it was already known that the film had been misunderstood and rejected by mainstream audiences but reanimated by queerdos and other outsiders. I was magnetically drawn to it from the very first poster I saw promoting the film. My first *Rocky Horror* screening was the first time I was around a large group of other queers, which was a revelatory experience because the film expanded my understanding of what queerness could be, and also revealed the nature of the queer community, showing me when and how we gather. In the midnight darkness in San Diego, California, that screening transformed an otherwise "normal" place, the single-screen Ken Cinema, into a vibrant, creative queer space created by the audience callbacks and shadow-cast shenanigans.

Since the beginning of cinema-going, there have been different live elements to some film screenings, from live musical accompaniment during the silent movie era to William Castle's incorporation of live gimmicks and effects (such as vibrating seats and audience props) in the 1950s. The 1970s saw the rise of midnight movie culture, including the participatory screenings of *Rocky Horror*. These interactive *Rocky Horror* experiences make the film a key example of live cinema, or screenings that incorporate an in-real-life component alongside or in addition to a filmic presentation. The temporary nature of live cinema, as with live theater, takes on a particular significance in queer culture because this event format offers a cloak of safety to vulnerable, persecuted identities. Since queer people have often needed to exist under the radar to preserve individual and community safety, the impermanent, transitory nature of live shows is valuable *because* the performances and the spaces they create are fleeting and the lack of "evidence" helps queer people avoid persecution and violence for expressing or playing with gender fuckery, bodily autonomy, and sexual freedom. In other words, midnight *Rocky Horror* screenings create space for queer people to participate and express ourselves, transforming a moviegoing experience into an ephemeral live queer cultural event.

It makes sense that *Rocky Horror*, a queer story that takes place during the time "good" and "normal" people are asleep, would have been claimed and reanimated by queer audiences at midnight. The importance of midnight both in the film's text and its exhibition is not coincidental or simply a horror trope—*Rocky Horror* both reflects and creates queer time and space for queer audiences. It is rare to see films featuring liberatory queerness— queer stories that don't reinforce key parts of "straight" society, such as monogamous marriage, child-rearing, and "fitting in." (The tradition of LGBTQIA+ representation in mainstream films usually presents queer stories that are about unfulfilled desire, doomed love, and/or death by murder or suicide—when queerness has not been censored outright.) It's not only the onscreen queer characters but also the queer revelry accompanying a midnight screening of *Rocky Horror* that breaks all normally acceptable theatergoing behaviors. Queer audiences have enthusiastically joined the film's narrator, the Criminologist, when he invites us "on a strange journey," acting as the "unconventional conventionalists" who gather at midnight to revel in queer joy. Queer people and outsiders gathering under the shroud of midnight to watch and participate with a film that features boldly queer performances and celebrates outsiders, subverting mainstream expectations, continues even now to be special and transgressive. *Rocky Horror* teaches and incites collective queer rebellion against societal norms. If a queer person can throw toast and shout sassy responses in a space where they are generally expected to be quiet, they can build confidence to push back against normative society. Queers who go to *Rocky Horror* screenings can revel in both the queer world inside Dr. Frank-N-Furter's castle as well as the queer community that is forged at midnight inside the theater. We find our own "light over at the Frankenstein place," a light that leads to a space which continues to be a refuge and sanctuary for people who need it. That is why *Rocky Horror* has been embraced by queers for generations: Again and again, it facilitates the creation of a midnight queer space that brings nonnormative people together to be, to create, and to connect.

Rocky Horror represents a queer practice of fandom that I call "horrorboros," a circulatory process in which queer horror fandom takes sustenance from itself, continuing to grow ever larger and more visible the more people participate. The more we have discussed the need for queer spaces in horror fandom, the more we have created those queer spaces. And the increased queer spaces in horror fandom further nourish and embolden us. I am in conversation with other queer people who love horror, and my shared experience informs theirs. My work incorporates their voices. My passion feeds theirs, and theirs feeds mine. We are inseparable. There is no beginning nor end, just a circular process in which queer horror fandom feeds itself and continues to grow ever larger by such rich feeding. When queer people see ourselves reflected on the screen—even indirectly, even imperfectly, even monstrously—we reflect it back.

For generations, queer people around the world have seen our existence represented in the camp-horror midnight glory of *Rocky Horror*, a film which both reflects and creates queer space and time. Queer people have embraced the midnight world of the film, and continue to recreate it through reenactment and revelry, further deepening our connection to the film and perpetuating the horrorboros cycle. As Dr. Frank-N-Furter croons: "Don't dream it, be it." From the moment those iconic, disembodied red lips emerge from the dark and sing to us about the "late night, double-feature picture show," we know that, away from the oppressive light of day, we can leave behind the rigid boundaries of normative society and become creatures of the night together.

A Rather Tender Subject

Trey Burnette

MY BODY—thin and boyish, waxed and shaved. Sixteen. My skin—smooth and radiant, scrubbed and prepped, still moist from the shower. On the floor in my bedroom, in front of my full-length mirror, I sat.

Concealer, foundation, powder. Eye shadow—ivory, charcoal, and black. Black eyeliner. Lashes. Lip liner. Lipstick—Russian Red. Brown pencil enhanced the small mole on my left cheek. Duct tape gripped my chest. Cleavage. More duct tape over thong underwear flattened my crotch. Nude, sheer-to-waist pantyhose slipped over my firm, young legs. I stepped into my black French-cut bodysuit, zipped the front, and fastened the hooks up to my breasts. My crown of glory, a dark brown wig that fell just below my collarbone, anchored by a black headband. Black four-inch strappy heels. Black gloves stopped just above my elbows.

In front of the mirror, I was six feet in heels and 120 pounds. My hair was soft and sultry. Smoky eyes were inviting and vulnerable. My skin glowed with youth. My arms were thin and undefined. My bosom was full. A twenty-seven-inch waist to put an arm around. And atop two perfectly shaped legs, an ass that could get someone arrested.

Everything that made me weak as a man made me powerful as a woman.

One thing was missing: jewels.

"Wanny, I'm coming down. Are you ready?" At that point, just a couple of months after her daughter's death, Wanny was ready for anything. The worst had happened.

Wanny—my grandmother—and Aunt Skeeter stood in anticipation at the bottom of the staircase.

"Here I am."

Their eyes blinked and squinted. They smiled, intrigued and fearful. I couldn't help but think of Janet Weiss and Brad Majors seeing Frank-N-Furter for the first time in *The Rocky Horror Picture Show* when he came down in the elevator to greet them. The movie was released before I was born, but I had recently seen it with my best friend, Dan. We loved the outrageousness of it and the freedom the occupants of the castle seemed to have.

"Well, then," said Aunt Skeeter.

If one had to play a part, Skeeter with her naïve and masculine beliefs, so anxious to maintain her square and in-control appearance, would have been Brad.

"I don't know what to say. You look pretty, I guess," said Wanny.

And Wanny, the feminine and curious Janet, ready for and delighted by something new, but discomforted when she remembered not to stray too far from what she has been taught to believe.

"What do you call yourself?" asked Aunt Skeeter.

"Foxy Girl Vivienne."

Skeeter hadn't quite figured out how to handle these moments; she was used to the quiet, perfect child Trey. The one who had hidden much of who he was while his mother was alive, the young man who went to school and got A's and maintained the finite amounts of family harmony. She wanted him back. Life had all changed so quickly, and she had had enough. She went back into the kitchen.

"Wanny, I need some jewelry."

"You can't wear my jewelry; you'll lose it."

"I won't lose it. Don't you have costume jewelry?"

Wanny was different; she was no fool. She may have lived a kind and Christian existence at this point in her life, but she knew the lineage of the family was far from traditional and most certainly never in a place to cast judgment.

"I do somewhere. Come in here."

I followed her into her bedroom, and from her drawer, she pulled out a small box filled with tiny treasures. I sat on the foot of her bed and emptied its contents on top of the bedspread. Wanny stared at me, contemplating her Christian duty to obey the Word and her Southern need for proper accessorizing.

She held up a pair of three-inch, double-row dangle rhine-stone earrings and one coordinating single-strand bracelet. Who knew she was so disco?

"Perfect."

"The Bible doesn't say anything about drag queens." Wanny fidgeted with the bracelet. "This reminds me of the time in the '70s when your Aunt Lanie took me to a club in Nashville. They had the most beautiful Asian singer there; you would have never known she wasn't a real woman." She paused. "I don't think I feel safe having you do this. I don't want someone to kill you."

"Girl, ain't nobody gonna kill me. I'll be safe. Here, I can't fasten this with these gloves on."

Wanny fastened my bracelet and silently prayed.

The stars appeared in the sky, and the warm air blew around me. The rumble of my Mustang's V-8 hummed at fifty miles per hour, and Madonna's voice filled the air: "Vogue." The song had been out for a while but felt more relevant that night. I had learned to escape the pain of life with my imagination, even if only for small moments. I thundered through the old Wood streets of Riverside and down Highland Place. The evening air and about three replays of "Vogue" had recharged me on my drive over to Dan's. The air smelled like semen on his tree-lined street. No one ever said anything about the smell, but I always noticed it. The tires hit the gravel driveway where the trees cleared, and his house sat in the clear overlooking a flood basin. I parked and felt the wheels settle into the loose rock. The music faded.

Dan's brown-and-tan, Craftsman-style house with detailed woodwork and stained glass had beautiful bones but needed attention. On the sturdy cement porch, there were unused items the family couldn't throw in the trash or give to Goodwill. The heavy overhangs needed a fresh coat of paint. I opened the car door, and my black stilettos planted into the rocks; my calves caressed the bottom of the doorjamb. I lifted myself out of the car, untied my headscarf, and tossed it on the front seat. I tousled my hair and crossed the lawn, putting my weight on the balls of my feet so that I didn't sink into the grass. The screen door was shut, but the front door was open, and I could hear the TV blaring while the family's thirty or more pet birds squawked as I sauntered up the steps.

"Hi, Ellen. Hi, Bruce!" Bruce and Ellen were Dan's White American parents who had adopted him when he was a baby still in Vietnam. Dan had six other adopted siblings and two, the oldest brothers, who were Bruce and Ellen's biological kids. His parents had also fostered numerous other kids. Bruce and Ellen had seen most everything and usually the worst of it.

"Dan, Trey's here," Bruce called out and opened the screen. He looked at me from head to toe and back up again, catching his breath. "Hello," he said in a slightly deeper voice than usual.

Ellen popped her back off the couch, sat up straight, and put her hands on the insides of her knees. Her mouth dropped open. "Oh, you look incredible. My, my. I wish I had your figure."

I spun, gave her a wink, and threw my right arm in the air as I fanned out my fingers like I had just revealed a magic trick—"Powder and paint will make you what you ain't."

Dan's bedroom door opened, prompting more squawks from the macaws. The clicks of his crutches on the wood floor grew steadily louder, and black hair bobbed from behind the cages. Dan appeared as Foxy Girl Bianca, my Vietnamese twin. Instead of a bodysuit, she wore a black bustier and black pants that hid her leg braces. Bianca stopped. She used her right hand to clutch her imaginary pearls, looked to her left, and batted her lashes at Bruce and Ellen, a debutant if I ever saw one.

"And where are you ladies off to tonight?" Bruce asked.

"Just clubbing in LA. We'll be home late," Bianca said, shaken by her dad calling her a lady. Dan often tried to be shocking, but he usually got a double dose of his own medicine from his parents' willingness to play along. At nineteen, he had more parental freedom than I did.

"I want to know how you got your boobs," Ellen declared while cupping her breasts to mimic a push-up bra.

"Mother," Bianca gasped.

In their joie de vivre, Bruce and Ellen had outwitted Bianca. Bianca's face flushed pink. She looked me dead in the eyes, placed her crutches in front of her, and said: "Girl, let's go!"

I flipped my hair, gave Bruce and Ellen a wink, and held open the door for Bianca.

"You two be safe," Ellen said, smiling. More seriously, she said, "Drive safely, Trey."

"Vivienne, Ellen. Tonight, it's Vivienne."

"Drive safely, Vivienne." Ellen tilted her head and nodded, agreeing to play along.

"Bye, Ellen. *Bye, Bruce.*"

We sat in the Mustang, wrapping our scarves over our hair and under our chins. I turned the ignition, took a deep breath, and turned to Bianca.

"Are you ready?" I asked.

She grinned. I threw the car in reverse, pulled out of the driveway, and proceeded down Highland Place at five miles per hour.

"Why are we driving so slow? Why is the music off?" Bianca asked.

I placed my finger over my puckered red lips. "Shhhhh. Take a deep breath and smell the night's air," I told Bianca as we crept down Highland Place. I took a deep, dramatic breath like I was smelling freshly ground French roast coffee.

"Girl, you have lost your mind." Bianca looked at me blankly, sniffing the air. "What am I smelling?"

I laughed.

"Your street, girl. Your street smells like semen. You never noticed that? It's the trees."

Bianca took a whiff; her eyes slowly grew bigger.

"Ewwww," Bianca cried out. "It does smell like semen. Oh my God, I never noticed that."

We stopped at Payless Drugstore for breath mints. We parked in a handicap spot and entered the store through the automatic sliding doors. It was overlit with harsh fluorescent light and almost void of customers. We had only a tiny audience that evening: a clerk at the customer service station and a cashier at a checkout station. We walked directly to the cashier and stood behind an elderly White lady buying canned cat food.

I sorted through the various types of gums and mints and settled on a pack of cinnamon Certs, mainly because Certs would go unnoticed tucked in my bra. A man walked in wearing ripped jeans, a rock concert T-shirt, and a ghoulish old-man mask. He had an eight-inch knife dangling from his belt. He headed directly to the back of the store and disappeared.

"Girl, did you see that?" I asked Bianca. "Let's go."

I threw the Certs back onto the shelf, took three steps, and stopped to see that Bianca had not moved.

"No. What?" Bianca asked. She couldn't get her eyes out of the *People* magazine she had her face plowed in, dead set on reading what Soon-Yi saw in Woody Allen.

"Come on, girl; some guy just walked in here with a mask and a knife."

"Girl, are you serious?"

"Yes. Hurry up. I really don't feel like being stabbed tonight."

She set the magazine on top of the candy bars, and we calmly and purposefully walked toward the exit. I wondered if anyone else had seen what I had seen. Was I just seeing things? Everyone was so calm. In the early evening, there were two drag queens in what looked like Dr. Frank-N-Furter costumes and a masked guy with a knife in a drugstore in conservative Riverside, and no one was alarmed. The glass doors opened and then closed behind us. Safe.

We got back into the Mustang.

"Girl, that was crazy," I said.

"I never saw him. What did he look like? Where'd he go?"

"He went to the back of the store. We need to call the cops." I left Bianca in the car and found a pay phone.

"911. What is your emergency?" the dispatcher asked.

"Hi. I was just in Payless Drugstore on the corner of Magnolia and Jurupa, and a man walked in with a knife and a mask."

"Where did he go?"

"Toward the back of the store, but I don't know exactly. My friend and I ran out. He hasn't come out of the store."

"Can you describe him?"

"A White guy in jeans and a rock concert T-shirt. I'll stay in my car until the police arrive and get his license plate if he leaves before they get here. By the way, we're in drag."

"What?"

"We're in drag. My friend and I are dressed as women, but we're not women." I hung up.

Bianca and I waited in the handicapped parking space with the car idling, watching the front door of the drugstore and waiting for the police. The store looked emptier than before; I wondered if he was robbing the place or maybe had people tied up. I finally saw one clerk on the phone through the window.

We watched what appeared to be two cop cars drive slowly with only their parking lights on. "I think the police are here. We can go." I cautiously reversed out of the parking space. Suddenly, four police cars surrounded us. Their bright white spotlights and red and blue flashing lights illuminated everything. Out of nowhere, a helicopter shined its spotlight from above.

Bianca and I looked at each other—*girl*.

"Put your hands up, and don't do anything crazy," I warned Bianca.

From a loudspeaker, a male officer said, "Get out of the car." We got out of the car. I left my door open and calmly stood there. Heels, bodysuit, headband. I had nothing to hide and nowhere to hide it. Bianca got out of the car a little less gracefully than usual and held herself steady by holding onto the side of the Mustang. Three officers approached us.

"I was the one who called 911. The guy with the knife is still inside Payless."

"Don't worry about that; just put your hands on the car," the oldest of the three cops commanded.

I turned around and put my hands on the side of the car. Bianca did the same on the opposite side. I looked down at our scarves, coats, and clutches scattered on the backseat. We locked eyes and stiffened our lips to keep from smiling. We hadn't even reached the freeway, and that was our evening. One officer came up behind me. Another, a blond, made his way behind Bianca. He was ripped and looked juiced and prone to roid rage. Under different circumstances, Bianca would've been flirting with him. The third officer rummaged through the car, only finding our feminine things on the seat.

"Do you have any weapons?" my officer asked. He was old, out of shape, and needed a haircut, which he tried to hide by using too much hair gel.

"No, I'm the one who called 911. We were just in the store buying mints. Didn't the operator tell you I called?"

I stood there with my hands on the car, looking over my shoulder, wondering how I could possibly look like a threat.

The officer behind me cuffed his hands on my glove-covered wrists. I felt the warm breath from his nostrils on my shoulder. His hands moved up my arms to my shoulders and down my back. They came forward around my rib cage and under my breasts. His fingers moved down against my stomach, and his thumbs pressed down my back. He got to my waist and slid his hands to the back of my hips. The palms of his hands continued down over the dimples of my butt cheeks. His hands seemed to enjoy what they felt as they slid down my firm thighs. I didn't think he noticed what I was concealing.

"What are these?" the other officer asked Bianca as he frisked her. He was either confused or defensive or both.

"They're my braces," she barked.

"She's disabled," I told the cop.

"Look, my crutches are in the car." Bianca pointed out the obviousness of two silver crutches resting against the front seat. The officer finally looked and saw the crutches. He seemed embarrassed but was unapologetic.

My officer stepped back, leaving me unsure of what he would do next. I kept my hands on the car. "I need your ID," the officer directed me.

I leaned into the car and got my ID from my small leopard-print bag. I turned and handed him my provisional license. "Here."

"I need *your* ID," he said while staring at me, slightly perplexed. He seemed to sink into some sort of quiet rage. "This isn't yours."

"Yes, that's mine. I'm a man, and that's me. I told the operator that we were in drag. This—" I motioned my hands, pointing out my clothes and my figure, "—is a costume."

I looked over at Bianca, and her officer looked more puzzled than before encountering her braces. I was terrified and proud, proud he had thought we were real women and terrified he had thought we were real women. Over his shoulder, I saw other officers had the would-be robber sitting on the curb in front of the drugstore. I figured everything would be over in a few seconds and Bianca and I would finally be on our way to Hollywood, where we belonged.

"Sit in the car." The officers took our IDs and walked over to their patrol cars. The robber stood up and left the scene. I looked at Bianca.

"Are you okay?"

She nodded. "That cop is an asshole. Motherfucker."

"It's not easy having a good time," I said to Bianca, a line from *Rocky Horror* we had begun quoting to each other when we experienced any sort of backlash for just being ourselves. "Excuse me," I yelled to the cops. "Why are we still here while that guy just left?"

"Just a minute," the officer said, throwing his open hand in the air while not looking at me.

"I was the one who reported this."

"Be quiet," he said, snapping his face over his shoulder and staring at me.

"You're just mad because you realized I'm a man."

"I said be quiet."

He turned and walked toward me. The office handed me our IDs and a ticket for parking in a handicapped space.

"Are you kidding me?" I rolled my eyes, already writing the letter I'd be mailing city officials to complain about his behavior.

"You don't have a parking placard," he said. At some point, Bianca's handicap placard had fallen out of the car.

Bianca chimed in, "We're going to report this and you."

I started the car and drove out of the shopping center. Bianca turned up TLC on the radio. I punched the gas on the on-ramp of the 91, moved to the fast lane, and headed west.

An hour after our criminal adventure, we were in Los Angeles and had added to our names, *Foxy Girl Vivienne and Foxy Girl Bianca: Môdel-Spies.* We exited the 101 at Santa Monica Boulevard, and Riverside and the cops were a distant memory. I was still going to write that letter, but we were free and where we felt safe. I turned left, and we made our way into West Hollywood. I pulled into the parking lot of the now-familiar French Market Place. The place, our pit stop, was where we were always allowed to eat, people-watch, and use the restroom without harassment.

We sat in the car, ensuring everything was in place: makeup, wig, duct tape, and jewels. Hoping not to need either, I put my money and my driver's license into my bra along with my lipstick. I closed the mirror on my visor and closed the roof. "Ready?" I asked Bianca.

"Ready."

Bianca got out and adjusted herself in her braces. I got out and opened the trunk. Bianca couldn't see me.

"Girl, look at this," I said as I stepped from behind the open trunk. Bianca's eyes widened. *Snap*—I cracked the whip that I pulled from the truck. The handle was six inches long, hard, and wrapped in leather. There was a wrist strap on one end of the handle and nine twelve-inch straps of leather at the other end.

"Girl, what is that?"

"It's a whip, a cat-o'-nine-tails."

"What are you going to do with it?"

"I guess I'm going to spank someone." I closed the trunk. "Can you imagine if the cops looked in the trunk and found this?" I said, laughing, and Bianca shook her head.

Outside the club, there was a line of *creatures of the night* that we would not be waiting in. People dressed mostly in black, either bobbing to the bass vibrating through the walls of the building, smoking cigarettes, or talking nonsense to each other, all pretending that they weren't waiting to be judged worthy enough to get inside. The hostess smiled, unhooked the rope, and ushered us in.

"Welcome to Sin-A-Matic."

Inside, it was dark and sweaty. Bodies were pressed together, voluntarily and involuntarily, at the bar and on the dance floor. There were people in leather, in vinyl, in denim. Participants and observers. People who belonged, people who wanted to belong, and people who were curious. Cigarette smoke and chalky fog filled the air. Colored lights—red, blue, and green—diffused in the smoke. Cocktail glasses clinked at the bar, and ice rumbled as it poured into sinks from buckets. People scanned the room, looking for the right person to fill their wants and needs.

We made our way to the back, to a smaller, slightly darker room. The music was softer, and the bodies moved at a slower pace. A couple of people pressed against the wall with partners spanking and whipping them with various instruments. A White middle-aged man in a black jockstrap was lying on a bed of broken glass. A petite blond woman in a red patent-leather bra, a red patent-leather miniskirt, and red patent-leather, thigh-high stilettos walked on top of him. Shadowed figures walked around, observing the activities. Groups of twos and threes made out in the dark pockets of the room. Leather-chapped and shirtless men meandered.

I turned to Bianca. "Are those two having sex?"

"Where?" She turned her head around to find the couple. "I don't know; I think so. I'll go see."

A three-hundred-pound man with brown curly hair, wearing baggy beige corduroy pants and an oversized red T-shirt, stared at me like he wanted me to help him find his mommy. He seemed lonely and out of place. I was out of place too, but I was better at pretending not to be.

"Will you spank me?" he asked as he looked down at my whip.

His sadness and desperation disgusted me, but I had no reason to say no. "Put your hands on the wall." I spun him around. "I said, put your hands on the wall." He was a slow learner, or maybe he was just scared.

I ran my whip over his giant back. I cocked my right arm back and released it forward—the whip snapped. I repeated the motion. Not knowing what I was doing, I only mimicked what I had seen others do in the last ten minutes. I found a natural rhythm, and whipping him became a meditation only broken when Bianca and I caught each other's eyes. She was across the room, beating a man in a black leather harness and Levi's with one of her crutches. We smiled, and I gave Curly another whack.

I wasn't sure how long the whipping was supposed to go on, but I had an audience at that point, and Curly seemed to enjoy everything. I felt a large masculine hand on my left shoulder. I turned, and my eyes locked into a pair of piercing blue eyes. I stopped.

"Yes?" I stepped closer to him. I could feel his breath on my face.

"You're beautiful. Can I have a turn?" His eyes cut deeper into mine. We didn't blink; we grinned. His voice was calm, clear, solid. "I noticed you when you came in," he said. "Are you real?"

He was six feet tall with dark blond hair that had been lightly highlighted and skin that was lightly tanned. He probably liked the beach. He was about thirty-six and attractively muscular. He wore a royal-blue polo shirt and blue jeans. He didn't fit in there per se, but he was here for the same reason we all were—an escape. Whatever it was that brought him to the club, he had found me. Well, he had found Foxy Girl Vivienne.

I rested my left hand on top of his firm chest. "Am I real?" I asked softly. There were so many ways I could have been real; I just had to figure out which real he wanted.

"Are you a woman or transsexual?" he asked me as if he knew which answer he wanted.

"Neither," I said, confused as to why those were the only two options he gave me. I stared deeper into his eyes. Paused. I let him feel my silence. I let him feel his discomfort. I let him feel how badly he wanted the safe answer and how badly he needed the dangerous one. My hand moved down his arm and squeezed his right hand.

"I'm a drag queen, honey," I said softly, knowing what he wanted regardless of how I answered.

"Well, you're beautiful."

"I know." I smiled.

Of course he thought I was beautiful; I was everything he couldn't say he wanted wrapped in a package of what he could want.

The fat guy moaned. "Hey, don't forget about me."

"Shut up!" My arm swung forward—*snap*—the whip landed on the center of his back.

"It's a real turn-on," my new friend said. At first, I thought he meant me whipping the guy against the wall, but he meant he was turned on by everything I was.

"What?" I asked, making him say it out loud.

"A beautiful woman with a cock," he said. He smiled. He felt safe. We had had our moment, and he was safe. It was baby steps with him.

"Are you gay?"

"No, I am straight; it's just something I like." He paused. He wasn't fooling me. I knew what he was. But he certainly didn't know who I was. "Do you want to leave?" he asked as if I had already agreed.

"This is just entertainment for me. I wouldn't have sex like this."

"That's okay," he said shyly. He looked down. And there it was, his shame.

"I thought you weren't gay?" I leaned in and felt him.

"I'm not, but I am willing to try."

I knew the truth; he had done this before. He had always found the queens willing to leave on their wigs, their heels, their armor of paint, and probably their duct tape. No one had ever taken it all off for him; no one had ever made him reveal himself. He had always had sex in the comfort of denial. They were never exposed, so he was never vulnerable. The other queens let him have what he needed and nothing he couldn't handle. But that wasn't me; that bored me, and he seemed to have grown bored of his safe ways. It's why my intolerance of his fear was so appealing to him; I wasn't going to let him get away with being scared.

"Are you going to be okay with me looking like a man?" I asked.

"I think so. I am curious to see what you look like."

"Just a minute." I released his forearm from my hand and turned to find Bianca.

Bianca was on a pedestal on her hands and knees, being spanked by the guy in leather—presumably for beating him with her crutch. I stopped the guy from spanking her. She popped up her head, and I leaned to her ear.

"Girl, doesn't that hurt?"

"Yes. It. Does. Girl. He almost pulled off my wig with his belt." She stopped. "Is it on straight?"

"Yes. You better be careful; remember, you bruise easily. Will you be okay if I leave for a while?"

"Where are you going, ho?" Bianca looked shocked and jealous.

"That guy wants to take me home."

"Girl, he's fine—f-i-n-e—fine. Does he know?"

"Yes. I'm not going to do anything too crazy, so I won't be gone long. If you leave here, meet me at the French Market. Are you going to be okay?"

"Yes. I'll make this guy buy me something to drink. Are you going to have sex like that? With him?"

"No, not like this. Can you imagine? Whatever I do, it won't be in a wig and duct tape."

I followed his BMW to his apartment, a few minutes away, in the less desirable part of Beverly Hills. The traffic was light. It was late, but not late enough for most people to be heading home from the bars. His third-floor apartment was small, clean, an executive studio. It could have been nice, but it wasn't what I expected. It was somewhat empty.

"Did you just move in?" I asked.

"Almost a year ago."

"It seems like you haven't settled in."

"No." He held my hand. "I keep expecting to move, but then I don't."

"I guess what we expect is different from what we get. I need to change."

"The bathroom is on the right," he said as he released my hand and touched the small of my back.

I shut the door and pressed the lock. The lighting was harsh, bright and yellow. If he couldn't buy furniture, he could have at least done something about that lighting. I took off my wig, then my jewelry, and then my clothes. I slowly peeled off the duct tape. I half-filled the sink with lukewarm water and washed my face. I had to scrub my face a couple of times to remove the stain of the Russian Red lipstick, black eyeliner, and mascara. I looked into the mirror; my eyes were bloodshot from the late hour of night and the cigarette smoke from the club. My skin was flushed from the removal of the thick makeup. There was still a light smudge of eyeliner on the rim of my eyelid. I stood back. I was nude and naked. My pile of clothes in the corner was the only explicit trace of Vivienne. I put my hand on the door handle, grasped it firmly, and took a breath—*Dear God, please don't let this guy have a knife or do anything crazy to me.*

I turned off the bathroom light and opened the door. He waited for me near the bed. The shadows allowed me to make out his well-defined body. There was nothing in his hand to harm me. His hands rose and arms opened, ready to embrace me when I got within his reach. He squinted, and his brow furrowed.

"Oh my God, you're just a boy."

I was just a boy. I was sixteen. I handled myself in a way that let others forget that. I often forgot myself.

Brief Encounters with
Dr. Frank-N-Furter

A. Ng Pavel (吳慧靈)

CW: sexual assault

THE YEAR IS 2009 and "that's so gay" is the most scathing diss in the hallways of my middle school. I am on the cusp of twelve, wolfing down a Reese's Peanut Butter Cup Blizzard at the only Dairy Queen within the Chicago city limits. I have deprived myself of my favorite treat, the Butterscotch Dilly Bar, because I was afraid I'd be accused of copying the birthday girl. Jealous, I watch her pink tongue lap up shards of caramel coating and vanilla ice cream.

The week prior, I dreamed I kissed a girl, and woke up terrified that I would end up being the lesbian friend. Even the word "lesbian" denotes filth, and causes real fear in me. I've never heard it said without revulsion. "One in five people is gay," Birthday Girl had said a few weeks ago, examining all of us at the lunch table. "That means one of us is a lesbian." We all cringed and ew-ed and wrinkled our noses. I burned with the foreboding sense that it would be me.

I stop myself from staring and look across the street at Chicago's Music Box Theater, an early twentieth-century theater with a white awning featuring film titles in thick black letters. Posters for the week's film screenings are displayed on the brick walls of the building. One of them catches my eye: In the center of a black background, a giant pair of bright red lips surrounds the figure of a woman (that's a woman, right?). The awning advertises a midnight screening. I steal glances at the poster, heartbeat thrumming, chastising myself every time, incapable of resisting the pull. I want to ask the other girls: Is that a woman? But I'm afraid. I scan the faces of my friends, wondering if anyone has caught me. Red liquid drips from the bubble letters that read *THE ROCKY HORROR PICTURE SHOW*, like the drip of ice cream running down Birthday Girl's popsicle stick.

The year is 2012 and *Should the gays be allowed to marry?* is a mainstream topic of debate. At dinner, I defend gay people's right to marry, and a family member says that gay love is to straight love what masturbating is to sex. I put my fork down, remain quiet for the rest of the evening.

I am fourteen years old and I watch *The Perks of Being a Wallflower* for Logan Lerman and definitely not for Emma Watson. Two years earlier, I was confirmed as a Catholic, and in my heart, I know that I am going to hell. You could say that I am like Susan Sarandon's Janet before her reeducation: naïve, eager to please, virginal. I want to be normal, and I do everything in my power to act the part. I love to hate on Emma Watson's pixie cut as I brush my waist-long hair. At night, I fantasize about shaving it all off. I fantasize about a lot of things that I pretend to hate the next day.

I watch *Perks* with a mixture of want and shame as Watson puts on the burlesque show, dancing in front of a screening of *Rocky*, singing the praises of sexual liberation and giving yourself over to absolute pleasure. I wonder what it's like to be able to dance in front of other people. I know, at this point, that the Music Box hosts regular screenings of the film, but I can't imagine asking my churchgoing mother for permission to attend a midnight screening of a movie about a transvestite. I can't imagine lying to her about it, either, even though I lie to her about myself every day.

The year is 2020 and the world has been placed under lockdown, courtesy of a microscopic virus that will kill millions of its human hosts. In my neighborhood, an elderly Asian man is nearly clubbed to death. He is the victim of one of the many violent attacks happening all over the country. With the president calling COVID-19 the "kung-flu" and the "Chinese virus," Asian faces like my own have become monstrous. I fear for my health and safety in a way that I hadn't known was possible in this century.

When I suggest to my sister that we watch *Rocky Horror*, she says, "I don't think you're ready for that movie."

I am sitting on the couch in the living room of our apartment. I am twenty-three years old, still recovering from sexual assault. To cope, I tell myself I am sexually liberated.

I push back a little. "What do you mean? It's a cult classic about being gay and trans and flamboyant." This is the impression I have gotten from mainstream culture.

Concern clouds her face. "It's super problematic."

I blink at her. "Like, racist?" I know the main cast is all white, and I am used to white queers drawing the line of their progressiveness at race.

She sighs, then tells me the inevitable. "No, like weird consent stuff."

The word "consent" triggers a chain reaction in my body: ice in my chest that spreads to my throat, which was once ravaged by unwanted hickeys that took a week to heal. The freeze spreads to the rest of my body, my arms limp by my sides. I understand, dimly, that we won't be watching this film tonight. I am rooted to the couch, trapped and immobilized like Daphne fleeing Apollo.

It is spring 2024. Seven years since the assault, and every cell in my body has been replaced. I can live with the confidence that he never touched this new body of mine. Mine, mine, mine.

I am on the verge of twenty-seven. I can dance in front of other people. I am in awe of life, the possibility of decades unfurling before me. I kiss people because I want to, not because I feel obliged. I know how to say, "No thanks." I do not bite my tongue. I have new standards when it comes to sex: It has to feel 100 percent good, 100 percent of the time. I pay attention to my heart, not just my crotch. If there is even the slightest twinge of anxiety or doubt, I stop, no matter how much I think I want it. Maybe if I'd been dealt different cards in my twenties, I wouldn't care. But as I am, absolute pleasure is the only thing about which I can be certain.

I pop my *Rocky Horror* cherry one Friday night in my apartment in Oxford, Mississippi. I need to know what the big fuss is all about. When Susan Sarandon starts singing, I say to my roommate, "I didn't know this was a musical."

I am pleasantly surprised. I didn't know the film was a genre mash-up. I laugh gleefully at the proliferation of camp—the bad costumes, the visibly drawn-on tattoos, the over-the-top recreation of the original Frankenstein's monster's "It's alive!" scene for the birth of the titular Rocky, replete with a ridiculous amount of levers pulled, buttons pushed, and knobs turned in the scientist's laboratory. Not to mention the entire film's story-within-a-story frame of a detective trying to figure out the narrative. I love Janet's goody-two-shoes characterization, her unabashed naïveté, and the frequent visual references to Grant Wood's "American Gothic" in the first part of the film.

I laugh along with the flamboyance, the varying degrees of parody—Rocky's Aryan features, the nods to Dr. Strangelove and Dr. Frankenstein, the Weimar Republic aesthetics crossed with a Victorian haunted manor and space travel. I am perturbed by Dr. Frank-N-Furter's fascist regime at the castle, but am moved by his final performance of "I'm Coming Home." The anxiety that flared in my body during the seduction of Janet and Brad is soothed by their depiction as nothing but earthworms as the castle-turned-spaceship blasts off into space.

When the film ends, I feel a sense of satisfaction at now being "in" on the joke, finally understanding what everyone's been talking about for so long. But I don't feel relieved of my lost ignorance.

Don't get me wrong, the film is fun: It's gay and trans, and it's a musical for crying out loud, with a pretty good soundtrack too. It's an homage to genre itself, to giallo, to B movies, to low-budget sci-fi.

And yet—I feel a little betrayed.

To be clear, I don't think it's useful to hold art to unattainable standards of morality. Art, just like its human creators, can make diverse political statements.

But it pisses me off to know that for nearly fifty years, everyone's been celebrating a movie about "queer sexual freedom" when, at the moment of the so-called sexual liberation itself, the question of whether consent is granted or not is *extremely* murky. While we celebrate Janet's and Brad's sexual awakenings, it's unclear whether either of them *consented* to being sexually liberated by Dr. Frank-N-Furter.

In the film, Janet Weiss and Brad Majors, a newly engaged couple, are stranded in a storm and seek shelter in a nearby castle, where they are invited to spend the night. That night, both Janet and Brad are seduced in succession by Dr. Frank-N-Furter.

Janet is sleeping when Dr. Frank-N-Furter, disguised as Brad, enters her canopy bed, parting her virgin-white curtains. They make out, and there is clear tension between Janet's desire to stay virginal and the temptation of sexual pleasure. The seduction is typical: Dr. Frank-N-Furter (as Brad) tells her that it's okay, that she wants it, that there's no reason to be ashamed.

When Janet realizes that "Brad" is actually Dr. Frank-N-Furter in disguise, she screams and struggles against him, while also moaning in pleasure. Initially, she vehemently refuses his advances, but eventually submits to the pleasure of his caresses. The scene repeats itself with Brad, the dialogue nearly identical, only this time Dr. Frank-N-Furter is disguised as Janet. The juxtaposition ridicules the prudishness and lasciviousness of each member of the couple.

My older Gen-Xer friends explain to me the significance of the film in their own lives. *Rocky Horror* was a coming-out film for many young gays of the '80s and '90s—there just wasn't anything else around that simultaneously expressed and embraced queer culture and sexual liberation. They describe a time when sex was taboo, the concept of "consent" didn't really exist, and in order to even have sex, people had to get wasted. (This bewildered me but I'll take their word for it). They tell me that in the '70s, sexual liberation for straight and queer sex *meant* playing along with a script of a forceful, "liberated" pursuer and a timid, "repressed" pursued who says they don't want it, but really they do. The pursuer convinces the pursued to give in to pleasure, and everyone orgasms and has a great time. This is the logic of sexual liberation that animates the scenes of Janet's and Brad's seductions, with both of them playing the role of the pursued and Dr. Frank-N-Furter playing the role of the pursuer. And because the pursuer's role relies on coercive tactics, unfortunately, so too does Dr. Frank-N-Furter. The result is that Janet and Brad's seductions reproduce the era's script of sexual liberation, coercion included.

The problem, I think, lies in the conflation of sexual awakening and liberation. Dr. Frank-N-Furter's role in Janet's and Brad's sexual awakenings and initiations has been described as pedagogical.[1] Sexual education is at the core of the film's message, songs, and dances. A virgin learns from an experienced elder the pleasures of the flesh. But I want to acknowledge the power imbalance inherent in the student-teacher relationship. If knowledge is power, and the role of the teacher is to bestow such knowledge upon the student, then it follows that the teacher, who holds the knowledge, also holds power over the ignorant and powerless student. In the act of sexual initiation, sexual knowledge is conceived of as power. Thus, teaching is synonymous with the initiation of the powerless by the powerful. The sex scene in *Rocky Horror* reproduces these power dynamics. To me, this scenario sounds like a nightmare—the product of a culture that treats sex as an expression of power. Sex doesn't have to be one person pushing themselves on another, believing that the other's resistance will turn into arousal. In fact, that sounds a lot like assault.

The problematic aspects of the seduction, which I consider to be coercive, could be waved away by the film's overall campy tone. If it's a satire with a queer mega-villain, then discursively, the film doesn't necessarily condone coercion. But even if the scene is supposed to be camp, the dramatic irony still betrays Janet, and the scene's humor is at her expense. Dr. Frank-N-Furter *is* an over-the-top queer supervillain. We can laugh at and with him, and that is liberatory for us as queer people living under heteronormative media that often villainizes gay people. But the problem is that even though this humorous characterization of Dr. Frank-N-Furter subverts villainous representations of queers, it *still* throws Janet under the bus.

Dr. Frank-N-Furter tricks Janet, then Brad, and seduces them. We get a satire of sexual repulsion and desire in both Janet and Brad: They both seem not to know that they desire Dr. Frank-N-Furter (because of their sexual repression), and the joke is that we, along with Dr. Frank-N-Furter, supposedly know that they actually do. Following the pedagogical metaphor, the scene's dramatic irony sides with the teacher and betrays the student, who, according to the joke's logic, doesn't know what's best for her. (When is it ever funny for a woman to be told she wants it, when she clearly doesn't?) Through this joke, the film aligns the audience against Janet. In the logic of the film, Janet is about to receive an education that will lead to her sexual liberation, and we get to watch her to learn her lesson.

Later in the film, Janet prepares to recount the night's events to Brad, rehearsing her shock and disgust. This is supposed to be funny, campy. The irony is supposed to diffuse the violence. As viewers, we're meant to be in on the joke: *Haha, it's so funny that Janet is struggling between her goody-two-shoes prudishness and her desire. Haha, it's so funny that Dr. Frank-N-Furter thrusts himself into Janet's opened legs, saying "Do you want him to see you like this?" It's so funny. Ha ha ha.*

It's December 29, 2024, and I'm at the historic Balboa Theater in San Francisco, California. Around me, people are dressed in fishnets, Doc Martens, and sequins. I buy a three-dollar "kit," a brown paper bag that contains toilet paper, newspaper, a glowstick, noisemakers, a party hat, a nylon glove, and a sheet of detailed instructions. A volunteer offers me a tube of red lipstick to draw a *V* on my cheek. I decline politely, not wanting to attract too much attention to myself. I sit in the middle of the theater, sharing the row with another *Rocky Horror* "live cast virgin." Over the loud music, I convince him to buy himself a kit. He returns, waving it like a goody bag from a children's birthday party. Together, we conspire to fully embrace the experience. Before the showrunner begins explaining the participation rules, Chappell Roan's "H-O-T-T-O-G-O" blasts over the theater speakers as cast and audience dance together. The room is filled with warm energy and my concerns about the film's depiction of consent are momentarily suspended.

"Here's to the bawdy-humored queers, creeps, and weirdos!" the showrunner gleefully exclaims before the show begins.

A round of laughter and applause echoes through the audience, and I happily cheer along.

Much like Janet and Brad are initiated into a world of sexual pleasure, so too are new audience members initiated into the subculture of *Rocky Horror* live cast shows. Before the show begins, the cast invites some of us "virgins" to join a competition of gift-wrapping show props. I can see how young queers could feel like they were being welcomed into a new community that celebrates itself for being queer in every sense of the word; I know I would've deeply appreciated this as a young queer craving belonging.

Finally, it's time for the show to begin. Before ceding the stage to the performers, the showrunner reminds the audience that while bawdiness is an essential part of audience participation, there is no tolerance for racism, homophobia, transphobia, or misogyny.

The performances are hilarious, as well as respectful of the audience's boundaries. But almost immediately, I am appalled by the vehemence of several of the male audience members' misogyny as they call Janet a "slut" and a "bitch" over and over. Prior to the screening, I'd thought that audience members called out "slut" whenever anyone says her full name, but at this screening, these men consistently shout with strong vitriol words that we must remember are originally slurs, at Janet, whenever she appears throughout the duration of the film.

The sense of delight building within me is quickly replaced by discomfort, fear, and disappointment. Any hopes that the showrunner's speech would deter people from using slurs are crushed.

There is a line between bawdiness and belligerence, and that night, that line is crossed many times, without any interference from the showrunner, the cast, or other audience members. A couple times, I find myself wishing that someone would yell back at the belligerent men, but at the same time, I know that the reason no one did is the same as my own: Their anger is frightening, and we are afraid of its potential for slipping from verbal to physical violence.

The rest of the time, the participation has a recited quality to it, a kind of ritualistic repetitiveness—it's clear the audience members are simply reciting words back at cues from the film. A particular moment of this recitation stands out to me: Audience members unanimously call Riff Raff and Columbia "slaves," when they are referred to as "servants" in the film's script. During this moment, the audience's tone is complacent rather than belligerent, almost bored. In many ways, the audience's complacency strikes me as being equally disturbing or worse than belligerent: The habitual recitation of the script prevents audience members from questioning the usage of the term.

During the seduction scene, the audience adopts both attitudes—energized belligerence and bored complacency—and unquestioningly sides with Dr. Frank-N-Furter.

"Don't fuck with her hair!" several men shout, some of them with glee, others with recitative boredom, while Frank-disguised-as-Brad hovers over Janet.

Frank-disguised-as-Brad touches Janet's hair, and his disguise disappears.

"We told you not to fuck with the hair!" the audience reproaches, as Janet screams in horror.

Just as the scene repeats itself for Brad, so do the audience's warnings to Dr. Frank-N-Furter. "Don't fuck with the hair!"

In both Janet's and Brad's cases, the audience sides with Dr. Frank-N-Furter, warning him that if he touches their hair, he will lose his disguise, and his unwitting partners will be made aware of his true identity. The audience therefore roots for Dr. Frank-N-Furter not to be discovered, for the seduction to continue with Janet and Brad unaware of their deception. Ice circles around my throat once more.

I recognize the film's cultural significance—in 1975, a musical film about a Gothic cross-dressing mad scientist[2] who shows two unwitting normies the path to sexual pleasure and liberation likely made a defiant statement to conservative pearl-clutchers, disarming harmful stereotypes about queer people at the time. But I nonetheless maintain that it's time to make some well-needed adjustments to our relationship to the film, as well as to the audience participation script.

Don't get me wrong—I am by no means suggesting we should stop live-cast screenings altogether or give it all up. But as we celebrate *Rocky*'s fiftieth anniversary, we should also seriously reconsider the audience participation script, as well as how we frame the film.

Yes, *The Rocky Horror Picture Show* is for self-professed "bawdy-humored creeps and weirdos." Yes, it's part of a long-standing queer tradition.

At best, ritualistically screaming "slut" at a screen could represent some kind of postmodern exorcism of internalized misogyny wherein ironic slut-shaming relieves the participants of their own shame. But even if the use of the slurs "slut" and "bitch" was intended to be reclaimed as ironic or feminist, then why, at the particular midnight screening I attended, were the people who were actually performing that "reclamation" older men, the very demographic that the words are allegedly being reclaimed from?

I couldn't help but feel, instead, that this midnight screening provided an outlet for angry older men to take out their misogyny in an environment that encourages otherwise socially unacceptable verbal abuse. The experience was bewildering and alienating, and I can't even imagine what it would've been like for a younger version of myself who still carried fresh shame and guilt after my assault.

This begs the question: Shouldn't we also draw the line somewhere, celebrating bawdiness but also acknowledging the inherent violence of men yelling "slut" and "bitch" at the top of their lungs at a screen whenever a certain female character appears?

As significant as it may be to queer culture, at its fiftieth anniversary, we can see that *Rocky Horror* relies on a flawed portrayal of consent—or lack thereof. Viewing the film in 2024 perhaps makes this flaw all the more noticeable. In 1975, it's evident that the film—through its use of camp and, later, by the gleeful audience participation it spurred—flipped the script on queer villainy and sexual liberation. I wonder if it's now time for audience participation to flip the script again by acknowledging the film's flaws and refusing to reproduce misogynistic and racist habits of the now fifty-year-old participation script.

Audience participation is fluid and joyful, and could so easily reflect progressive ideals. As a cult classic, *Rocky Horror* could easily take the route of other infamous films, like *Gone with the Wind*, and include a historical contextualization at the beginning of the film. Likewise, a new audience participation script better adapted to today's sensibilities (literally just not using slurs), could easily pave the way for *Rocky Horror*'s continued success, without alienating so many community members.

At the end of the day, the core message of the film, the motto "Don't dream it, be it" still resonates, especially as we face Project 2025 and the new conservative backlash. More than ever, preserving and creating inclusive queer community matters, and updating our engagement with *The Rocky Horror Picture Show* might be part of that endeavor. In the meantime, we'll fight for queer liberation, remembering that to see blue skies sometimes means looking through the tears in your eyes.

Notes

1. Zachary Lamm, "The Queer Pedagogy of Dr. Frank-N-Furter," in *Reading* Rocky Horror: The Rocky Horror Picture Show *and Popular Culture*, ed. Jeffrey Andrew Weinstock (Palgrave Macmillan, 2008).
2. For a further discussion of monstrosity in *Rocky Horror*, see Linda Badley's *Film, Horror, and the Body Fantastic* (Praeger, 1995).

On the Queer Morality of *Rocky Horror*

Holly Joy Wertman

THE FIRST TIME I realized that my mom might have been more involved with *The Rocky Horror Picture Show* than she let on was on my thirteenth birthday. She took my sister and me to a warm midnight showing at the Nuart Theatre in Los Angeles. Dressed in a red tutu and a Disney hat from my underutilized costume closet, a few *V*'s drawn on my face in crimson lipstick, I followed orders when the shadow cast asked everyone in the audience to stand up. "If this is your first time at a midnight show, take a seat," someone dressed as Columbia instructed, so I sat. "Now sit if you've been to five shows or less," and most of the audience was out. "How about ten?" My mom remained standing. When my mother was still up for "one hundred," my jaw dropped to the floor.

Although it was my first time at the Nuart Theatre, it was not my first time watching the film. Before my mom would bring my sister and me to the theatre, she insisted that we watch the movie at home. I should have been suspicious when she silently mouthed the lyrics and lines alongside the characters or when I recognized familiar phrasings in my household being quoted directly (If I ever petulantly yelled "I asked for nothing!" it was invariably met with "And you shall receive it in abundance!"). However, I was distracted, captivated by freedom beyond my imagination, still young enough that I had to ask permission to use the bathroom at school. At the end, my mother engaged us in an extensive discussion about the film's lessons: a call to prioritize pleasure and a serious caution against its excess.

My mother was adamant about the moral foundation of *Rocky Horror*. While my friends' families prohibited their children from watching the movie due to its R rating and controversial reputation, my mom had no concerns about us following in those high-heeled, studded footsteps. However, she did not support shock tactics just for the sake of stirring controversy. She believed the film had an important message, so she made us wait to see it until we were thirteen. She wanted us to be mature enough to grasp that beyond all the innuendo and overt campiness that defines the film's schtick, the crime for which Frank is ultimately punished is allowing his excessive desires to hurt other people.

This is how my mother raised me and my siblings: to enjoy life and not hinder others' abilities to do the same. In the moral underpinning of my childhood and *Rocky Horror*, rules were in place for protection, and anything before the line of danger was fair game. The other so-called rules regarding what we should and shouldn't do could always be questioned as long as they didn't result in harm. My mom wanted us to understand Frank's downfall extends beyond parties and indulgence. Instead, the film serves as a cautionary tale about how Frank-N-Furter discards and mistreats those around him in his pursuit of hedonism.

My mother was a teenager in Manhattan during the 1970s. Growing up in the city involved contradictions: Her strict Italian and French immigrant parents imposed an early curfew but expected her to ride the bus to school alone beginning at age six. It took me years to get the full story from her about her *Rocky Horror* past because she was concerned about me getting ideas. Rules had not been up for negotiation in her childhood household, as she made them in mine. If I disagreed with my curfew, I was allowed to make my case. By contrast, at sixteen, my mother had to sneak out of her apartment building every week on Friday and Saturday nights dressed in a corset and fishnets to join the inaugural shadow cast of the 8th Street Playhouse in New York City.

The shadow cast concept was invented in New York, at the Waverly Theater. After a man named Louis Fares started shouting at the screen, a woman named Dori Hartley showed up dressed as Frank. (Fun fact: She looked so much like him that Tim Curry had her play the role in his "Paradise Garage" video). New Yorkers were devastated when the Waverly closed—and launched shadow casts at the Festival and the New Yorker—but then six months later, the 8th Street Playhouse began to show the movie and became the central hub of *Rocky Horror* innovation for some time. People would begin lining up outside the theater around 9 p.m., and the three-hour wait was a significant commitment during a New York winter. It became a running joke that there was so much competition to be in the shadow cast just because people wanted to be allowed in early without needing to line up.

My mother was hooked and went twice a week, consistently enough to earn her a spot on the cast. It may have helped that her name was Janet, and that, as a sixteen-year-old, she had a look of wide-eyed innocence that mirrored Susan Sarandon's performance. My mom, however, knew what she was doing was particularly risqué and kept her last name hidden from her new friends, since she was considering a career in law or politics. Although she spent much of her free time with her crop of *Rocky* friends for years—even smoking cigarettes with Little Nell, who played Columbia—after she went off to college, she lost touch with them. It wasn't until around the time she started taking me to the Nuart shows that she found those friends once again on Facebook, after discovering herself in an old picture that Dori Hartley had posted, tagged only as "French Janet."

And so it was that in 2009, I stood in line at midnight across the country from where my mom had first watched the film when it was released in the mid-1970s. At thirteen, I wore less clothing than I ever had outside the beach, and the bold, costumey outfits were ones I had never dared to wear before. At that age, I was relatively sheltered and always wore a uniform to school. In this new context, I got to wear whatever outlandish outfit I could imagine: tulle, leather, lace, and experimental makeup that was so outrageous, it often landed on the opposite side of sexy. The thrill of being out at such a late hour, dressed in clothes I couldn't wear during the day and shouting whatever I desired at a screen, was so exhilarating that it made me dizzy.

Strangely, even with the revealing outfits that we all wore, the experience didn't strike me as overtly sexual. At that time, in my eyes, sexuality as a concept had largely been shrouded and presented as something to fear. The idea of lust existed outside of me, happening to me from a dangerous other and posing a threat I needed to be wary of. At the Nuart Theatre, I was introduced to a different form of human physicality, one that was much more lighthearted, less mired in shame, and that afforded me agency over my body. In a sea of people screaming profanities at a screen and air-humping a crowd to devirginize them, I felt empowered to express myself, including saying no and knowing it would be respected.

As I started to frequent the Nuart and recognize regulars, the whole affair began to feel like a celebration of weirdness, creativity, and self-expression. I would often bring new friends to devirginize, and we would enjoy our hours beforehand getting dressed up in whatever we wanted. Once we arrived, I would be greeted by *Rocky* friends of all ages who would exchange compliments, outfit ideas, handmade pins, and DIY tips. We celebrated our hard work, showing off the shoes and jackets we had spent hours studding. Getting there early was the best part—spending that time in line and getting to know people who ran the whole gamut of human experience.

This was the first time I experienced such a range of people considered eccentric or unusual. People of all ages; punks; artists; stoners; fans of horror, musicals, and anything else could find a home there. Despite being one of the youngest attendees, just like my mother, my age was never a cause for concern. This community was open to everyone—outlandish and potentially off-putting, but unfailingly kind.

Although the midnight *Rocky Horror* experience may outwardly reek of hedonism, there were codes of conduct in both the planet Transsexual and the shadow world we created beneath it. True, there were few limits on what you could say—screaming a new callback at the screen was fair game, and it might or might not be picked up based on whether it was sufficiently funny or outrageous—just don't be an asshole or ruin the experience for anyone else.

As I would learn, these rules also form the basis of queerness. Radical queer leader, thinker, and poet bell hooks once defined the word as follows: "'Queer' not as being about who you're having sex with (that can be a dimension of it); but 'queer' as being about the self that is at odds with everything around it and that has to invent and create and find a place to speak and to thrive and to live."[1] Queer thought leaders like hooks understand queerness to be a radical political viewpoint that challenges the structures we live within. The concept of gender and the rules that come with it (who to be attracted to, how to be attractive, what to wear, when and how and with whom to have sex, etc.) all fall away in both queer spaces and in the galaxy of Transylvania.

I was raised in such a queer state of interrogation and imagination, partly due to my mother, who believed that a child still had the right to an opinion. I was often at odds with the world, which didn't function as I did. Rules frequently did not make sense to me, seeming arbitrary or counterintuitive, in which case I would likely break them. I spent a lot of time in trouble for things like leading flash mobs, organizing protests during recess, and "practicing" kissing with other girls in the locker rooms. The message I received from the world around me was clear: Something was wrong with me.

There is an emptiness to which queerness serves as both the cause and the solution. The expected order of our days and lives is exposed to be completely arbitrary, and the future becomes open to possibility. To embrace queerness is to find meaning in a complete lack of hard truth. Under the queer gaze, no expectation is beyond challenge. This can be untethering, as freeing as it is terrifying, to let go of the order that society imposes and declares proper.

Leaving behind the singular way we were taught that life is supposed to unfold can lead to a breakdown of the building blocks that form a worldview and sense of self. Returning to "normalcy" is hard once that concept has been disbanded. It calls into question what happens after the credits roll, when Brad and Janet return to their everyday lives. Were they able to go to tea with Betty Monroe and dance with people who only knew the Madison?

Philip Roth defines satire as "moral outrage transformed into comedic art," a definition in which each word on its own is a fitting description of *Rocky Horror*. In a 2000 op-ed for *The New York Times* to promote a Broadway revival of the original play, Richard O'Brien said he was called to write "a rock 'n' roll show that combined the unintentional humor of B movies with the portentous dialogue of schlock horror."[2] *Rocky Horror* was always intended to parody science fiction as a cinematic genre, but thematically, it set its satirical sights on the American puritanical sexual hang-ups of the 1970s.

The England-based creative team for the play set the naïve Brad and Janet in the fictional American town of Denton. By choosing to set the film in America, they highlight the stark contrast between the sexual liberation of the 1970s and the restrictive, puritanical image that America portrayed to the world. The moral decline of our protagonists subverts various elements of puritanical hang-ups: same-sex attraction, infidelity, premarital relations, gender nonconformity, and unrestrained feminine desire.

Frank-N-Furter was cast as the ultimate foil to this heteronormative culture: flamboyant, androgynous, hedonistic, and undeniably sexy. An actual alien, Frank eschews the human performance of gender and the repression of desire. In both the original play and the film, Tim Curry delivers a dynamic performance that beautifully balances exuberant femininity and masculinity, embodying the raw power of naked desire. I believe that the resulting magnetism is what my mother was referring to when she got in trouble at fifteen for tagging "Tim Curry is God" on all her desks at school.

Frank defies categorization but finds definition through his desire. I, too, have shaped my identity based on what I want, navigating various identities over the years, including straight, bisexual, lesbian, and queer. I have dated individuals with diverse gender identities and been a partner to people transitioning between them. While these experiences at times left me questioning what they meant for my own identity, ultimately, I took Frank's lead in deciding that categorization was unnecessary.

Instead, I am shaped by my curiosity for the richness of human experience, constant search for good people, and boundless capacity for love. I am strictly governed by a politic of compassion and joy. The only times that I feel genuinely unhappy with my sense of self are when I stifle my desires due to rigid self-image or expectations. But as I work to live a life by my own ethics, Frank's exaggerated self-indulgence and resulting destruction also warns that this pursuit can be taken too far.

"Don't dream it, be it" is not just a song, but the moral thesis of *Rocky Horror*. During the floor show, the characters chant the phrase in cultlike fashion as they abandon legitimate grievances and follow Frank into the "warm waters of sins of the flesh." They cast aside their ethical codes for the raw pursuit of carnality. Each one is so tempted and tortured by what has held them back for their whole life that they finally release, surrendering to the thrill after suppressing their urges for so long.

Years after my first watch, I am still unpacking what it means to me. I have come to understand the first part of that phrase, "Don't dream it," as a warning against restricting desires. The scene cautions against the extremism created in response to extended restraint. After performing a series of highly authoritarian, controlling, and downright barbaric acts, Frank-N-Furter describes how much he ached to be dressed like Fay Wray, to be free. He attempts to justify what he did by pleading; he couldn't help himself, he just wanted to create a space where he belonged.

In recent years, the concept of a "second adolescence" in LGBTQ+ adulthood has emerged as part of understanding a differentiated queer lifespan—that queer individuals undergo self and identity development later in life because of the impacts and limitations of shame, trauma, and concealing their queerness. Therefore, they experience the heightened emotions, indulgence, and rebelliousness that typically characterize adolescence later in life.

The idea was born out of a viral tweet from @IamGMJohnsons in 2017:

> Many of us who are LGBTQ go through a second adolescence because our first (5–18 yo) is about suppressing identity.
>
> So when we do get into our 20s we make A LOT of mistakes that most attribute to younger people because we never got to be younger people in our true identity.[3]

Shortly after, responses came, such as one from Brianna Suslovic, LMSW, who cautioned against distorting this concept to "justify immaturity, recklessness, and unjustifiable harm-doing." She wrote that part of adolescence often involves a healthy dose of narcissism, entitlement, and rebellion as young people assert their independence and learn to understand themselves as individuals. Therefore, "adolescence" experienced as an adult with no guidance or natural limitations could be especially dangerous and harmful.

Given the peculiar yet more restrained nature of the other Transylvanians doing the Time Warp, it seems that Frank has always been a bit of an outcast. Only when he came to Earth did he feel able to embody a more honest version of himself. The outrageous nature of his commitment to pleasure echoes the equally radical depth of his desire. A second adolescence might help us better understand Frank's creation and destruction of lives, but it does not justify it.

Frank gets close to creating a world in his image and forcing that on others. He and his followers dive into the pool, where he floats above a representation of the painting *The Creation of Adam*. A wide zoom-out reveals Frank between the outstretched hands of Adam and his creator, just as Frank positioned himself in our human world as an all-powerful giver and taker of life through Rocky and Eddie. In these acts, Frank committed a cardinal sin: to play at being God.

So Frank is punished. Even in another dimension, far removed from the social structures of normative gender, concepts of harm and goodness remain moral pillars.

Rocky Horror set ablaze a culture that it mocked, and in doing so, created a space for those who did not fit into those same molds to find and celebrate each other. Fans have connected so deeply with this movie that they created an entire community around it. On opposite coasts, spanning multiple decades, these spaces provided both my mom and me with a place to belong. We may not fit into polite society by day, but we have found other creatures of the night. This community taught me that I can be whoever I want . . . as long as I am kind.

I was fortunate to receive this lesson as a gift on my thirteenth birthday: There are infinite avenues to move through the world with kindness, and we are only limited in pursuing them by our ideas of self and what is considered normal. I choose to follow in the footsteps of those who possess the bravery to stand against a puritanical culture, who dedicate themselves within a capitalist society to prioritizing play and mischief, and who take pride in the love they feel for someone else, even when it doesn't conform to societal expectations. And I am grateful to my mother who shared with me this secret to life (itself!) when she pressed play.

Notes

1. bell hooks, "Are You Still a Slave? Liberating the Black Female Body," conversation with Marci Blackman, Shola Lynch, and Janet Mock, May 6, 2014, posted May 7, 2014, by The New School, YouTube, https://youtu.be/rJk0hNROvzs.
2. Richard O'Brien, "The Job He Found Was Writing a Hit," *New York Times*, November 5, 2000, https://www.nytimes.com/2000/11/05/arts/theater-the-job-he-found-was-writing-a-hit.html.
3. George M. Johnson (@IamGMJohnsons), "Many of us who are LGBTQ go through a second adolescence because our first (5–18 yo) is about suppressing identity. So when we do get into our 20's we make A LOT of mistakes that most attribute to younger people because we never got to be younger people in our true identity," Twitter (now X), November 10, 2017, https://x.com/iamgmjohnson/status/929080973660180481.

Calling All Aliens

Lindsay Katt

I WAS THIRTEEN years old, sitting in the basement of my conservative childhood home, holding fast to our family's newly acquired cable TV remote as though it were a magic wand capable of transporting me to the outside world. I typed the number 1401 into the parental lock screen and was met again with the now all too familiar "Error, incorrect password" message. I remained optimistically unfazed.

To call our home rural would be an understatement. We lived in a large house on forty acres of land bordering thousands of acres of tree farm in the Rocky Mountains of Montana. My parents wanted to give all of us a full and innocent childhood. Their ethos was informed by the dogma of their Christian values: that children should never be exposed to any outside influences or media that could harm an impressionable young mind. My siblings and I were homeschooled, sheltered by a parenting style that on a good day could be viewed as overprotective and on a bad day as isolating, indoctrinating, and repressive. Our social lives were generally oriented around church, community activities, and gatherings with other (mostly homeschooled) families, some of whom held values that were even more strict or fundamentalist than our own. In our late childhood years, we were permitted to attend the local Christian day camp—a well-manicured brainwashing facility masquerading as wholesome family fun. It hosted "worship services" that included activities like the laying on of hands and altar calls, in which people were manipulated through music, lighting, and emotional language into "speaking in tongues" and going up to the altar to dramatically "accept Jesus into their hearts."

The worship services included screenings of anti-abortion propaganda and "educational films" discussing the consequences of homosexuality, featuring "success stories" of recovered queers who had been through conversion therapy. These videos outlined how and why LGBTQ people were sad, damaged, and worthy of our pity. They emphasized how accepting homosexuals as they are would be a disservice to *them*, and insisted that rejecting and condemning their harmful lifestyle was the truest form of love.

At home, my parents reinforced these values by constantly monitoring and censoring all media that entered our space. My mother carefully screened every radio station, movie, and book to determine if it was "appropriate" for a child's consumption. Sexuality was an especially guarded topic, the mere mention of which could elicit a reprimand more commonly reserved for expletives of the four-letter variety.

These reproaches, heavy with subtext, did their job well. We all knew the rules, and I knew how to follow them. If I wanted to maintain my standing as a "good kid" and avoid social exile, I must refrain from expressing any interest in sexuality outside of marriage. I felt begrudgingly prepared to do so, despite my curiosity.

Sexism was my first real wake-up call: listening to the boys in Christian youth group pervasively refer to all girls as "heifer" in place of their names while the adults laughed it off, telling the girls not to let it bother them and that boys would be boys. The only thing more jarring than discovering sexism in the first place was realizing how hard people would work to deny its existence or rationalize it away. Their denial of the problem only fueled my frustration. If women were naturally submissive to men, why had it historically been necessary to violently force them to be submissive? It didn't make sense.

Up until that point, I had been a diligent rule follower, trusting my parents to protect me from harm and believing they held some integral key to ensure my well-being. When they instructed me not to watch a film, I didn't watch it. If there was a radio station I was not permitted to listen to, I didn't listen to it, no questions asked.

When I started to push back more at home, my mother would say, "There are a lot of kids whose parents don't care about them enough to monitor what they watch. Would you rather I didn't care about you and just let you do whatever you want?" The message felt abundantly clear: To reject or criticize their control or authority was to reject their love, and to deserve any resulting consequence.

The hypocrisy present in my parents' beliefs continued to crack and fracture the facade of their "Christian values," making it impossible for me to ignore. I watched them decide which Bible verses to follow and which to explain away or ignore. The erosion of this fundamental trust was agonizing and disorienting. As I grew older, I began to recognize how my emotional safety and social standing with my family and the church community was contingent on my willingness to contort or conceal the truest parts of myself. If I looked like them and acted like them, I was safe.

After a lifetime of being performatively encouraged to "question my faith" as part of religious practice, my parents had not accounted for the possibility that their inquisitive, unknowingly transgender child would double down on another family value: the ability to think fully and critically for oneself. Slowly, I lost my ability to trust them and began to trust my own intuition for the first time.

I gave myself permission to transgress and transcend beyond the confines of my family's rule book without guilt or shame. The tipping point had come: that beautiful collision that happens when preparation meets opportunity. I had enough information to know that I wanted more, and that I would need to go find it myself. What I needed was a plan, and I had one.

On this early summer day in 1999, I found myself home alone. My approach was simple enough: bypass the excessively prohibitive parental lock system my parents had purchased as an add-on to our cable subscription, with the hope of discovering . . . something. Something that I imagined might exist on the other side of the wall separating me from the secular world. Something that my parents and the adults around me seemed to fear—a fear I did not share. I had a burning desire to know things, to know everything. I was holding onto a feeling that somewhere, in all that everything, there would be something like me.

So I sat facing the TV, holding a notebook where I had written all the possible four-digit passcodes sequentially, crossing out the disqualified combinations. 1402, 1403, 1404. I pressed the buttons on the remote, typing each digit into the lock screen in an almost meditative state. I had crunched the numbers and determined that even if the code was 9999, a highly unlikely outcome, if I attempted between seventy-five and one hundred combinations a day, within three or four months, I would succeed. If I stayed focused, methodical, and persistent—qualities that came as naturally as breathing to my young autistic self—I would be only months or even weeks away from earning my freedom. It was a mathematical certainty.

So I pressed forward: 1405, 1406, 1407, and then, like a prayer answered, the world changed.

I stared at the screen before me, awestruck and slack-jawed, unsure of exactly what I was looking at. I had succeeded, and what met me in that moment was a scene I could not begin to compute. A screen filled with a lascivious, decadent exhibition of . . . what exactly?

Music blasted out of the TV speakers as anxiety about being caught in this willful act of disobedience flooded my nervous system. I lowered the volume while the adrenaline and endorphins coursed through my body, the images flashing before me a visual feast of elaborate costumes and colorful gyrating figures. But *what* was it? Pornography?

I knew about pornography and was old enough to have noticed the magazines tucked securely behind gas station counters, rumored to cause blindness in the boys and men who succumbed to their lustful temptations. I had even indulged my own sexual curiosity on the family computer, exploring the early internet's version of nude centerfolds, going as far as to type "what if I'm gay" into the Yahoo! search engine, frantically closing the browser window at any hint of sound or movement behind me. But this couldn't be pornography, could it? I didn't know much, but I felt sure that my parents would never have brought pornography into our home. Sex was off-limits, something private, a lauded "gift from god" intended only for husband and wife. The word "sex" alone was enough to send my mother into a sneering grimace of disapproval.

I navigated away from the debaucherous scene to the TV Guide. I checked the name of the channel, hoping to gain more insight about what I had seen, and recognized it as VH1, with MTV listed just above it. The program title was *The Rocky Horror Picture Show*.

VH1! My mother had unlocked this channel countless times to watch music videos and interviews with musical artists. I recognized some of the film's actors, like Susan Sarandon and the infamous Tim Curry, who I knew well from the children's film *Muppet Treasure Island*.

I returned to the program, where the dancing man in fishnet stockings was singing with a confidence and bravado unlike anything I had ever seen. I stared in bewilderment, the fruits of my unyielding commitment to transformative rule breaking laid out before me. My mind was made up: This was not pornography but something else, and whatever it was, I wanted more.

A new thrill of possibility began to take root inside me, violating every Christian boundary and shattering every conservative ceiling. This strange alien character, so artfully and joyfully vocalizing self-expression, had expanded my world by inviting me into his. A world that welcomed me, and people like me, into its fold.

There were people like me! People who wanted to be touched and fucked, seen and desired. People who wanted to wear fishnets. This decadent, sometimes outright silly exhibition of self-love was not projected through a lens of shame or embarrassment, but with a formidable humor and an integrity that I have come to recognize as raw queer pride, unmitigated and untamed. Whatever "this" was, I knew with increasing certainty that it was made for me, by strangers expressing themselves the way I longed to: free, unbridled, and unrestricted by the arbitrary condemnations of religion. *These* were my people, and they existed not in the corners of some sleazy dark alley but out in the open . . . on VH1!

What followed can only be described as unadulterated obsession. I watched the spectacle as though I were watching some missing part of myself, a puzzle piece from my own blossoming identity appearing in front of me through the dazzling grandeur of queer representation. I couldn't look away. I could feel my body responding to the images, growing emotionally excited and sexually aroused, a tension building in my genitals. The film ended, followed by a documentary-style commentary. What I was watching was a show, a film, a musical, that had existed since the '70s. It played in theaters all over the world to packed audiences who dressed up, yelling dialogue at the screen and celebrating their sexuality with reckless abandon. The film had a full soundtrack that I wanted—no, needed—to purchase as soon as possible.

My very small hometown was an hour-and-a-half drive from the nearest city, so I knew there was nothing to do but wait. I informed my older sister (a then-closeted queer teenager in her own right) that I had hacked my way into our cable TV. She was the only sibling I trusted not to immediately tattle to our moral overseers, and she agreed to swear a vow of secrecy before I disclosed the sacred numbers.

The following week, on our family's monthly drive to Missoula, I casually requested that we stop at Best Buy so I could get some CDs and was met with an unsuspicious "Sure."

I entered the store like a boy buying condoms for the first time, making my way past the larger electronics to the CD section, wearing an expression intended to convey that I was a serious person looking to make a completely reputable purchase.

I flipped thoughtfully through the sleeves of random CD cases, the familiar sound of the plastic covers clicking between my fingertips. *Where would it be?* I thought. *It must be here somewhere.* I mustered the courage to approach an employee standing nearby and performed my most confident and adult voice: "Where would I find a musical soundtrack?"

The man shot me a friendly smile. "You bet," he said. "Should be in Aisle Two. Are you looking for anything in particular?"

I began to lose my footing, my internal monologue running at high speed: *Be cool, be cool be cool, it's fine, everything is fine, it was on VH1, it's famous, this is his job, you can say it out loud.*

"Ummmm, I think it's called *The Rocky Horror Picture . . .* something?" I lied, forcing my voice to be as neutral as possible. "I've never actually seen it . . . A friend recommended it to me, so I thought I'd check it out."

The man responded with a glint of recognition. "Oh yeah, that's a classic, we definitely have it. That's probably under Classic Rock, or in Musicals." He gestured for me to follow, and I picked at my thumbs as we wound through the display racks. He flipped through the CDs, spotting the requested album and whisking it out, placing it in my hands. "There you go!" he said. "Can I help you find anything else?"

"Ummm . . . no, thank you," I said, my voice cracking a bit. "I think I'm just going to browse for a while."

I pretended to peruse another section for five minutes before selecting some albums I felt sure my parents would not question. I have no idea what those other CDs were, but I was grateful to have them when I rejoined my family and my mother immediately asked to see what I had bought. I was a terrible liar. I believed in honesty, experiencing pangs of guilt any time I found myself ensnared in a falsehood. But this deception felt different; it felt like I was entitled to this, and I was unwilling to have it taken away.

I listened to that soundtrack like it was oxygen, breathing it in and out, over and over and over, a stim that my fellow AuDHD comrades will surely understand. I would snap the CD into my Discman, don my slightly broken foam-covered headphones, and walk the property that granted me reprieve from my parents' relentlessly watchful eyes. I fought to recall the images from the film as I sang out loud to myself, dancing along with the instructions: "It's just a jump to the left / And then a step to the right / With your hands on your hips / You bring your knees in tight / But it's the pelvic thrust / That really drives you insane / Let's do the Time Warp again."

I jumped to the left, I stepped to the right, and I thrust over and over as a long-festering thought began to develop in me like a photo making its way to the surface and revealing an insight about my family's values that I could no longer avoid: I was the thing my parents were trying to protect me from. My parents were never worried that exposure to images of sexuality and gender nonconformity would disgust, damage, or confuse me. Quite the opposite: They were worried that I would like it. They were afraid that it would appeal to me, that I would see myself in it, and they were right.

Months later, on a family road trip across the country, I passed the hours in the car with Tim Curry and my new friends. I would listen over and over, trying to recall the images, filling in my own details and fantasies. Later that night, I found myself on the couch of our family friends, my brother and sisters sleeping on various pieces of furniture throughout the sprawling living room. I covered my head with the large blanket, waiting until the room was thick with the staggered breathing of sleeping bodies, before beginning what was now a well-established bedtime ritual. Cocooning myself away from prying eyes, I secured my headphones, clicking through the tracks on my Discman as quietly as possible and arriving at a song titled "Touch-a Touch-a Touch-a Touch Me."

As quietly as I could, I began sliding my right hand down under my pajama bottoms and touching myself over my underwear. I moved my fingers back and forth to the rhythm of the music in absolute pleasure, climaxing into a hope so powerful I could feel it in every part of my body. This hope continued to grow in me, and over time became my resistance. I felt powerful and bold, part of something bigger.

I eventually took classes at the local public high school, where a friend in my art class informed me that his work was banned from the upcoming gallery exhibition due to the subject: two men engaging in a romantic kiss. Only his was banned, though another student's piece featured a passionate heterosexual kiss between a prostitute and a poet, and another student's work depicted violent scenes of self-harm and intravenous drug use. I was enraged. This was overt prejudice and discrimination masquerading as concern for children.

I was ignited by the injustice and wanted to take action, to push back, and I promised my friend that I would try. I wanted to fight for him, but can see now that I was also fighting for myself, hoping to speak truth to power and effect change. The step you take when you realize you too can pick up the torch and join the fight.

I sat in the principal's office, politely trying to explain to this adult man that his personal morality or prejudice did not give him the authority to discriminate against a student based on sexual orientation. I asked him why he thought that was okay. He was dumbfounded, face red, voice shaky, eyes bulging with anger as he blurted out, "BECAUSE IT'S . . . IN THE BIBLE!"

There was silence. We stared at each other, unsure what was supposed to happen next. "Please don't scream at me," I said calmly. "I am speaking to you with respect."

I watched him collect himself, realizing how this could look from the outside and what consequences he might face for screaming at a student. He went on to tell me that *he* was the sole authority here regarding student safety. I could feel his indignance and disdain, his anger at the audacity of a child

challenging him. I pressed on, unrattled. "You have no authority to impose your personal religious beliefs on students in a
government institution. If you are unwilling to compromise
here, I intend to contact every news outlet, LGBTQ resource
center, and civil institution I can find and let them know that
you are unwilling to honor the rights of your students."

It felt like a scene from a movie, the underdog standing up
to an unjust theocratic rule. The reality, of course, was much
different, and while the principal did eventually agree to a
compromise, we had to agree to their framing of the situation:
that gay people were controversial and dangerous. In the end,
he agreed to provide curtained-off space in a separate room for
all potentially controversial art pieces, telling us, "This way,
parents can still protect their children." His message was clear:
Your queerness may be allowed to exist, but *only* in the context
of something controversial, distasteful, and wrong.

Despite this setback, I allowed myself to enjoy the success
of my resistance. When you expect nothing, something can feel
like everything.

The Rocky Horror Picture Show has proven to be more than
a subversive, status-quo-defying art film. For this rural queer,
the film provided a symbol of something far deeper than fishnet
dress-up and jaunty sexual proclivities. Watching this film was
the first time I had encountered a mirror in which I could see
my own sexual identity reflected back, providing an awareness
that even in my separateness from others, I was not alone.

That is the power and importance of diverse representation
in artistic work. The legacy left not only for the benefit of those
who journey but as a guidepost for the generations to come. A
trail marker communicating the presence not only of a path
forward but a well-traveled one.

I still marvel at the sheer odds against my first encounter with this inimitable classic; how unlikely it was that my
thirteen-year-old self unlocked this specific film at that specific
moment in time. I cannot help but view it as an invaluable gift,
an offering built by the queers and weirdos who came before.

To this day, it is difficult for me to express the full extent of my gratitude for the character of Frank-N-Furter and all that he represents. I am so thankful to this beautiful, unapologetically perverse antihero for singing not only to the two travelers seeking shelter but directly to me, a fellow alien misfit, temporarily marooned on my own lonely planet.

I had been waiting with anticipation for a sign, any sign, that my dreams could, in fact, become real. And the transmission that I happened to receive was a message from a sweet transvestite from transsexual Transylvania, quietly whispering, "Don't dream it, be it."

And I did.

A Cinnamon Role

Victoria Provost

CW: gynecological procedures, menstruation,
sexual trauma
Names and details have been changed to
preserve privacy

SHIT, you think, *shit shit shit shit shit.*

It is the evening of your debut performance in the New York City *Rocky Horror* shadow cast. You stare at the red blots in the toilet bowl, willing them to disappear. You can't perform on your period. You cannot don black underwear and fishnet stockings and do high kicks with blood leaking out of you. In a panic, you call your friend.

"What do I do?"

"Do you want someone to cover for you? I can't do it, but I can help you look."

"No . . ." You want nothing more than for someone to cover for you, but you have been eagerly anticipating this night for months. You have invited friends, made arrangements to perform alongside specific castmates. There is no way you are postponing this.

"Just use a tampon, and wear an extra pair of underwear. You'll be okay."

You hold back a quiet sob. "I don't know how," you say, almost in a whisper. "I don't know how, I was never allowed, my mom never told me how, she wouldn't let me."

There's a beat of silence on the other end. "That's okay," your friend says. "I'll bring some and show you."

When you arrive at the theater, your friend meets you in the women's room.

"Okay, so. I got you the smallest size. This is how they work." They open the tampon box and hold one up for you to examine. "You insert it," they say, using their fingers to demonstrate, "and you use this plastic sliding part to push it up inside. Then, you pull the plastic part out," they say, demonstrating again, "and you leave the string hanging. That's how you take it out later. You can keep one in for about six hours." They discard the plastic part. "Meanwhile, this part"—they refer to the cotton entrails of the tampon—"expands out and absorbs everything, like so." They use their fingers to spread out the cotton and show you. You chew on the inside of your cheek. "Now, wash your hands, go into a stall, and try it. I'll be right here with you."

You enter a stall and lock it, and hold up your adversary. It's so *small*, hardly wider than a mechanical pencil. And yet, you are intimidated. You let out a deep breath. You are eighteen years old. You are stronger than this tampon. *I can do this.*

You inhale, bring your hand downward, and push.

Nothing happens.

It is as if, where there is supposed to be some Georgia O'Keeffe painting of an orifice, there is only a hard wall of skin and pelvic bone that will not yield. The plastic applicator digs into your skin, and you bite your lip to keep a sob from escaping your chest.

Your friend does their best to coach you from outside the stall. "Try sitting down . . .Take a minute to relax and try again." It just isn't working.

"Do you have any pads?" you ask, with more than a note of panic and desperation in your voice.

"No," they tell you. "I don't use them, and you won't be able to perform with them. I believe in you, and you *can* do this."

You hold the tampon, close your eyes, and retreat into your mind to address yourself. *It's just you and me, in this theater bathroom stall. No friends, no Mom.* Slowly, fighting the stinging sensation, you insert the tampon. You exit the bathroom stall, weary, teary-eyed, as if emerging victorious from a duel.

"I did it," you say, as if in shock.

"YOU DID IT!!!" exclaims your friend.

Your castmate walks into the bathroom. "Did what?"

"She just figured out tampons for the first time!!"

She gives you a cool smile and a nod of respect. "Yas, Queen." You smile, relieved, a little shaky. You did it.

I was too young to remember my first exposure to *The Rocky Horror Picture Show*. A local movie theater in our college town had the infamous burning red lips outside the entrance. Unlike the other posters, which rotated with the schedule of new releases, the lips never moved. Being a creepy little witch girl, I was enamored with all things "horror," and begged my dad to take me. "When you're older," he would curtly placate me, buying us two tickets to the newest Pixar heart-warmer.

At twelve, still too young to see *Rocky Horror* in a theater, I attended the Johns Hopkins Center for Talented Youth, a summer program for gifted middle- and high-school-age students. That was the year I watched the film for the first time, on the screen of my roommate's iPod Touch. We learned the steps to the Time Warp, my roommate enthusiastically thrusting her pelvis at the air while I gingerly mimed the movements, as much as my prim demeanor would allow me. It was my first time away from home; no one was going to round the corner to reprimand me, yelling about how I was acting like a slut. Instead, that small voice was coming from inside my head.

As I grew up at Center for Talented Youth, surrounded by rainbow and trans flags and members of the Gay, Lesbian, Or Whatever (GLOW) Club, I felt safe enough to claim my own flag, the black, gray, white, and purple asexual Pride flag. It was unlikely to garner me much discrimination from the Catholic Church or the supreme court, and it was a banner that comforted me. I could think of few things more horrifying and gross to me than sex.

Despite my aversion to sexuality, *Rocky Horror* quickly became one of my favorite activities to participate in during high school. I painstakingly taught myself the Time Warp tap solo in my carpeted dorm room. I put corsets and fishnet stockings on my Christmas wish lists. When my dad finally brought me to see a live *Rocky Horror* cast at fifteen, I pretended not to already know every lyric and audience participation line by heart. During my final year at CTY, I was cast as Columbia, and I helped our student director herd our classmates through the choreography of "Hot Patootie."

The day I turned eighteen, I drove to New York City, moved myself into my NYU dorm, and dropped off a filled-out application form to an NYC RHPS cast member before one of their shows.

I quickly began spending every Friday and Saturday night at the theater, arriving at ten p.m. and lingering until four in the morning. At first, I was a lowly crewbie—a "prop-tart" in charge of loading in and out of the theater each night. Despite being the youngest on the cast by about three years, I knew some parts better than some of the veteran cast members. And yet . . .

I was eighteen, a college first-year, and I exuded the energy of a wide-eyed prepubescent girl. My chest never developed the way I hoped and prayed it might, and I felt I had no right to act in a way that exhibited sexual independence, or even knowledge. Twice a week, I watched dozens of unwitting *Rocky Horror* "virgins" fake orgasms into a microphone. On occasion, I was even an emergency fill-in for Trixie, the character who performs a striptease for the audience during the movie's opening credits. I screamed phrases like "WOULD YOU LIKE TO FUCK ME?" and "SIT ON MY FACE!" at a movie screen and its audience, and I still felt that those phrases had no application whatsoever to me. My castmates established me as the sweet, innocent "cinnamon roll" of NYC RHPS, "too good for this world, too pure." Despite my debaucherous environment and friends, I was content to be so. I had been accepted into a cosmopolitan, alluring, generous community, and that was the role they had assigned me. I projected that sweet, innocent persona in every interaction I had, both onstage and off.

One night, I was an emergency fill-in for Riff Raff, the butler at Dr. Frank-N-Furter's castle. As he enters for his solo in "Over at the Frankenstein Place," the cast and crew typically shout, "OH SHIT, (S)HE'S/THEY'RE HOT!" When I popped up from behind the first row, however, I heard my castmates shout "OH SHIT! SHE'S CUTE!" As the cinnamon roll of the cast, I could only laugh and bow to my role as the pure, chaste, and demure little girl. As a college student experiencing a burgeoning queer awakening, it was hurtful and demeaning. We were supposed to be upholding unconditional body positivity—but how was it body positive to infantilize me at nineteen? In a community where everyone was supposed to be celebrated as hot, I wasn't.

I was coming to terms with the fact that I no longer identified with asexuality; however, I was finding my *Rocky Horror* cast to be an out-of-bounds place to admit that. Everyone *loved* me as the sweet cinnamon roll of the cast. It made me unique; it made me special. If I wasn't that person . . . Who would I be then? Would my castmates still love and dote on her?

I lost my virginity after spring semester finals week, to one of my childhood best friends. I told almost no one, even though it was something I had very badly wanted. Having sex seemed to me like riding a big roller coaster, knowing it would be fine and that I would have a lot of fun, but still feeling frightened to do it.

I knew it was supposed to hurt, and indeed I expected it. During the act itself, however, I could think about little else than the searing pain. It felt good to have crossed this line, for someone I wanted so much to want me back in the same way, but the feelings in my mind were intensely disparate from those in my body. I felt victorious, to have acted outside the bounds of my role as the kid sister of all the people around me, who slut-celebrated themselves with pride. In the light of day, however, nothing had changed. I had the growing, nagging feeling that everyone doted on me, but no one took me seriously.

Over a year and a half later, it was a different bed, with a different man. Albert was a usual suspect in the NYC RHPS circle. He was not a performer, but he regularly attended shows, parties, and other cast functions. He once greeted me at a concert we attended with a breezy "Hey, beautiful" and kissed my hand.

"Oh, my goodness," I said, "no one's ever done that to me before!" He smiled jauntily at me and spun me around with one hand. I have no doubt in my mind that, had circumstances been different that night, Albert would have tried to take me home.

Later that week, Albert asked if I had a crush on him.

I replied yes, maybe, if he had been about ten years younger. He told me that, if it weren't for the years between us, he would totally seek a more intimate connection with me, with his only reservation being his "unconventional" approach to relationships and sex, and his concern that we might experience a disconnect in that area. He called me super sexy and smart, and reacted with playful indignation until I admitted that I found him nerdy and adorable. He told me that it would still be fun to think about each other, at the very least.

But of course, that wasn't the end of it. I was lonely and vulnerable and starved for physical affection, and he was attractive and charming and knew all the right things to say to me. He was someone from *Rocky* who didn't just see a cute-as-a-button prop tart when he looked at me, but who actually wanted to fuck me. I also found myself quickly forming a deep emotional bond with him that was rooted in our shared adverse experiences. He and I had both had abusive mothers. We spent hours talking to each other about it, relating the memories that were unspeakable to everyone else, even to our therapists, even crying about our mutual grief over maternal love we had never received. I trusted him.

I found myself routinely spending nights at his apartment, watching TV and drinking while working on our laptops at first, then talking and cuddling until the sun rose, and then making out on his couch, in dwindling clothing.

"I have to make one thing clear," he said at dinner, early on. "I will never be your boyfriend." Sipping my root beer, I nodded.

That night, we were both a little drunk, and he was on top of me, my legs wrapped around him as he kissed my neck.

"I don't wanna have sex right now," I said to him.

"That's fine," he said. "We don't have to do anything you don't wanna do. But it would be really nice if we did." His hand started wandering, too close to my underwear. "These are nice . . ." He bit my neck, softly. "I want you."

I sat up, put a hand on his shoulder. "Calm down," I said. "Don't rush me." He laughed, and he sat up too.

"Sorry." We kissed some more. "Can I ask you something though?"

"Sure." This was a common exchange between us.

"Why not? Am I making you uncomfortable in some way?"

"No, you're not," I said. "I'm just scared of it hurting."

That was the end of the conversation. As I continued to get to know him, however, I started to get more comfortable with the idea of being rushed.

After a few months of this, we attended a Halloween party. He wore a red smoking jacket, while I shimmied into a black bustier complete with bunny ears.

On the train back to his apartment, he whispered in my ear: "If I fuck you, you should keep that corset on." I laughed.

And yet, once again, something wasn't right.

We were back in his bedroom, where Albert had turned off the big light. He'd ripped open a condom packet with his teeth, something I'd only read in seedy fan fiction but never thought anyone actually did. He was on top of me, as I lay back, biting my lip, trying not to yelp. For the first time in our short-lived tenure of sleeping together, he was the one who was hesitant.

"What's wrong?" I asked.

He sat up. "I don't think we can do this."

"What? What do you mean, why?" I sat up too. He looked at me.

"I'm barely doing anything, and you're already whimpering."

"So what? Like, I know I'm sensitive, and things hurt, but I don't mind, I'm fine," I said, all in one rush. "I'm fine if you're fine."

"No, but like, you might have a thing, like a medical thing."

"What does that mean?"

"You might have a condition, some people have it, it means sex is painful for you." I looked at him, looked down at myself, at my clothes that were lying in puddles around his room. It was all I could do to repeat the question: "What?"

He shook his head. "C'mere, it's okay." My head was swimming, from the alcohol and the adrenaline and the cold October air through the window on my skin, but mostly just from that single question: *w h a t ? ? ?*

He pulled me downward so that he could spoon me as he rubbed my shoulders. I could feel myself starting to hyperventilate. I felt like a parrot, stripped of my vocabulary. *"What?"*

"I'm sorry, I'm sorry." He kissed me on the head and continued to hold me. "You can see a doctor about it. You can see a gynecologist."

"A *what?*" I had never been to see a gynecologist before. My mother had always forbidden any medical care that she feared might "lead to promiscuity," even preventing me from receiving the HPV vaccine. Gynecology was a fearful, daunting concept in my mind.

The next morning, I arranged to have lunch with Parvaneh, my friend, Our Patron Saint of Tampon Instruction. They were the shining jewel of our cast—they played every role from Frank to Trixie, they had an established drag career, they were popular and sought-after, and they were classically stunning. Every Instagram post of theirs was peppered with comments like "STEP ON ME." I met them at my favorite restaurant. My mind was still swimming, still processing flashes of the night before.

"I have two things to tell you," I said to them. They nodded, their perfectly contoured face serious as they put a hand on mine. "One, I went home with Albert last night, and we hooked up." If Parvaneh was surprised by this revelation, they didn't show it. They nodded.

"Did you enjoy it?"

"Well, yes," I said. "Sort of." I lowered my voice to just barely a whisper, not only because we were seated in a room full of Sunday afternoon diners, but because the words were hard to say, as if I was under some invisible gag order.

"I think I have a condition where I can't have sex. Like, it's really painful for me." I took a sip of water and a few deep breaths. "Albert said he wasn't gonna do anything with me if it was gonna hurt me. Even though I said I didn't mind. And he said I should see a gynecologist, which is a little scary since I've never gone before." I paused to take a breath. "My mom never let me, she got mad at me when I asked about it." Parvaneh nodded.

"I've had friends who have the condition you're talking about. It's called vaginismus," they said. I sounded out the syllables in my head: *vaginismus.* It sounded like a curse, like a pestilence in a fairy tale that I had to rid myself of. Parvaneh continued.

"As I understand it, a great deal of it is psychological. Have you talked much about your sexual experiences with your therapist?"

"No, I haven't." I sighed. "It's probably about time I did . . ."

"Yes, I think that would be a good idea."

I found a GYN on the Upper East Side, and arrived at my first appointment fifteen minutes early, trying not to let my apprehension show. The waiting room had piano music playing softly and unique art hanging on the walls. I made myself a tea from the Keurig machine as I waited for Parvaneh to arrive.

When Parvaneh walked in, I was poring over the intake forms they had given me to fill out, and already some questions had stumped me.

When was your last OB-GYN appointment?

I looked at Parvaneh helplessly. "It's okay to write 'never,'" they said. "Just write that." I did.

How many sexual partners have you had?

I looked at Parvaneh again.

"How many people have you had sexual interaction with?" they asked. They had only rephrased the question and said it aloud to me, but it made all the difference.

"Two?" Parvaneh looked at me. "Two," I repeated, numbly,

as if I were a calculator spitting out an answer. It should have been an easy question, but once again, that inexplicable gag order weighed on me.

Have you ever been sexually abused or assaulted? Explain.

I was starting to hyperventilate. As if I were a character in a video game, my surroundings began to feel computer-generated, artificial. I fixed my gaze on the yellow-and-peach couch upholstery. I skipped the question.

Dr. B. was kind and matronly, and spoke with a vague Eastern European accent. "Hello," she said, "Just relax, do not worry, Dr. B will take care of you. Is this Mom?" she asked, referring to Parvaneh. Par was only three years older than I.

"No," answered Parvaneh, "I'm a dear friend."

"How wonderful," said the doctor. She perused my chart. "You are twenty?"

"Yes."

The doctor looked back down at the chart. "And this is your first visit?"

"Yes."

"Okay. And you listed on the form, you are experiencing painful intercourse?"

"Yes," I said, my voice barely above a whisper.

"Has it always been like this?" she asked. "Or did something happen? Sometimes there is a specific event, an event of sexual assault or abuse, that causes conditions like this to flare up."

"No," I said. "It's always been like this. I . . ." I paused and gripped Parvaneh's hand. "I can't even masturbate. It's not just sex, it's everything, everything is painful."

"Okay," she said. "This could be vaginismus"—Par shot me a glance—"Or, it could be something else." She snapped on a pair of gloves. "I am going to examine you." I looked at Par.

"Can my friend stay?" I asked.

"Yes, of course; so nice that you have such a good friend." Par took my hand in theirs. Dr. B. showed me each of her instruments before she used them: a speculum, a metal device that looked like a torture instrument ("But we will get a pediatric one for you, so it will not be so much pressure"), and a long plastic stick that she would use to get a pap smear. I gripped Par's hand harder.

"I will be very gentle," said the doctor. Slowly, she began to probe me. Without consciously thinking about it, I began to sing: the Gimmes's punk-rock cover of "Science Fiction / Double Feature." Not missing a beat, Par joined in. When we ran out of "Science Fiction," we started singing "Dammit Janet." *We can sing Rocky Horror until the appointment is done*, I thought, *everything will be fine.*

"How are you doing?" the doctor asked. "How is the pain, one to ten?"

"Um, about a seven," I said. "Maybe a six."

"Good, good."

A few moments later, the doctor did something, used too much pressure. I sat straight up in the exam chair and screamed. *"Can you please get out of me right now!!!"* The doctor froze. Parvaneh froze. I sat, my mouth open—I hadn't meant to shout that way.

An attendant knocked on the door. "Everything okay in there?"

"Yes," all three of us answered. Dr. B. took off her gloves and threw them in the trash. "It's okay, it's all right," she said. "We can conclude the exam." I curled up into a ball on the chair, wrapping my thin medical gown around myself.

Why? I was spiraling. *Why would I react that way? What am I remembering? It has to be fake. That can't be real. I must have made that up. I must be lying to myself. I'm a liar. That can't be real. That goes too far.* Tears streamed down my face and made dark blue dots on my hospital gown.

"So, you definitely have vaginismus," she said. She produced a bottle of water, which Parvaneh opened for me. "I am referring you to a pelvic rehabilitation doctor." *Pelvic rehabilitation.* A cold, slippery phrase. "I think he will be able to help you a lot with physical therapy and medication for this condition." I nodded. She left.

"I'm glad I was here," Parvaneh said. "I love you."

"I love you too," I said. I still felt impossibly numb. Par guided me out of the waiting area and into the elevator. I was glad they had come with me. They had known all the right questions to ask.

I went alone to Pelvic Rehabilitation Medicine. I couldn't bear to come unwound in front of a close friend again. Dr. Roger, a tall man with a booming voice, gave me another painful exam and confirmed that I had an extreme case of pelvic floor hypertonia, a condition indicating an abnormally high level of muscle tension, and often comorbid with vaginismus. "I've been doing this for ten years, Victoria. Your case is one of the most severe I've ever seen in my career. Your pelvic muscles"—he held up a tightly clenched fist—"are like *this*." I nodded. I don't know if hearing that I was a medical marvel was supposed to make me feel better, but it certainly didn't.

Dr. Roger wrote me a prescription for diazepam and baclofen—essentially, Valium and an added muscle relaxant. "You can't drink on these medications," he said. "They don't interact well with alcohol." *Great*, I thought. I couldn't go home from a bar with anyone, and now I couldn't even drink at one. *Probably a good thing,* I thought. Since that night at Albert's, I had been drinking too much.

I've always had a hard time taking pills. These pills were so enormous I would have to chase them with glassfuls of water, fighting the impulse to retch them up. The medications made me sluggish and uncoordinated. It became harder to stay up doing homework at night, and harder still to wake up for class in the morning. I was chronically late to my lectures. If I ever skipped a dose, I would wake the next morning to find myself paralyzed with pain from withdrawal. For months, I struggled with those symptoms and side effects as a full-time student, in addition to working about thirty hours a week between five different part-time jobs. Unsurprisingly, my grades suffered. The meds didn't even seem to be helping my pelvic condition.

I could hardly see the point, but I continued to take them, not knowing what else I could do. Swallowing those pills each day was the only action I felt was in my power to make things better.

After my date with the gynecologist, and the realizations that I'd had about my past, Albert had gently but firmly told me that the "fooling around" part of our relationship was over, at least for the time being. I had physical therapy to go to, and meds to take, and he told me I didn't need pressure from him weighing on me to get better. I couldn't disagree. It felt like Albert had begun to play a different, darker role in my life; all things considered, it was a good thing we were no longer sleeping together, at least not in the euphemistic sense of the word. He was still there for me on nights when I could not bear to be alone with myself, nights where I fell asleep in his bed, nudged into the crook of his arm. But we had drawn a demarcation line, and that is where the line stayed. However, this wounded me. I longed to have a partner who would be supportive and present, rather than distant or inadvertently pressuring. I wished that Albert would be the former, but I never should have been surprised that he was the latter. I had become another girl who got tangled up with an older man and paid a price.

Albert didn't make it any easier for me to be present and watch as the other people in my *Rocky Horror* community, Albert among them, flirted and stripped onstage and took each other home. I was never particularly interested in hookup culture, but now more than ever I was aware of how much it permeated the culture of my *Rocky Horror* cast. I was *physically incapable* of participating in it. My *own mother* had caused me the sexual trauma that was manifesting itself physiologically in ways that prevented me from doing so, even if I wanted to. This chain of events felt too bizarre and its implications too great for me to comprehend at age twenty. I thought that I could feel what had been done to me in my body—not just the shame and guilt that lived in my brain, but the physical violation. My body was a place where wrong had been done to me. I felt that pain in class and in bed and walking to and from work. I carried it with me.

Performing no longer gave me joy. Rather than empowering me as it always had before, now I was too caught up in my insecurities to feel unencumbered onstage. It felt like all my anxieties that I was undesirable and unsexy had come true. After one performance where I cried for nearly the entire duration of the show, forcing an open-mouthed smile through my makeup and tears, I took a voluntary two-month leave of absence. I could not perform if I didn't feel sexy, or for that matter, happy.

I should have taken longer than two months. My depression was a constant that permeated every aspect of my life. Without the biweekly *Rocky* shows, however, I became utterly isolated from my castmates, the people from whom I most craved validation.

Albert's ending of our sexual relationship had affected me more than I was willing to admit; if I couldn't sleep with anyone, how would I be able to tell if I was getting better? How was I supposed to find a partner, or even swipe through Tinder, if I was *literally* unable to have that form of intimacy with people? How and when was I supposed to tell a new person about my condition, and at what point in a relationship would someone leave me for it?

I began to notice stinging sexual references everywhere; in advertisements, in jokes, in *SNL* skits. My entire social circle existed in a context of sexual freedom that my own body had excluded me from. The concept of sex taunted me.

It was a cruel irony. My mother had always staunchly opposed any sort of sexual or even romantic expression on my part, policing what I wore and the male friends I had, and even keeping me home from school whenever she knew I had gotten my period. She had never outright said so, because that would have required her to say the word "sex" out loud, but it was an absolute, unspoken rule that sex was bad, and should never be discussed or even alluded to. My vaginismus at once felt like a validation, a physical confirmation that *yes, Mommy really was that bad and did those horrible things to you*, and an awful parting gift from her: *I told you so.*

Maybe she had been right. Maybe fishnet stockings and premarital sex *would* send me to hell. Was all this just God's way of calling me to be a nun? I found myself attending church instead of *Rocky* on the weekends, searching for answers and clarity that I never found at Saturday evening Mass.

I only wanted to exercise the basic right of human sexuality, but it felt wrong to desire that. My mother had drilled rejection of that part of me into my mind from a young age. I had demons who no longer only wanted me to procrastinate and self-medicate and starve and die, but who told me that I was bad, that I was *sick* to feel this basic human urge. Often, I felt so ill that I dissociated for hours on end to cope with the pain, both physical and mental. I shook with the unfairness of the sexual abuse that had led to my vaginismus condition, which had occurred before I knew what sex was, or even what a vagina was, and that I had one. My wings had been clipped before I knew I had them.

That all happened years ago.

In the midst of this reckoning with myself, COVID-19 descended, shuttering theaters and sending me home from my final semester of college. The pandemic gave me extended time and space away from *Rocky*, which I could not bear to choose for myself but that I badly needed. I was still freshly wounded from my experiences with Albert, and my self-esteem was in the gutter. When I most craved reassurance and physical closeness with other people, it was taken away from all of us. The forced hiatus from *Rocky* in particular caused me anguish and heartbreak—this weekly, irreverent congregation of queer acceptance and love that I needed to hold me was no longer gathering. However, this also gave me the distance to see everything that had happened from a bird's-eye view.

This is the hard truth: The *Rocky Horror* community was and is a space that gives inexperienced, impressionable teenagers exposure to older adults. Some of these adults are inspiring, positive influences on young queer individuals, helping them to become the best iteration of their true selves. Some are not.

In the years since these events transpired, I now believe that Albert should not have been welcome in my *Rocky Horror* community. He did not directly inflict harm upon me; however, through our relationship, he had managed to make connections with other, even younger women in our cast. This made me feel even more broken and undesirable, and later overcome with guilt for the other girls I did not think to warn, who fell in with him and later spoke out against him. My relationship with this man led me to my vaginismus diagnosis, as well as a diagnosis of PTSD. Throughout this experience, I was devastated that Albert had ceased supporting me through my ordeal, only to move on and mistreat others.

In time, I came to realize it was not only the lack of support from Albert, but that of my entire *Rocky* cast which led me to feel so despairing and abandoned. No one provided me with support that was meaningful enough to prevent me from taking a leave of absence from the cast—a measure that was almost as mentally damaging as the circumstances that led to it. I had become detached from several cast members whom I had considered my close friends—seemingly in the wake of my association with Albert, who had developed a harshly negative reputation amongst the cast. I felt like I was being unfairly treated as an accessory to all of Albert's repugnant activities, even though I felt I was a victim of his attention. I felt shunned instead of supported, and I felt the absence of the protection I had previously felt stifled by when I was being treated like an innocent child. It felt like my secret fear had come true: Once it was known that I was not the pure "cinnamon roll" everyone had labeled me as, but a slut like the rest of them, I was no longer worthy of all the attention I had once received. What's more, after all I had done to shed that label, I had no desire to celebrate myself in my newfound sexual empowerment. I only felt new, more experienced layers of shame. The events of that year destroyed what little self-esteem my participation in *Rocky* had given me, and exposed how my relationship with performing in *Rocky Horror* had constrained me from self-actualization.

When my vaginismus finally did improve, it was not because of the medication, or the physical therapy. It was not because of the support of my *Rocky* cast, even though it should have been. I have since learned that I was not the only person on my *Rocky Horror* cast who had vaginismus, but I was the only person who had sought support from the cast for it. Few people seemed to know what to say when I confided in them, and still fewer seemed to recognize that at the time, I was crying out for help. I had not known what to expect in the wake of this diagnosis, but I did not anticipate having to relearn how to exist in my community. This period of desperately seeking fellowship and empathy is how I discovered who my real allies were in my *Rocky* cast—those who treated me as an adult and an equal, and those who didn't know how to. For a community that prides itself on body positivity, disability representation, and open discussion of sex, whose members claim to keep a broad definition of what sex can be, so few extended the same understanding or openness for someone whose body was incapable of having sex in the way they wanted to. It just wasn't sexy.

As far as villages go, the *Rocky Horror* community that contributed to raising me was unconventional and strange; it was neglectful at times, painfully oppressive at others. It was also, at several points in my life, necessary for me. I learned to use a tampon backstage at *Rocky Horror*. It was where I learned about how people have sex, how they can talk about it casually and without fear or gravitas. It was not the best environment where I could have learned those things; however, in the queer community, we often don't have a better one.

Every October and every June, NYC RHPS receives a flurry of applications from college students and other young people who want to join the cast. Many of them are gay. Many of them have families who do not support them. Not all will stay, but many will come to regard the cast as a family, to rely on us for tangible support. I worry that this gets taken for granted. I worry that we enjoy the concept of found family without any regard for the responsibility that must come with filling that role for those who need it. I hope that, as radical acceptance for gay and trans children might grow, the need to rely on found families might become supplementary. Until then, for now, like many queer communities, the *Rocky Horror* circle acts as a safety net. It saves lives. Because of that, its members must actively strive to keep its overall influence a positive one.

Despite all the dysfunction that my involvement in the *Rocky Horror* community has brought to my life, I am still a member of the New York City *Rocky Horror Picture Show* cast, though I struggle to learn the names of anyone who joined post-2020. I am still grateful for its existence, and proud of the small part I have played in it. I don't discuss here the lifelong friendships I've made, or the unforgettable moments I've shared with my castmates and the inexhaustible audiences who see the show with new eyes each week. I chose to tell this story instead of any others because, like any dysfunctional family, a found family has stories it does not easily pass down or talk about. Like a family, I still love the *Rocky* community in spite of these stories, but in order to keep our community safe, they cannot be made into secrets or rumors. They need to be shared.

The year 2023 was the first Halloween season since I was thirteen that I did not attend any screening of *Rocky Horror* whatsoever, not as a performer or an audience member. This was not intentional, and when I realized that the holiday had come and gone without a single slice of toast or playing card thrown at me, my reaction was small. I queued the soundtrack on my phone and listened to the opening strains of "Science Fiction / Double Feature." For once, the *Rocky* soundtrack was just a fun album, one I could listen to without concentration. It was absolute pleasure.

Your tampon secure, you head out of the bathroom to greet the rest of your castmates, who are starting to arrive with slushies and hot dogs, luggage full of costumes in hand. You gently remind Garrett, your dance partner for the evening, that you need to rehearse your dance lifts one last time before the show.

"Okay," says Garrett. "I'll show you how it's done." He winks at you, sets down his 7-Eleven Big Gulp, and cues the song on his iPhone.

You hear the familiar saxophone riff that begins "Hot Patootie" as you put your hair up, feeling an edge of adrenaline. On your cue, you dance like you've known the steps all your life, which you almost have. Garrett is a considerate and sure-footed dance partner; he has been doing this since he was eighteen, same as you. Of course, many more years have passed for Garrett since his first show than have passed since yours.

When Garrett does sidecar lifts with you, it's fantastic. He throws you from side to side, catching you with his left arm, then his right. You scream, a short, high-pitched squeal of joy. He might be cocky, but you trust him to catch you every time.

Garrett locks your hips in a vice grip and lifts you up. You feel your abdominal muscles engage, the same way you feel them kick in when you are on a swing, pumping your legs to get higher and higher. You are suddenly vertical. You feel the blood rushing to your head. You let go of his shoulders and spread your arms out like wings, feeling your body pivot on the fulcrum of his hands and your torso. You balance, and as Garrett turns, holding you over his head, you are flying.

Meeting My Mom at the Frankenstein Place

Birch Rosen

For my mom, in memory of Tim Buckner

WHEN MY MOM came back from the library with a *Rocky Horror Picture Show* DVD, I was excited, but I had no idea how much it would come to mean to me.

It was the late aughts, and I was an older teen in the suburbs of Seattle. My mom frequently borrowed library DVDs for me, usually movies I'd heard were classics: *Citizen Kane*, *Psycho*, et cetera. I watched them obediently, even though I frequently fought with my mom. I considered the movies part of my cultural education, and watching them with my mom was a safe way to spend time with her without her yelling at or insulting me. I don't remember us ever talking about the movies afterward; in fact, when I cared about one of the movies, I pulled further away from her.

We usually watched the movies together upstairs, but I wanted *Rocky Horror* all to myself, to keep it from my mom even as she tried to share it with me. She set the DVD down on the half wall near the front door, and sometime later I quietly took it down to the basement to watch.

I'd never seen *Rocky Horror* before, but it was already special to me. It had held an esoteric aura in my mind ever since I'd read Stephen Chbosky's *The Perks of Being a Wallflower*, which prominently features midnight shadow-cast screenings. I had been maybe ten or eleven, reading about things I didn't understand in a sort of dazed awe. *Rocky Horror* was a mystery, shown to me only in glimpses through context clues, but the characters in the book loved it. It represented a transformative kind of belonging. *Rocky Horror* wasn't just another movie; it was an experience that made you part of something bigger.

I'd never thought to check it out on my own, possibly because I thought of it as invite-only. Although I was often drawn to queer media, queerness always felt just out of reach. I was a "girl" (by default and lack of knowledge of other options) who dated boys. Sure, I was also sexually attracted to girls, but I hadn't had a crush on one and wasn't interested in casual sex, so that was purely hypothetical. Queerness, much like the Gay-Straight Alliance at my school, was a club I didn't feel cool enough to belong to. But now, finally, *Rocky Horror* had come to me, and I was about to be initiated. Now it was my turn to belong.

The movie was and wasn't what I'd expected. (Could anyone really expect *Rocky Horror*?) It was lively and raucous, with the same allure as all the queer things I thought could never be mine. It was a musical, which I hadn't fully realized going in, and the songs grabbed me and didn't let go. The plot was no less confusing to watch than it had been to read about, and it dragged a little at the end, after all the catchiest songs. Still, I wanted more: the shadow cast, the props, the costumes, the full spectacle. I wanted to be part of it.

I had the perfect opportunity a few years later, in 2012. Seattle's Neptune Theatre, which had first opened in 1921 and had had one of the country's longest streaks of showing *Rocky Horror*, had recently undergone an extensive renovation, and its grand reopening would be a shadow-cast screening. By then I would have moved into my dorm for my second year at the nearby University of Washington, but it would still be a few days before the start of classes.

As soon as I heard about the screening, I knew that I was going to dress up; that was never in question. But as who? I pragmatically decided on Magenta—a relatively minor character, but one that suited my body type and didn't come with too revealing an outfit. I bought cheap red hair spray at Party City and thrifted a black velvet wrap dress to turn into a maid costume, both of which I brought with me to college.

I was edging ever closer to recognizing myself as queer, having had what felt a lot like a crush on the first genderqueer person I'd met, a classmate in a literature course called The Queerness of Love. Calling myself straight didn't feel quite right anymore, but with no experience acting on queer attraction, I wasn't calling myself anything else yet either.

On the day of the showing, I went over to a friend's house to get ready. In the time that I knew her, she never identified as queer or anything, but she *did* write me a poem about my smile and try to give nude photos to Amanda Palmer at a concert. Her boldness captivated me.

While she dressed up as Columbia, complete with sequined jacket, hat, and bralette, plus a human-hair wig, I donned my dress, ratted my already-big Jewish hair, sprayed it red, made a little apron out of towel scraps and safety pins, and put on dark eyeshadow and red lipstick.

When she finished, we went to pick up another friend, this one costumed as Columbia in her late-night outfit of Mickey Mouse ears and striped pajamas. This second friend had been my first girl crush, although I hadn't realized it yet. When we had been in high school together, I'd thought it was fascinating that she was bi, and I had wanted to listen to all her favorite music, and she'd once mentioned wanting a zebra-striped bra, so I had always kept an eye out when I was shopping.

The three of us took poorly lit photos in the entryway of her house. In my costume, I portrayed a confident (if menacing) sexuality I'd never been able to access in my "real" life, wielding a feather duster as if I might use it on my friends.

We had all chosen our costumes independently, and I hadn't decided to be Magenta out of a particular connection with the character, but now that we were together, it just felt right. As Magenta and Columbia(s), we belonged together—not just because we were in the same movie, but also because there was a special intimacy between our characters in the "Touch-a Touch-a Touch-a Touch Me" scene. We were a pair, like Brad and Janet or Frank and Rocky.

When we got to the theater, there were hordes of Brads, Janets, Rockies, and Franks, and fewer Magentas and Columbias. It was as if there were a place just waiting for us. My friends and I took seats at the front of the balcony and took more pictures as we waited for the show to start. To my relief, there was no pre-show virgin ritual. When the movie started, my eyes bounced back and forth between the screen and the shadow cast. My (also *Rocky Horror*–virgin) friends and I did our best to keep up with the audience participation.

It was thrilling. I felt alive and included and part of it all, at the center of my own life, in a way I rarely did. Most of the theater-provided props (toast and playing cards, among others) left our bags for good at some point during the show, but I gratefully saved a plastic whistle. After the show, I got a picture with the shadow-cast Magenta, and then my two Columbias and I went out for frozen yogurt, still in costume. Being together made it safe to be weird. As she drove us back to her place to sleep over, the Columbia I'd gotten ready with stripped off her sequined top, giving me a final thrill to end the night.

In the next couple of years, I finally came to understand myself as an actually queer person, and the discovery upended my life in a way that caught me completely off guard. I came out as pansexual in the spring of 2013, after making out with a woman from my feminist club a couple of times to test my attraction to women.

The LGBT media I had seen had led me to think coming out would be the hardest part, but it wasn't. My mom had raised me with knowledge and acceptance of gay people as far back as I could remember. I knew she'd had a close gay friend named Tim until he died of AIDS-related illness, years before I was born. When I was in my teens, I'd watched shows (e.g., *Glee*, *Modern Family*) that had major LGBT characters and aired on mainstream networks to huge success. I'd always lived in liberal places. Sure, certain people at my school threw the word "gay" around as an insult, but among the people who mattered to me, it went without saying that it was fine to be gay (or bi, or whatever—although we didn't really talk about transness). I had no fear that any friends or family would react poorly to my coming out, and none did.

But once I understood myself as queer, all the homophobia in the world suddenly felt personal, and it was crushing me. The movie adaptation of *Ender's Game* was coming out soon, and people in my classes and dorm were buzzing about it without ever acknowledging that the author of the book was a notorious homophobe and that some of their ticket money would likely go to anti-LGBTQ causes. In my lifespan development course, I had to read about old dead white men's theories of what must have gone wrong in my life to turn me queer. A drunk man on a bus touched my hair through the back of the seat, ranting loudly about gay people, and even worse, no one else supported or even acknowledged me when I pulled away and argued with him. I felt alone and powerless.

I didn't tell my mom any of this. She wouldn't have gotten it. She accepted my queerness but didn't understand its importance to me. She didn't see why my opinion on queer representation in media should matter more than hers as a straight person, or why I cared that certain celebrities or fictional characters were bi. She asked me questions about my chosen label, "pansexual," but also referred to me as a lesbian, not understanding that the difference, to me, was profound. She seemed not to believe that I was still attracted to men, and my attempts to explain nonbinary gender never seemed to stick, which was additionally upsetting because I was beginning to think I might *be* nonbinary.

By 2015, when Fox announced its forthcoming remake, *The Rocky Horror Picture Show: Let's Do the Time Warp Again* (2016), starring Laverne Cox as Dr. Frank-N-Furter, my life looked much the same as it had in 2012, but I was a changed person. Following my queer crisis, I'd dropped out of school, moved in with my first girlfriend and gone almost no-contact with my mom for nine months, broken up with my girlfriend, moved back in with my mom, and gone back to college (a condition of my mom allowing me to live at home again). I was emotionally wounded and still struggling, jumping from one bad living situation to another as necessary to maintain the barely sufficient livability of my life.

The rift in my relationship with my mom was wider than ever, thinly papered over with casual conversation when we weren't fighting about how many chocolate-covered almonds I was eating or how I was wasting my life. We barely acknowledged the year I'd tried to escape my life as I'd known it. Despite the tension (and definitely contributing to it), there was an unspoken family rule that if my younger brother or I weren't working on homework, we'd all be in the living room watching TV together.

Our family culture put a huge value on any show or movie that the three of us, or even two of us, could agree on. My mom and I both liked musicals and enjoyed Laverne Cox in her breakout role on *Orange Is the New Black*, so as soon as *Let's Do the Time Warp Again* was announced, we knew we'd watch the premiere.

My hopes for the remake were high, while my expectations were less certain. The original *Rocky Horror Picture Show* meant so much to me (and many other people) that it would be difficult to live up to. Could anyone faithfully replicate that ecstatic weirdness?

There was one scene I saw clear potential for improvement in, though. When Tim Curry's Frank-N-Furter comes to Janet, then Brad, in bed, he initially appears to each of them as the other. Through the veil, he engages them each in ambiguous but decidedly sexual activity before revealing his true identity. While there's humor in the scene ("What have you done with Brad?!" "Nothing. Why, do you think I should?") and neither character ultimately seems harmed by the experience, the dubious-to-nonexistent consent troubled my newly articulated feminist sensibilities. I hoped the remake would take the opportunity to keep Brad and Janet's queer and sexual awakening while replacing Frank-N-Furter's sexual deception of them with more informed (though still naïvely virginal) consent.

When *Let's Do the Time Warp Again* aired, I was underwhelmed. The remake was framed within short scenes of an audience watching *Rocky Horror* in a theater, participating as audiences do. The depicted crowd is colorful and excited, but the sense of personal connection that I'd witnessed in *The Perks of Being a Wallflower* and experienced for myself with my friends was missing. It felt like being told I was being shown something special instead of actually seeing something special. Talking during the first commercial break, my mom and I agreed it was disappointing so far.

The sets for the first few songs were sufficient, but the castle interior was surprisingly spare for a movie. It looked empty and unlived in, which wasn't helped by a self-referential wall hanging that read "Be it" with a rainbow Pride flag, or a huge pop-art portrait of Cox's Frank saying, "Ooh, Rocky!" The "Time Warp" scene struck me as a disappointment rather than a spectacle.

As for consent, the remake kept all the dubiousness of the original while removing some of the most delightful and clearly consensual touching, between Magenta and Columbia in the "Touch-a Touch-a Touch-a Touch Me" scene. I remembered the original scene as a sort of frenzied pansexual orgy montage. The Fox version of the scene left me cold. Where had the fun, transgressive sexiness gone? The scene that had become so important to me had been moved from the realm of fantasy to the land of the uninspiringly mundane.

My mom and I finished the movie, quickly agreeing it had been a letdown, before I went downstairs for bed.

Over the next few days, I tried to put into words why the remake disappointed me so much. At my desk in our little-used basement where I did my homework, I repeatedly rewatched

YouTube clips of the scene in each version of the film to confirm my initial perception and to see exactly what had been changed.

In the original, Columbia and Magenta start the "Touch Me" scene having fun together while watching Janet singing in her underwear and seducing Rocky. While their voyeurism isn't consensual, their intimacy with each other is a rare scene in the movie in which two people fully understand the circumstances of what they're doing sexually with whom. The two are touching from the beginning of the scene, Columbia painting Magenta's toenails and Magenta blow-drying her hair while they gossip about Janet's virginity. When Janet hits the first chorus, Columbia first clutches then strokes Magenta's leg.

After the second chorus, the scene cuts from Rocky massaging Janet's breast to Columbia holding Magenta's leg and shoulder, bringing their faces together as she sings, "Touch-a touch-a touch me." Magenta laughs, grabbing Columbia's breast, then pulls her in by the unbuttoned pajama top as she echoes "I wanna be dirty" in reply. Columbia leans her whole body over Magenta's, her face briefly dipping into Magenta's neck.

Magenta points her blow-dryer at Columbia's chest, and Columbia cries out just as the visual cuts to Janet's moan at the beginning of the third-chorus climax. As Rocky and Janet switch positions so Rocky's on top, we see Columbia get directly on top of Magenta again, her body between Magenta's spread legs, both characters laughing and writhing in ecstasy. It's a sweet moment and also an undeniably sexual one, as the parallels between the couples make clear. It had been a scene of sapphic possibility to me before I knew I was queer.

The song finishes with a final reminder that this is a promiscuous, pansexual sex scene, with the "creature of the night" montage giving us Janet on the bottom, arching her back and grasping at the air, and flashes of all the other characters on top.

Fox's remake of the scene opens with femme-friend-fucking potential that quickly dries up. Columbia and Magenta share a bed, Columbia again in pajamas and mouse ears, Magenta in a short dress and fishnets. They both suck blue lollipops while watching Janet and Rocky on the monitor, and they exchange a glance as the song begins. Magenta's legs are wrapped around Columbia's waist, although the characters aren't facing each other. When they gossip about Janet's virginity, they're lying side by side, touching only incidentally.

The remake gives most of what had originally been Magenta and Columbia's screen time during the song to Janet and Rocky, even during Magenta and Columbia's brief echo of the "touch me" line. There is a moment of Magenta and Columbia standing in bed, Magenta sliding her body down Columbia's, but the shot quickly cuts back to Janet and Rocky. Lest anyone find too much woman-on-woman sensuality in this, our final view of Columbia and Magenta is of them standing in the bed, applauding for Janet and Rocky, not touching each other at all, with Magenta fist-pumping and whooping. This version of the song has no montage; Janet and Rocky are the only creatures of the night here. Whereas the original builds the enthusiasm and intimacy between Columbia and Magenta throughout the song, the remake gradually reduces their intimacy to nothing. The gal-pals version of "Touch-a Touch-a Touch-a Touch Me" chilled me a little, but it certainly didn't thrill or fulfill me.

(To be fair, it's not just the more sapphic characters who got such a desexed "Touch-a Touch-a Touch-a Touch Me" in the remake. With Rocky flexing, bicep curling Janet, and thrusting her into the air rather than thrusting on or into her, it looks like his muscles are all that might grow while he poses.)

Even the *Glee* rendition of "Touch-a Touch-a Touch-a Touch Me," with its substitution of "heavy sweating" for "heavy petting" and its bedless, school-campus setting, gives its bi and lesbian couple more sexuality and intimacy than *Let's Do the Time Warp Again* does. Brittany and Santana, *Glee*'s Columbia and Magenta, have all of the screen time for their own lines as they spy on Emma, the guidance counselor, seducing Mr. Schuester, the choir director, in a classroom. They clutch each other's arms and shoulders throughout the scene and each moan just before the second chorus. For their echo of the "touch me" line, we see them joyously dancing through the halls, Santana twirling Brittany around. They're clearly into each other and turned on by what they've seen. The bland unsexiness of the Fox remake was even more surprising because *Glee* had also aired on Fox.

A much earlier draft of this essay, the product of my 2016 analysis of the three versions of "Touch-a Touch-a Touch-a Touch Me," concluded there. But as I started updating and building out that essay for this anthology, I realized that the story of my relationship with *Rocky Horror* is also the story of my relationship with my mom. She was, after all, the one who physically brought it into my life.

In the years since we watched *Let's Do the Time Warp Again* together at arm's length from each other, she's worked hard to mend our relationship. I don't know the full extent of the work she's done internally, but she started restoring trust by finally believing me about how she'd treated me throughout my life and apologizing for her actions. As my identity and understanding of myself have continued to evolve, she's continued to ask me questions, and over time those questions have become more attuned to who I am as a person. Throughout my transition, we've revisited past periods of my life and finally talked about what I wasn't telling her at the time. She understands what being nonbinary means to me and that queerness is more than an incidental detail of my identity. And now that I can finally really talk to her about my life, I've become curious about hers.

Why *was* my straight mom into *Rocky Horror*? She would've been a teenager in the Midwest when it came out and grew into a cult classic. Was it just a movie to her, or did she have a personal connection to midnight screenings? She'd mentioned her late gay friend, Tim, now and then throughout my life, and we'd talked more about him in the National AIDS Memorial Grove in San Francisco while she was staying with me to help me recover from bottom surgery. He sounded vivacious, and he had liked to take my mom to gay bars. Had he introduced her to *Rocky Horror*, too?

When I started revising this essay, I called her to ask about her relationship to *Rocky Horror*. To my great satisfaction, I'd guessed correctly about her seeing it with Tim. As she told it, she'd been a teenager in semirural Michigan, and Tim was the first openly gay guy she knew. When he took her to a *Rocky Horror* showing, it was her first time being around a bunch of queer people. She described the experience as socially and culturally transformative, and the sexuality of the film as "fucking mind-blowing."

I felt like something had come full circle. I never knew Tim, and I'll never know what my mom would have grown up thinking about queer people if she hadn't known him, but I feel like I owe my mom's easy acceptance of queerness to him. He brought queerness into her life with all the campy audacity of *Rocky Horror*, and she shared it with me.

The Rocky Horror Picture Show, in all its messy glory, showed me a glimmer of queer life before I knew I could have a queer life of my own. It was sexy, resplendently alive, and old enough to connect me to a queer legacy, while still feeling utterly novel in its weirdness. My mom, across decades, states, sexualities, and genders, loved it largely for the same reasons as I did. The same fever-dream spectacle of a film that beckoned me toward queerness in my youth had welcomed her as a guest when she was young. There was a light in both our lives, and it was *The Rocky Horror Picture Show*.

A Wild and Untamed Thing: How Performing in a RHPS Shadow Cast Helped Me Discover My Bodily Autonomy

Aliya Bree Hall

CW: sexual harassment, mentions of
sexual violence and trauma

THE CAMERA ZOOMS in on the face of the Criminologist, whose tie is being climbed by a Transylvanian on a quest to find the Criminologist's nonexistent neck. Shouts and laughter from the audience drown out his final words, "It was a night out they were going to remember for a very long time." A dramatic clap of thunder—my cue.

I rush onstage with my scene partner, another Transylvanian, and kneel in front of our version of Brad and Janet, waving my hands over my head to the steady pace of *Asshole, Slut, Asshole, Slut*. I am a windshield wiper.

My castmates shout out directions that I know by heart. *Windshield wipers on weed*, I slow my wrist movement; *windshield wipers on speed*, I wave my hands as fast as I can; *windshield wipers on acid*, I undulate my arms as the crowd laughs and prepare for the final callback before I leave the stage. *Windshield wipers on molly*! I turn to my scene partner and run a hand down her arm as her body leans into mine. We fall into each other and roll off the stage, stifling giggles. It's just like rehearsal, except this time I'm in a corset and she's in her bra, and our bare skin touches in many places.

There's nothing particularly charged about the moment, but my body is still a live wire. I just debuted my first prop role. In lingerie. In front of a room full of mostly strangers. There isn't time to sit with the weight of that because "Over at the

Frankenstein Place" is starting and I want to chime in. But I can feel every inch of my body, and it's a beautiful thing.

I can't remember a time where I felt like my body belonged just to me. Even before my body matured, I was sharing it with the world. With adolescent boys who engaged in boundary-testing games like "fire truck," where they inched up the leg from the knee when I gave them the "green light," stopping only when I got uncomfortable and said "red light." The goal for them was to see how far up the leg they could make it. The flaw with the game that I didn't realize came from the name: When I said "red light," the boy said "fire trucks don't stop for red lights," and snaked his hand all the way up to the crotch of my jeans.

"Bean dipping" was another trend that took off in middle school that didn't require even the illusion of consent. Boys would run around and scoop underneath girls' breasts to brush a hand against their nipples.

While these experiences weren't unique to me, they did reinforce to me that my body was only my own until someone else wanted to play with it, an obviously harmful mindset to form in puberty.

From fourteen on, I was the perfect storm of doe-eyed, trusting, and disinterested in sex; a deadly combination considering that at the time I was also a 32DD bra size. I was told that if I were a Disney princess, I'd be Snow White because I was naïve enough to eat an apple from a stranger. Growing up in conservative rural Oregon, I fit the stereotype of a nice, nerdy girl with big breasts, and that was *extremely* appealing to a certain demographic of boy—and man. I swallowed a lot of discomfort, thinking it was normal for a senior several years older than me to ask if I masturbated (I didn't) and if I would do it that night for him. (I didn't, but as a chronic people pleaser I lied, hoping that would end the conversation.) He eventually stopped, writing me off as a tease. My embarrassment wore off quickly as the relief set in that I wouldn't have to talk with him again.

I didn't want to change how I looked or acted, and I hated the baggy clothes that could possibly hide my chest. I rarely wore spaghetti straps or strapless dresses, but so much of the clothing I wanted to wear for my own enjoyment showed a hint of cleavage. So I put up with the whistling when I walked into a classroom of freshmen, and with the thinly veiled comments in the hall. Even years after high school, a former classmate clarified who I was to a friend of mine by miming a large chest with his hands—even though I had been the only person with my name at our school.

In high school, I didn't know yet that I was a lesbian, but my adolescence had already affirmed to me that my body was created for the male gaze, an object I was only allowed to borrow when I wasn't being perceived, fondled, or coveted by cishet men.

For those outside of the *Rocky Horror* community, it could appear to invite the same type of objectification to join the shadow cast for a movie all about sex and desirability, where cast members in skimpy costumes yell vulgar things at the screen and about themselves. But for the two years I was involved, I carved out a space where I could, broadly speaking, "give [myself] over to absolute pleasure." I began the journey of taking back ownership of my body and redefining what being viewed as an object of desire meant to me.

By the time I headed to college at the University of Oregon, I had come out as bisexual and had already seen *The Rocky Horror Picture Show* multiple times. I was enamored with Frank-N-Furter, who struck me with his beauty and confidence in embracing raw femme sexuality. As he had for many others, he contributed to my gay awakening. Even though I arguably had more in common with the virginal Janet, it wasn't her journey that stood out to me; I longed for the fully realized sex appeal and command Frank had over his body.

Unfortunately, I wrestled with deep-seated shame and resentment toward my figure, despite the societal expectation that I should be thankful for my proportions. The perception that I was lucky only made me feel more guilty. Who was I to complain when I had a conventionally attractive body type that so many other women longed for? But all the attention was never about *me*. It was only ever about my *body*. I was dissected from the neck down. My personhood was so easily extracted from my physique that I removed myself from it as well. I retreated into my mind, distancing who I was from the flesh that held me, as a way to disassociate from the realities of what was happening *to* me.

It didn't matter that the majority of this behavior came from a gender I wasn't attracted to. I didn't come out as a lesbian until I was twenty-six and in a relationship with a woman. Before that, I was so entrenched in compulsory heterosexuality that I missed all the signs, all the cues my body was trying to give me that I wasn't attracted to men, until finally my brain stopped registering them. Discomfort seemed normal, because straight girls often talked about how much they didn't like giving head to men. I thought I simply didn't produce enough natural lubricant on my own. Even though I knew I liked women and femmes and pursued dating them, I just assumed men had to be part of the equation.

That was still my mindset as I attended my first *Rocky Horror* shadow-cast performance. A friend of mine was playing a Transylvanian and invited me to watch. It was exhilarating to be marked with a red lipstick *V*, the first step toward initiation. I attended the show alone, but didn't stay that way for long. I immediately gravitated toward two other women who were also virgins, and together, surrounded by a theater full of college students, we experienced the chaos as one. However, when the show ended, I knew I was on a different wavelength when I asked the women what they thought and they responded, "It was weird," followed by an uncomfortable laugh. I remembered thinking that of course it was weird—that was part of the magic. People of all body types and stages of undress layered a new dimension of humor over the film by breaking the fourth wall. It was a joke we were all in on, and I wanted that laugh.

I saw the Forbidden Fruit Shadow Cast again the following night, and auditioned two weeks later by playing "Happy

Birthday" on my ukulele. I hadn't realized this when I joined, but the majority of the cast was queer. While I recognized how integral queerness was to the film, seeing that reflected in the cast itself was a profound experience. I had never been in a queer-focused environment before, where I could let that part of myself live so loudly and openly.

I spent my first year as a Transylvanian learning callbacks and playing minor roles onstage as props. It was intimidating at first, but meeting twice every week for rehearsal quickly solidified my trust in the cast. My comfort grew as I played with and explored aspects of sexuality that were divorced from the concept of strictly male pleasure. Everything was on the table: There were jokes about masturbation, STIs/STDs, bodily fluids, gender fuckery, abortion, kink, and queerness. All of the lines were presented with a levity and silliness that took the pressure off of sex. Plus, none of it was mandatory. There were enough of us that we could opt out of specific callbacks we might not feel comfortable with. There were cast members who didn't like the abortion jokes ("As it clung to her thigh," *like a homesick abortion*) or who had family in the military and didn't appreciate *Semper Fi, suck him dry*. For the first time in my life, I knew my voice and concerns were valued and heard.

Every aspect of the shadow cast was informed by consent, from choosing my Transylvanian costume to our emcee sharing the rules with the audience members before every show. They would infuse humor while strictly upholding the safety of our cast. Performers weren't allowed to be touched, and we asked for consent before engaging with the audience. As the living, breathing representations of the film, we bridged the gap between fiction and reality, creating a bubble that allowed for hypersexuality and reclamation of queer language. We could set the context for the fantasy everyone was participating in, and we made it extremely clear that if you weren't willing to adhere to these rules, then you could—with all due respect—"get the fuck out." While the movie operated in blurred lines, we flourished within explicit boundaries.

The safety of this queer-focused community gifted me the realization that being perceived as an object of desire was different when I was an active participant. I was never once uncomfortable with having my corseted body on display or being used as a prop, because it was my choice. Performing in a predominately queer space helped create that sense of safety. It didn't matter if cishet men were there because, for once, they were an afterthought. I was performing for myself first, and for the queers in my audience second. It was liberating, knowing I could feel sexy and respected all at the same time. I could bask in the attention without there being an expectation that I had to follow through on.

My courage only grew in the second year. I took on a larger role as a femme, gender-bent Eddie—adorned with "bend over" gloves and a spiked bra. This was a big step for me, because at least the corset had provided ample support and covered more skin. This costume showed off my midriff and pushed my breasts up to expose everything above the nipples. As someone who still only wore tops that concealed my bra straps in day-to-day life, I somehow wasn't self-conscious in this costume at all.

That was a relief considering I was stepping into a role that drew all eyes toward me. "Hot Patootie" is a *moment*. It disrupts the plotline and is the catalyst for the second half of the film. Plus, it's fun. I ran around the entire audience on an air-motorbike, played a deflated plastic saxophone, and danced with Columbia. I even reprised my role during the dinner scene, when I hid under a sheet and mimicked having a boner until our Frank ripped the sheet off and revealed my "corpse"—blowing kisses to the front row. I looked hot, felt hot, and fully experienced the power and beauty in my body that Frank-N-Furter reflected back onscreen, coupled with the reckless audacity Eddie lived his life with. I've never yearned for the spotlight, but those moments onstage reminded me that I was worthy and deserving of attention, and I could be known for so much more than just my physicality.

When I found out later that a girl in my journalism class had attended the show, instead of internally cringing, I was filled with pride and excitement. I didn't care that I had put myself on display, or worry about that defining me. I contained multitudes. I wrote features for the university magazine, which included profiles of vagabond musicians and refugees, all while performing in *Rocky Horror*. Through this self-discovery, I had built a foundation for myself to trust and learn to love my body again.

This journey hasn't been linear. I eventually left the cast to study abroad and focus on completing my journalism degree. The safety and security that protected me on cast didn't follow me when I left the stage. I experienced sexual violence multiple times after I first performed. In 2023, I uncovered past sexual trauma I didn't realize had been locked inside of me. I have over a decade of disassociation from my body that I am still in the process of healing.

Rebuilding a healthy relationship to my body is something I grapple with daily. It's easy for me to want to slip back into numbness, but I have deliberately chosen to try to understand my body again. I am thankful to be in a healthy relationship that has given me the breathing room to engage in this level of body work, and I know now what safety and trusting my voice look like.

On Halloween 2023, I took my fiancée and two of our friends to see *Rocky Horror* at the Clinton Street Cabaret and popped their cherries. I hadn't seen the show in years, but in many ways, it was like no time had passed. Most of the callbacks came back to me instinctively, I lost myself in "Time Warp," and I even recognized a former cast member.

I dressed up as Janet, the rusty hinges on that era of my life creaking tentatively back open. I had a lot of anxiety and second-guessed myself leading up to the show, but the moment we joined the line of audience members, I shared smiles with other slip-wearing attendees and was buoyed by the joy that only this community can bring. As I sat in my seat, the trill of the piano introducing a pair of luscious red lips to the screen, I felt it: *"I'm going home."*

Becoming a Regular Frankie Fan

Roxy Ruedas

I'VE BEEN FASCINATED with the culture of *Rocky Horror* ever since I saw the film for the first time, when I was twelve. My mother showed me the film on an inspired whim—she had ordered the DVD for us to watch together, since I loved being in my middle school's plays and since my teacher had let me read her well-loved copy of *Sweeney Todd* a few weeks before. My mom was certain I would love this old movie that she had seen once when she was seventeen and only vaguely remembered. As we sat in our living room with my ten-year-old brother, who was hardly paying attention, my mother quickly discovered that *Rocky Horror* was a fabulously fun rock musical movie—but also that it had *far* more sex than she had intended to show her preteen children.

Though I didn't really know what being gay was, and I *definitely* didn't know what being trans was, I was utterly enraptured. The second the movie ended, I looked it up on my cell phone—on a private browser, *just in case* my parents decided to check my browsing history. Wikipedia informed me that there was an entire *Rocky Horror* community out there! The movie itself might have changed my world, but I was captivated by the idea that there were people who *dressed up* and went to theaters to see people *performing it*. I imagined a dazzling world of people in elaborate costumes with full sets, perfectly mimicking the film behind them. I wasn't quite sure why it felt so important to me at the time, but I did know I *really* wanted to see it one day.

As a native New Yorker, I was thrilled to discover at age fifteen that there was an active *Rocky Horror* shadow cast in Manhattan, and I dreamed of going to see it. By seventeen, I was a closeted lesbian who didn't want their parents knowing that they secretly wanted to be as indulgently queer as Frank himself. One of my close friends and I made plans to see the show together, telling our parents where we'd be. I got annoyed at my mom—not because she didn't want me to go, but because she wanted to *come with us*. I was vehemently against this, as my mother's presence threatened my ability to be openly queer. Even though I knew that in theory she was fine with expressions of queerness in other people, I was uncomfortable sharing a very queer space, with hedonistic displays of queer sex and identity, with her. My mother pouted: Wasn't *she* allowed to have fun? I told her she could have fun with her friends, whom she could attend the film with separately from me if she wished. And she did, to prove a point. Although I was desperate for independence and wasn't thrilled with the idea of her tagging along, my mother always supported my interests to a fault.

My friend and I dressed up in cute little outfits that weren't revealing but that also certainly weren't what we'd wear in our everyday lives. We approached the line nervously, since we were the youngest people there. We knew that we were *technically* allowed to see this movie alone, but weren't sure if they'd require us to be eighteen due to the nature of the performance in front of the movie. We had our IDs ready to prove how old we were. We were carded, as predicted, and the guy who checked our IDs told us we couldn't enter unless we had a parent with us.

Although that night could've ended in disaster, what I thought was going to be my nightmare ended up being my saving grace—my mother. After my friend and I were denied access to the theater, I sheepishly joined my mother at the back of the line and informed her that she needed to tell security that she was my mother. And then I watched my mother give a blow job to a banana in the preshow, which is exactly why I didn't want her to be there that night.

After I turned eighteen, I started going to see the show more regularly—without my mother watching over my shoulder. I loved the film and had a delightful time every time I saw it. I developed a small crush on a performer who played both Janet *and* Rocky, which was endlessly attractive to me, especially since at the time, I had very limited exposure to expressions of gender fuckery in my daily life. While I wasn't a regular, I tried to go whenever I was home on break from college. But there was something looming over me every time I went to another late-night double feature. Even though I was becoming more familiar with the film and more comfortable participating in the culture, I felt insecure that I wasn't more knowledgeable about the callbacks, which are the funny, sometimes raunchy fan-created lines that people yell out in response to things that are said or done onscreen by the film's actors. I knew that it didn't make sense to compare myself to people who had been going for years, but when other people were yelling at the screen over every other line, it felt hard to edge into that. I also didn't have the timing down for the few callbacks I did know. I didn't have a feel for the beats of the movie yet—how the lines were said and when the audience would respond, or the visual cues for many of the callbacks. Often, I would find myself saying them too early, or remembering them too late, and then getting embarrassed when I said something "wrong." I didn't know anyone else who was into *Rocky Horror* to reassure me or teach me new callbacks. Most of what I knew about the culture and show came from my internet research among the remnants of old web forums and lingering Reddit posts. But since callbacks are traditionally learned while physically at screenings, the internet provides little help. The first few things that show up when you search "*Rocky Horror* callbacks script" is a sparse list of callbacks from playbill.com when the 2016 remake of the film was released, and an oddly formatted fandom wiki.

College was where my obsession with *Rocky Horror* truly flourished. I went to a small liberal arts school with many queer people, and in my first week there, I had already shown all of my new friends the movie in my room. I finally met other people who thought that *Rocky Horror* was as exciting as I did, and who also resonated with what I feel is the sort of "thesis" of *Rocky Horror*: allowing yourself to feel pleasure and joy amidst everything else that is happening in your life, a sentiment that was even more valuable to me after coming out as transgender to my friends in my sophomore year.

The film was so important to me that my best friend and I directed a student theater production of *The Rocky Horror Picture Show*. We created an immersive *Rocky Horror* experience, staged with the audience surrounding the stage, and incorporating audience interaction and participation. But what really made our production stand out was the script of callbacks that I created for the Phantoms, the ensemble members of the show. I had painstakingly combed through the internet to find many different versions of callback scripts and chose the ones that I found funny or clever and thought would translate well to the stage. We also sourced some from cast and crew members, in the spirit of the collaborative process that created the original *Rocky Horror* callbacks. Although we only had three weeks to pull the show together and were practically working nine to five each day, every minute that I spent working with my codirector, cast, and crew is something that I cherish. I loved getting to create a meaningful piece of theater in collaboration with more than twenty people. In the end, our hard work paid off—we sold out our entire run, and it was arguably the most talked about event of the entire year! Not only did I make tons of friends, but the whole process gave me confidence that there was actually a desire for more *Rocky Horror* among young people.

After the show closed, the members of our production team wanted to have a little fun, and we decided to organize a one-off shadow-cast performance where we played the roles that we had always dreamed of playing. It wasn't the most organized or put-together show, and we barely knew the movie cues or what they were saying, but it ended up beginning something much bigger than just a one-off show branching off from a staged production. Some of the participants and our audience members were interested in continuing these shadow casts and doing more of them, and thus my college's secret underground *Rocky Horror* shadow-cast society was born. We already had a script of the callbacks that I thought were the funniest, and had done a lot of the hard work of finding people who were willing to dance around in their underwear in front of an audience. We refined our craft of shadow-casting and figuring out staging and blocking, and I slowly learned how to become a better organizer of both the performance and the parties that would follow. Performers invited their friends and anyone else they thought would enjoy it, and it grew over time. Forty people attended my final performance—more than double what the attendance was at our very first event. When I graduated, I passed it down to my successors, and they've kept it going in my absence. I hope that the performance and the script that I pieced together off the internet continue to be passed down for years to come, and that they develop their own callbacks and traditions.

Since graduating from college, partaking in the communal aspects of *Rocky Horror* has looked a little different for me. In some ways, it's much more traditional than what I had been doing in years prior. In the months between my graduation and finding a job, I did what any bored young person would do and threw myself into hobbies. I became a sort-of regular at the nearest *Rocky Horror* cast, and was starting to really enjoy myself and have fun at screenings. I quickly realized that there weren't usually a ton of people who attended *Rocky Horror* regularly who knew the callbacks. I attended multiple screenings where I was practically the only person saying anything. While I didn't talk to many cast members in those three months, there were numerous times when audience members would come up to me after the show and ask me how I knew all the callbacks

I did or tell me how impressive or funny they thought I was. I shyly accepted their compliments, told them my story about directing and doing research on the internet to create a script based on other people's lines, and reassured them that everything else about timing came with practice. One time, another audience member told me that they had remembered me based on a very specific callback I had said nearly a year prior at a particularly quiet show. Although at first I was completely mortified to be recognized by a total stranger for something so seemingly insignificant, I was kind of amazed at the fact that I had made enough of an impact that someone was even able to recognize me. That was the first moment that I truly felt part of the *Rocky Horror* community. I gave that person the link to my digital script and told them that they should contribute too, if they liked, or just keep it in their back pocket. Anything to make getting into the world of callbacks easier for another person, so they didn't feel daunted by them in the first place.

When I had to move away from a place where *Rocky Horror* was readily available on a monthly basis, I still found ways to keep attending, sometimes going when I visited family in New York. I also started to travel for my job, mostly traveling to large metropolitan areas for extended periods of time, and I needed something to do for myself so I wouldn't go crazy in the weeks away from home. In the span of two years, I saw five different *Rocky Horror* casts, and not one was the same. There's something so enchanting about being in an area and deciding to go see *Rocky Horror*, and discovering how a new cast interprets it. I always try to sit in the first few rows so I can get the best view of the cast and try to hype them up as much as possible. I tend to draw attention to myself because of how actively I participate, but that's just part of the fun for me. When the lights in the theater turn back on, sometimes a cast member will come up to me to chat. It's always good fun, and I love connecting with people in different *Rocky Horror* casts and such, but they usually start by asking, "What cast are you in?" While it's endlessly flattering, it often feels like

I need to lie about my true experience, which is to say that I didn't gain my knowledge the "hard" way by attending dozens of screenings in person and connecting with seasoned *Rocky Horror* vets, but rather by doing research on the internet and scrapping together my own version of *Rocky Horror* community. I felt (and still sometimes feel) that this somehow isn't "enough" to be considered a "real" fan, despite how knowledgeable I am about callbacks. Despite my own internal conflict surrounding this, *Rocky Horror* screenings are always a place that I can go when I miss home after being on the road for weeks at a time. When I'm feeling isolated and alone, I can find kinship with people I've never met before and may never meet again who are all sharing in the joy of queerness and self-expression for two beautiful hours.

As the film reaches its fiftieth anniversary, it's important to ask the question: Who embodies *Rocky Horror* culture, and who is it for? Many fans have a complicated relationship with the film. While *Rocky Horror* was a revolutionary piece of media for its time, with its unabashedly queer characters who are allowed to experience pleasure in being queer, there are numerous elements of *Rocky Horror* that are deeply flawed. The film includes casual racism, including the Zen Room and the orientalist music associated with this fleeting moment. The leading cast is all white, with an assortment of ethnic background characters that don't actually say anything or contribute to the already sparse plot. These background Transylvanians don't even show up in the wedding scene, just in Frank's castle, which is painted as a den of degeneracy. The ableism in Dr. Scott's narrative is a common trope that still exists in media today: a character with a disability who can magically throw off their disability, moving his legs again for the floor show purely because it's funny.

The ways the film enforces rape culture is also a visible problem, with Frank "tricking" Brad and Janet into having sex with him. The actor who played Brad in my production told me that they watched the movie with their family, and when the sex scenes happened, one of their parents said "That's rape!" and was scandalized that their child was going to be performing that. The ways in which Frank is depicted as a transsexual who tricks the virginally pure heterosexuals, Brad and Janet, into following him into sexual deviancy are classic transmisogynistic tropes. Some people classify both Frank's coerced seduction of Brad and Janet and his generally seductive demeanor as biphobic as well, seeing as Frank is, in some ways, the slutty villain of the story. Frank-N-Furter's own identification as the "Sweet Transvestite" is not uncomplicated, especially given that the originator of the role, Tim Curry, is a cisgender man and that part is still often played by a cisgender man in drag. Even the use of he/him pronouns for Frank in the film becomes contentious when considering just how deeply rooted the transmisogyny is within the text of *Rocky Horror*. And while I personally don't think that Frank should exclusively be played by transgender women in staged productions (I think the role can be suited to anyone of trans experience if done correctly and respectfully), I certainly didn't always feel this way.

When people try to confront the film's biases, some fans commonly point to the fact that *Rocky Horror* is intended to be a satirical film that draws on B-horror films. However, this doesn't address the fact that those films are *also* perpetuating bigotry. There are countless people who are uncomfortable with the way that *Rocky Horror* handles much of this content, and some people who even refuse to engage with it because of the use of language such as "transsexual" and "transvestite."

There are also issues of bias and bigotry within the community, including historical racism and antisemitism in callbacks. One of the most pervasive examples is the infamous "Sieg heil!" callback whenever Dr. Scott's name is mentioned. Though this is less common than it used to be, it still shows up every now and again and makes for a deeply uncomfortable night, knowing that someone else in the audience is okay making that joke. There are some people who feel that they can relate to all the aspects of *Rocky Horror* without reservation; very often, these are the white queer people who revel in the hedonism that the film portrays.

My own relationship with the film and its community is complicated. I can count on two hands the other people of color I've seen at screenings who have been more involved than seeing it for the first time with a live shadow cast, and don't even get me started on the lack of people of color in shadow casts themselves. While it's definitely true that there are people of color who participate in all aspects of *Rocky Horror* culture (especially globally), it remains a very white-dominated space, which is reinforced by the content of the movie itself. I've personally witnessed unchecked bias while experiencing *Rocky Horror*: On the last night of the production I directed, when it was common for participants to introduce funny changes to the blocking and words of the show, our music director decided to change the already racist Zen-room music to the more famous and even more racist oriental riff (you know, *that* oriental riff). It was both uncomfortable and demoralizing as an Asian person—I can't imagine what it must've been like for people who were experiencing this show for the first time.

So much of my own discomfort comes from the way that white queer liberation and joy seem to take precedence over critical thought and discourse on the more problematic themes of the film and its culture, and the white fragility that makes people defensive when any of this is brought up, because discussion is seen as an attack on enjoyment rather than something that can and must coexist with enjoyment. And although I myself am not transfeminine, I have often struggled with how blatant the "man in a dress" trope is in the film and the ways that people even play into that in their callbacks (notably, when Janet says, "The owner of that house may be a beautiful woman," and the audience says, "He is!"). But when someone brings up that people may not be comfortable with *Rocky Horror* because of this transmisogynistic trope, people (especially on the internet) get up in arms about pointing out an aspect of the film that isn't perfect and brush off the critique by pointing out that the film was revolutionary for its time and has been an essential part of queer culture and community for decades, as if both things can't be true at the same time. It often feels like people who love *Rocky Horror* are more willing to criticize the film for being a "bad" film with a low budget than they are willing to critique the film for these elements that have always been harmful.

Despite all of this, *Rocky Horror* has given me some of my most cherished experiences with my friends, and has become a comfort that I feel safe returning to even amidst changes in my life. I go to see *Rocky Horror* when I'm traveling because it's important to me to keep this community and these traditions close to my heart. After every single shadow cast I visit, I take the time to write down any new callbacks I've never heard before but thought were funny or clever, keeping my script as updated and complete as it can be, even though there's no one correct set of callbacks—there are so many that differ from place to place and person to person. The tension between these very positive and very challenging experiences is something that I'm always navigating, and I desperately wish it was acknowledged by white queer fans in a more intentional way.

We can't erase the harmful aspects of the movie and the culture surrounding it, and though some of that is in the past, there are fans still engaging in harmful behavior in the present. I believe there are a couple things that are critical to the future of this culture that has come to mean so much to so many people. Being unabashedly open and queer is already a core part of *Rocky Horror*, but fans and shadow casts need to make it clear that this goes hand in hand with dismantling bigoted ideology. This doesn't mean talking about the technical flaws of the movie itself—which *Rocky Horror* fans are no stranger to—but rather the tensions that exist within our cultural spaces and in the text of the movie. It would be a welcome surprise if casts told people not to say anything racist, ableist, or antise-mitic at the start of their shows, and made it clear that they do not encourage bigotry. Even people who aren't part of the cast can tell someone who says a bigoted callback "That's not funny" without mincing words. We all talk during this movie, so we shouldn't be afraid to use our voices to make a more welcoming community. No *Rocky Horror* audience is passive, and we are all capable of being complicit in bigotry both as audience and cast members. If we can say that we're slut-loving and not slut-shaming Janet, we can certainly make it clear that we don't tolerate Nazi jokes—especially now as fascism is on the rise.

Another critical part of creating a more welcoming space for fans is better archiving and preserving what we do know about the cultural phenomenon of *Rocky Horror*. Partly this includes encouraging older fans to document their experiences, but it's so much more than that. Many people want to know more about *Rocky Horror*, its history, and its culture, but so much of what exists online now is decades old. While these older books and blogs are deeply important to the history of the *Rocky Horror* community, I firmly believe that there should be more reassurance that there is still community and connection now—especially for wannabe fans and people who may never aspire to be a member of a shadow cast. It would be great to see performers post written histories of shadow casts on their websites. More accessible starter guides to callbacks can be so helpful and welcoming to people who are just learning about *Rocky Horror*, and can even inspire them to get involved or to start their own shadow cast. And while creating and archiving digital resources is important, it's also important to have physical archival materials. Creating a history of our own culture is something that will ensure the longevity and continuation of it and help to create a more unified sense of community around the fandom. We should make it easy for new fans to discover *Rocky Horror*, and embrace being queer as loudly as we can.

So, who embodies what it means to be a *Rocky Horror* fan? It's a question that turns around in my mind whenever I see a shadow cast or watch the movie in my own home. I think about it when telling friends from other countries to watch it, or when convincing a friend who's seen the film maybe twice in their life to get up onstage with us. I think back to my teenage self, so desperate to connect with other queer people across generations; a kid who wanted to see the movie with a live cast so badly but didn't want to go with their mother, and who didn't think Asian people could be a part of that culture. When you ask who embodies the essence of a *Rocky Horror* fan and what it means to be part of this community, I give you the answer that I needed to hear:

Anyone has what it takes to be a *Rocky Horror* fan. There's no right way to exist as a fan in the *Rocky Horror* community. Your level of involvement and participation in the culture have no bearing on being a true fan. There isn't a set number of callbacks that people need to know, or a specific way you have to dress. You don't even have to know older fans if you're too shy—your experience is what you make of it. There's a place for anyone to become a devoted member of the *Rocky Horror* community because there *is* so much that still resonates with people about this film fifty years later, and if you are one of the people it resonates with, then you belong here. But it isn't solely up to newcomers to figure out how to navigate the ever-evolving community: Current community members need to be invested in creating ways for new people to join the community and to make the new folks feel welcomed. There's no right or wrong way to be a *Rocky Horror* fan, just being interested and wanting it is enough. You can make it up as you go, but if you find out it isn't for you, that's okay, too.

Regardless of what you make of it though, it's bound to be an experience that you remember (*for how long?*) for a very long time.

Rocky Horror and the
Performance Cults of Flloyd

Flloyd

THE FIRST TIME I went to *The Rocky Horror Picture Show* was in March 1980. I had read about *Rocky Horror* in an article about cult movies in *Time Magazine*, which also included *Eraserhead* and *Pink Flamingos*. Before I ever saw the movie, I ended up with the soundtrack—I must have asked for it for Christmas. From the first song, with its clever compilation of movie titles, I was intrigued by the rich tapestry of decadent ideas and concepts in the *Rocky Horror* soundtrack. Why was the transvestite "sweet"?

I was spending the night with my best friend Mike, and his brother said, "Let's go see *Rocky Horror*." I didn't even know it was playing in Atlanta. My first thought was *Now? I'm not ready for THAT*. But when you're a guest in someone's house, you can't say no to fun. He ran around giggling and putting things in a bag: a deck of cards, a squirt gun, some hot dogs. "Mother will kill me!" I wasn't even old enough to drive, so he drove us all there.

In Atlanta, *RHPS* played at the Film Forum, which was located in a strip mall. We were standing in line outside the theater when a lovely creature dressed as a housemaid with a feather duster started making her way down the line. She seemed to be judging everyone. When she got to me, she stopped. "Are you a virgin?"

What was she asking me? "That's kind of personal," I said.

"That's a yes!" she said. "Oh no, this will not do." She took me by the hand and led me into the theater, past the ticket takers, past the popcorn stand, past the water fountain, past the men's bathroom and straight into the women's bathroom. This was a new world for me. She introduced herself as Hayley as she pulled out a mascara wand and started putting it on me. A little eyeliner and "Voila, now you're ready!" We went into the theater where people dressed as characters from the film were milling about, setting props, and warming up their voices, which, by the way, they wouldn't be using.

"This is Ken." She introduced me to a man—a boy, really— wearing a corset, black fishnet hose and a lot of makeup. It said 4711 on his right leg. He looked at me and said, "Do you have any tattoos, Braaaaad?" I didn't get it.

She put me in a seat on the aisle and soon the theater was full. My friends sat next to me and asked me what was going on. I didn't know that my life would be changing forever.

What happened next was one of the most magical nights of my life. I had more of a reaction to the experience than to the movie. I had read about the shouting of lines and the throwing of things, but hiding under a newspaper so we didn't get wet was campy fun.

I grew up in the suburbs in Georgia. Life in the suburbs had a very dismal promise for me—I didn't imagine a future of happiness while living in the suburbs of Atlanta. This was the first time in my life I'd ever found a group of people that sort of thought the same way that I did. It was a real eye-opener to see this alternative lifestyle and to think that having a happy life could actually be possible. I felt at home.

Hayley gave me her phone number and said, "Call me." I still have that piece of paper with her phone number on it. I put it in my photo album and I saved it forever because it was a Moment—a life-changing moment for me. I'm more of an archivist than people would imagine.

I left with this feeling of elation, and all I could think about was, *When can I come back?* At the time, I was too young to drive, so the possibilities of coming back were somewhat limited. I really wanted to be a part of this world.

I decided at a very early age that I was not going to lie about who I was, so I was never in the closet. My parents have always been really great, very loving. I told my parents I was gay when I was fourteen, and they weren't sure what to do. They thought they would take me to get help. The first therapist they took me to said that he was going to cure me. He had a giant poster of Jesus on the wall. That therapist didn't work out.

Later, we started family counseling. I have a brother who's three years older and very straight. My parents didn't want my brother to know that I was gay. So we would go to family counseling, but it would just be my parents and me. The second therapist pulled me aside and said to me, "We're not doing this because there's something wrong with you. We're doing this because we need to teach your parents to accept you." And I understood that. I was like, *This makes sense to me, we need to help my parents understand that it's okay.* That made me feel like there wasn't something wrong with me, that I was okay.

I come from College Park/Jonesboro in Atlanta, near the airport, and it's very redneck. I was super gay, so in school I was bullied to the extreme. My best friend at school, Cheryl, was a really beautiful Black girl, and I would walk her to class after lunch every day, and eventually a crowd started to follow us. People would yell racist slurs. We would hold hands, asserting ourselves in a way, but in some ways we were probably provoking the other kids by holding hands. Eventually the principal would have to walk us down from lunch to our class every day because this angry mob would follow us.

I would drive her home from school. People would drive their cars at me in the parking lot, so I couldn't park in the school parking lot. I was too afraid, so I would park across the street at the Burger King.

Several times, bullies spray-painted my name on the water tower next to the school building. One time, it said "Bryan Chambers sucks the principal's cock." Another time, I came to school and there was new graffiti on the water tower, which said "Bryan Chambers is a [n-word] lover." It wasn't just embarrassing to me. I mean, I was being slurred, but not in the way that Cheryl was being slurred. It was much more offensive to her to have that word thrown at her.

I called Hayley, the girl that I had met at *Rocky Horror*, and we immediately hit it off. We became famous in my family for having conversations that would last for over twenty-four hours. We would be on the phone literally for twenty-four hours, and my brother would get frustrated, my parents would get frustrated, because they couldn't use the phone. It was before call-waiting. As a result of talking to Hayley, I got my own phone number, and a phone in my room, at age sixteen.

I started going to see the film every week with Hayley, and we became best friends. Eventually, after I had been going every week for a while and hanging out with the cast, Hayley took me to a cast meeting, and I told them I wanted to be involved. They said that what they were missing in the cast was someone to do Lips. They wanted me to paint on fluorescent red lips and hold a black light so my lips would glow in the dark. I was kind of shy when I was little, and I came out of my shell very slowly. I had been in high-school plays, and I had theater experience in school, but a lot of it was directing. I had always been very nervous. So it was a good step for me to do this one tiny part.

After being around the cast for a long time, I would fill in for people, stand in for Brad. I was nervous about that too. But you're lip-syncing to a movie that's already there; you can't forget the lines coming out of the screen. And if you fuck up, it doesn't matter. That's what was so great about it as an experience—you could fuck up and it wouldn't matter, because it's *Rocky Horror* and someone's going to throw a hot dog at you. Being part of the *Rocky Horror* shadow cast definitely helped me with my confidence. I was eventually able to get up onstage and not be nervous.

Cast members would have these arguments about who got to do which character, which would create competition and turmoil among the cast. Sometimes they would just both do it at the exact same time: There would be two Eddies onstage at the same time. There was more than one Magenta. And there were people in the audience who were throwing toast and hiding under newspapers, and we had squirt guns and stuff. It became my life.

I started going to *Rocky Horror* before I could drive, so my father would drive me to the show and then he would come and get me. We lived in suburbia, twenty-five, thirty miles away, and my dad would have to drive at two in the morning. It got to the point where I would just spend the night at somebody's house.

I guess in some ways I was kind of wild, because when I was sixteen, I would leave the house on Friday and come back Sunday night. I would just be gone all weekend long, couch surfing and sleeping at my friend Hayley's house and just being out.

After *Rocky Horror*, the cast would all go out to gay bars and watch the drag shows together—Atlanta has incredible drag, and in Atlanta, if bars serve food, they can stay open twenty-four hours a day. You can go out to a bar at five o'clock in the morning and see a drag show. So when I moved to New York and the bars all closed, I was like, *No, this is New York. What do you mean the bars are all closed! What do you mean?*

One of the people from *Rocky Horror* was the guy who worked the door at a gay bar, the Locker Room. He knew that I was sixteen, and he actually had a kit to help people with fake IDs. He had a white grease pencil and plastic laminating tape, and he would scratch out your birthday and fix it. He would fix my ID so I could get in.

These people became my family. This lesbian couple from *Rocky Horror*, Kim and Lisa, adopted me as their son. Kim was very masculine and wore a cap and looked like a truck driver, and no one fucked with her. And Lisa was really beautiful; she was from New York and had this really intense Bronx accent, and she would play Magenta. They looked out for me and took care of me and kept an eye on me. When we would go out to these bars, we would all hang around together, and I felt like I had this protection.

I went with *Rocky Horror* people to see the drag queens of Atlanta for the first time, including Yativa Antoinette and Lily White, who died recently. Lily White had a big influence on me. She was probably forty at the time, and we thought she was ancient, but she was a goth queen who would do these dark performances. In Atlanta, many of the professional drag queens are like Barbara Streisand impersonators, and some of the drag is very straightforward. Lily White was the weird one. She would come out onstage with an axe, wearing a wedding dress. Years later, without even thinking about it, I created this drag act where I smash up a bar stool onstage with an axe, and my costume is based on a wedding dress. It took me years to realize I'm doing Lily White, imitating this drag queen that I loved and worshipped.

She actually gave me a toilet. She did this show where she was drinking schnapps out of a toilet onstage. And I said, "Can I have the toilet as a souvenir?" And she was like, "Yes, of course." So I took this toilet home to my parents' house and my mom was like, "You're going to put a toilet in your room?" And I said, "This is a celebrity toilet." Later, when I moved out, they threw it away.

One of the things I love about *Rocky Horror,* and something that I took from it, was this comical, humorous aspect to drag. Frank-N-Furter is a drag queen, but it's very old-school drag—the way I grew up with drag—and that is: Drag's just a man in a dress. There was Jethrine on *Beverly Hillbillies*, and that was a comical drag-queen role. I had also seen and was a big fan of Monty Python, and they did drag all the time. They did housewife drag, but it was always tongue-in-cheek, and it was never meant to be serious. Frank-N-Furter is not tucking, he's not trying to pass. He's just a man in women's clothing. I think that's an important aspect of the film for me, because later when I started doing drag all the time, I was emboldened to just be a man in a dress. There's an ironic, tongue-in-cheek humor about it.

I don't think of myself as being innocent, but half of the Locker Room bar was actually a bathhouse, where gay men were having sex, and if they paid to get into the bathhouse, they could get into the disco for free. People were on the dance floor at the disco dancing in towels, standing at the bar and hanging out in towels. And I never knew that part of the Locker Room was a bathhouse where they were having sex. I never put two and two together.

I also had no idea what a bookstore was; I thought it was a place where you could buy books! I didn't know that there were glory holes and people were having sex in the bookstores. I was so innocent, I didn't know that all of this was going on. I didn't learn about glory holes and bookstores and bathhouses until years later, when I moved to New York.

Rocky Horror was my first family outside of the family that I grew up with. It was my first cult. I really felt loved and appreciated and encouraged to grow and to be who I was, no matter what kind of a freak that was. It almost felt like the freakier the better.

When you're young, you meet people and they have attributes that you like, and so you emulate those attributes, like trying on hats. You learn from people that way. So when you're in situations you don't know how to handle, sometimes you act like your mom or your dad. When I was in *Rocky Horror*, I was definitely trying on a lot of hats. I was young. I was experimenting with my sexuality, I was experimenting with my look. At the time, I was very avant-garde and into punk rock. I started going to *Rocky Horror* in 1980, so punk was still happening. It hadn't turned into New Wave yet.

I was doing punk rock things. Hayley and I used to hang out in the laundromat, and I would wear a Tide box as an accessory, and it was very camp. We would run around and act really crazy, and we would go into the grocery store and lay in the meats, in the meat department. We got in trouble for that.

In my everyday life, I was experiencing extreme prejudice and extreme bullying, having a terrible time in high school. I would drink Jack Daniels and smoke pot before I went to school. My car was driven off the road. So that's what I was experiencing in College Park. And then I'd go to *Rocky Horror*, and there were all these gay people acting freely, and they were very loving and supportive. It was my family for two years of my life. And that was sort of my entrance into the world of professional drag.

I lost touch with my friend Cheryl after high school. I came home from the last day of high school, got my crap, and left. The last day I was in my parents' house was the last day of high school. At that point, I was driving and had a car, and I had already created this life for myself based on the people from *Rocky Horror*. In June 1982, I left my family's house for good.

My friends and I were sitting on a bench in Piedmont Park one summer day in 1982, smoking a joint, and RuPaul came up to us, and we started talking. RuPaul fell in love with my best friend, and eventually, we became best friends and we lived together. He was part of another Atlanta clique, The Now Explosion clique, which was connected to this Atlanta-based music TV show called *The American Music Show*. When RuPaul and I met, this huge *Rocky Horror* clique collided with The Now Explosion clique. And when those two cliques came together, it became a scene that ruled Atlanta. It was this creative fusion that caused all of these other things. RuPaul's first band was two people from the *Rocky Horror* clique. There was this other queen that was part of the scene, Benjamin Smoke, who also used the name Miss Opal Foxx, and was part of the Opal Foxx

Quartet. There's a Benjamin Smoke documentary from years later.

RuPaul was very confident about talking to strangers and speaking up. He dyed my hair blond and put makeup on my face—real drag makeup for the first time. He taught me how to put on my own makeup. And then when we met Lady Bunny and she became part of it, the three of us were just this major force to be reckoned with.

That was sort of the end of my time with *Rocky Horror*—I transitioned out of *Rocky Horror* to being with RuPaul and Bunny. In 1980, I was sixteen, still in high school, and for two years I went to *Rocky Horror* every weekend. Then when I met RuPaul and we started doing drag shows and performing, I didn't go to *Rocky Horror* anymore, but a lot of those people were already embedded into my life. The important people from *Rocky Horror* remained in my life as real friends, even without the connection of *Rocky Horror*.

In some ways, I got the confidence to do drag by being forced to do drag by RuPaul. RuPaul collected people, he was like the Andy Warhol of our clique. He would name them, like my friend Laurie, who lived with us and was a very important part of the scene. RuPaul named her Laurie Nevada, and he directed two films of her as a superhero called Disco Isis. He would book these shows with us, and a lot of times he would tell us what numbers we were going to do, and he would set it all up and figure out the order, and he would present us as basically the House of RuPaul. It wasn't a phrase that was around, but we were essentially the House of RuPaul.

I was taking lots of drugs; I would buy acid by the sheet, a hundred hits of acid. And that would be just for my friends and me. I wasn't trying to sell that. That was just so that we had our share, and we would do acid every other day.

Me and Ru and Bunny were like groupies for The Now Explosion, and we would follow them around. I had a car, and so I would drive us to North Carolina to see them. We would follow them to Tennessee, and we would be in the audience, dancing, and we would get other people to start dancing, and get the party started, because we were so excited about the band.

The Now Explosion booked a show at the Pyramid in New York City, and the Pyramid wanted a whole weekend of Atlanta. And so Larry Tee asked us if we would perform. They called it the Old South Show. And Nelson Sullivan, who was part of this other clique, videotaped it. There's actually a video on YouTube of me and Ru and Bunny all performing together in New York City for the very first time in 1984. When Ru and Bunny and the rest of us came to New York and went to the Pyramid, they called us the Atlanta Drag Mafia because we just showed up and took over.

After that Atlanta weekend, Bunny stayed in New York, and me and Ru went back to Atlanta for a while. My father worked for Delta, and I got to fly for free. So whenever The Now Explosion would play in New York, I would go. I went several times before all of us went there together and stayed. I lived in Harlem in '85, and San Francisco in '86. I've only been in New York permanently since 1987.

I started having sex very young, when I was sixteen. I was hanging out with *Rocky Horror* people, but I was also hooking up with people. That was 1980, before people were talking about condoms. I don't think people started talking about condoms till, I don't know, '82 or '83. But when I first started having sex, when I was young, gay people never used condoms. We weren't worried about having babies.

When AIDS happened, people were really scared about it, and people stopped having sex—a lot of people became abstinent until we figured out what was going on. I really dodged a bullet, and I don't how I am HIV negative. I do know that at one point in 1986, when I lived in San Francisco, I sort of had to come to this conclusion, and it was this: If I have to stop giving blow jobs, I'd rather die. I'm going to keep giving blow jobs. And if that kills me, then it just kills me. Then that's going to be the story of my life.

I think a lot of us here in New York just somehow knew that this is where we had to be. When I came to New York, I went to the Pyramid Club, which was kind of like *Rocky Horror*—another place where I was like, *Oh my God, I've come home.* I'd walk into the Pyramid and there'd be all these drag queens dancing on the bar. There were drag queens who were not trying to be pretty drag queens, who were just doing crazy things. This one queen did this act with these two raw chickens on her hands. It was very much up my alley.

The Pyramid wasn't a gay bar, it was this freakish place where crazy people hung out. There were straight people like Lady Miss Kier from Deee-lite and Samoa Moriki and Kembra Pfahler from the band The Voluptuous Horror of Karen Black up on the bar. And you could see crazy shows. Nico from the Velvet Underground played there, and Genesis P-Orridge's band. And it became my job—I survived by dancing on the bar at the Pyramid. I think we got paid sixty or seventy dollars to dance there, and I would try to do it three nights a week, and I would live on whatever that was. I didn't really have a permanent place to live. I couch surfed and stayed at people's apartments until around 1990, when I got my apartment.

I became a Club Kid, and that was when the Limelight became my home, as part of the group of Michael Alig and his freaks. My history with Monty Python and that absurdity, and my avant-garde aspects really came in handy for being a Club Kid. I would wear just insane things. I actually found a bag of little girl costumes, and for about a year in the '80s, that was all I wore: these little girl outfits where the dress would stop at my belly button. I would be riding the subway in my underwear, a tutu, and a little girl's dress. But that was another family that I was part of.

Later, in the '90s, I was involved in the Blacklips Performance Cult, which was another family of freaks. It was very inspired by the Cockettes—they were doing plays, and they were taking lots of drugs and drinking, accepting the fact that taking drugs and drinking alcohol was just a normal part of life.

It wasn't something that you avoided before you went onstage. In fact, in a lot of situations, it was something you partook in specifically to go onstage.

In the early '90s, at Wigstock, I performed a Pete Seeger song, "I Come and Sing at Every Door," by This Mortal Coil. Afterward, ANOHNI and Lily of the Valley came up to me and were so excited that someone had done something weird at Wigstock.

ANOHNI asked me to be in Blacklips. I thought that ANOHNI was like Andy Warhol or John Waters, and she knew who I was from being a famous drag queen in the East Village. They were all going to ETW, the Experimental Theater Wing of NYU. At that point, they were performing at a bar that I was boycotting, so I said no. When they moved to the Pyramid, my home away from home, I said that I would be willing to come by.

When I went to Blacklips, I got that same feeling that I had when I went to *Rocky Horror*. The first night I went to the Blacklips, ANOHNI said, "We don't have anyone to videotape the show. Can you please?" So my first experience with Blacklips was seeing the play through the eye of a camera.

I said to myself, *This is a real scene here. They've got something going on here.* So I asked ANOHNI, "Can I please be involved?" They started writing me into plays, and they were excited to have this East Village drag queen that had sort of an underground gothic feeling.

It felt very similar to my experience with *Rocky Horror,* of having this family. I've been really blessed to find these cliques of people where I can be myself and be encouraged to be whatever that was.

When I met RuPaul, I had all this confidence inside of me already from *Rocky Horror*. I learned confidence about being onstage and not having to worry about fucking up, which is really important to learn. I think if you come to performance through the world of theater, there's so much pressure to not fuck up that it can be really intimidating. So to have learned the ropes at a place where it's a free-for-all was quite liberating. I built my foundation of performance in this relaxed environment of being able to fuck it up and still come back to it.

I learned so much from *Rocky Horror*, playing all the different parts and being able to adjust and adapt to whatever's happening. You never know what's going to happen at *Rocky Horror*. I built this ability to perform in a rainstorm indoors. It really was the groundwork on which I built my career, whatever career that may be. I have changed it a million times, but that metaphor of not being afraid to fail, I've taken into other categories of my life. Whenever I've done anything, I've been able to go onstage and be willing to fail, to fuck up, to tell the joke wrong, or to not get a laugh, or to feel the audience hating you. I've been able to take it in stride because I'd been through it; I'd had that experience.

When I met RuPaul and moved on to my next cult, I had all of this experience of stage time that didn't involve a lot of pressure. A lot of times I would be performing numbers that I wasn't even that familiar with, and maybe I'd just heard it the day before and didn't even know all the words, but I was able to perform without the fear of fucking up. And that's something that carried over into Blacklips—a confidence that you can only learn onstage. You have to live through these fuckups onstage and not be destroyed by them.

I'm not afraid of failing, which is such an important thing in performance. When you're backstage and you feel like you're going to throw up, thespians always say "You're not nervous, you're excited." I've learned that if you're not nervous, then there's something wrong. You should be nervous! You should be excited! You should be putting a little pressure on yourself to do a good job, and you should care. I think that that nervousness is an expression of care.

After my experience with *Rocky Horror* and RuPaul and the Blacklips Performance Cult, I feel like if I was at the Super Bowl and J-Lo said, "I'm running late, can you go out and vamp?" I feel like I could do that.

It was an incredible experience to have at such a young age, to be learning stagecraft at the age of sixteen, seventeen. I never would've been able to do all the things that I have done in my life without it. I give *Rocky Horror* a lot of credit for educating me, and not just in stagecraft, but in dealing with people, with the audience, talking to people. People coming up to you afterward and saying, "Oh, I thought you were great." When I was younger, I'd be like, "No, I wasn't. I was terrible." You have to learn to take the audience on and to say, "Thank you." Whether you believe them or not, if they had a great time, you don't want to ruin it for them by saying, "No, I was terrible." The audience is part of it.

Since moving to New York City, I have been to *Rocky* a few times, but I never spoke to any of the cast members. I would just go randomly, and I felt like an outsider. It's interesting to me that they would yell different things. A lot of the old callbacks have disappeared and have been replaced with other things.

When I've gone to *Rocky Horror* in New York, I didn't feel like that was my family. I already had a family at the Pyramid, and I had so much going on, I wasn't really in need of a family. I think if I had been lonely, I would've been more likely to talk to them and say, "Hey, I have experience with this. I know how to do this." But I never did.

It's funny—watching it, I could see the interactions of the people, and I could sense the conflict of who gets to be Eddie. It felt like I was watching my whole life, my past life, up there.

Who Lives in the Old Dark House?

Benjamin Larned

WHEN I WAS six years old, I asked my mother for permission to watch *Frankenstein Meets the Wolfman*. This began a life-long love of monster movies, especially the Universal films, from James Whale's *Frankenstein* to *Creature from the Black Lagoon*. Though they were made decades before I was born, I felt a strange kinship with these pictures. I wouldn't realize until many years later that the kinship was queerness.

In 1932, Whale debuted *The Old Dark House,* the second horror film he made for Universal, "one of the director's most flamboyantly gay and least seen."[1] A terrible storm traps a married couple and their bachelor friend, Penderel, inside the secluded Femm mansion. The heroes must contend with these madmen and women—particularly Saul, a homicidal brother locked in the attic—before they can return to normalcy.

A morsel of pre-code depravity, *The Old Dark House* is full of potentially queer characters. The Femm siblings—played by Una O'Connor and gay actor Ernest Thesiger—both come on to the visitors of their sex. Horace Femm is a self-pronounced "nervous man" who sees prayers as "strange tribal habits," while Rebecca Femm taunts the young female visitor with tales of "laughter and sin . . . lustful red and white women." The dying patriarch of the family is played by actress Elspeth Dudgeon in drag. Neurotic pyromaniac Saul is "a repressed homosexual as theorized by Freudian psychoanalysis: paranoid to the point of trying to eradicate the unacceptable desire"[2]—and Morgan is intensely devoted to Saul.

Even Penderel can be read as queer, in his dandyish dismissal of societal norms. But by the end of the film, "[he] has overcome the queerness of *The Old Dark House* (and that within himself) and been 'reborn' into a heterosexual union."[3]

Despite its censor-pleasing resolution, *The Old Dark House* is more progressive than most films of its time. In Paul Jensen's essay on James Whale for *Film Comment*, he notes, "Many films at the time used queer stereotypes for humor or horror. Few had compassion for them like Whale did. The inhabitants of *The Old Dark House* are quaintly eccentric, and even the homicidal maniac is helpless-looking and ingratiating."[4]

Whale's most famous films are, at their core, "ingenious and creative attempts to come to grips with the horrors of the Great War." Going further, Jensen finds that Whale has "the ability to transform grief into redemption." And "eroticism—specifically homoeroticism—can be a redemptive experience in the face of horror and trauma."[5]

Born sensitive and artistic to a large working-class family, traumatized by war, ignored by Hollywood for his open homosexuality, Whale was a lifelong outsider. His compassion for "monsters," unusual and discarded members of society, is apparent in his films. His *Old Dark House* is a haven for the strange. It gives "eccentric" people a place to exist as themselves, without being hounded by the ignorant masses.

If it escaped me as a child, this sensibility is clear to me now. From Frankenstein's laboratory to Dracula's foggy castle, Hill House to Manderley, the old dark house is a sort of queer paradise. A filmmaker like Whale understands that what is strange and horrific to one person is beautiful, even vital to another. He knows that someone rejected by society might feel at home in isolation.

Though for the Femms, the old dark house is also a trap, a personal hell where demons roam in the flesh. They find no solace there, only a living death.

As a kid obsessed with both musical theater and monster movies, *The Rocky Horror Picture Show* fascinated me. I heard "Time Warp" for the first time on a Halloween-themed cassette tape. "He stared at me and I felt a change / Time meant nothing, never would again . . ." The idea of being forever altered by a single stare was terrifying.

While Universal fare was deemed safe, my parents would not let me rent *Rocky Horror*. I remember my dad describing Frank-N-Furter as a vampire so aberrant, he couldn't seduce his victims—he had to trap them in his castle. This sufficed to keep me away for a while.

I finally saw the film at sixteen, attending a cosplay convention with a new group of nerdy friends. I couldn't follow the plot, but the blatant queer joy and flamboyant sexuality lit a fire in me. When it ended, I remember admitting for the first time that I wanted to sleep with a man; Tim Curry, to be specific.

After decades of anemic representation, queers have become adept at reclaiming media on our own terms, particularly horror films. From *The Old Dark House* to modern slashers, we find ourselves in the subtext. "And ultimately *The Rocky Horror Picture Show* (1975), which was not successful on its initial run, but which quickly developed a cult following, laid bare the queerer implications of the genre for all to see."[6]

In revisiting *The Old Dark House,* I find endless parallels to *The Rocky Horror Picture Show*. Both are tales of heteronormative characters who, by acts of God, are stranded in remote estates and subjected to the whims of the residents. Brad and Janet could stand in for the lost married couple; Riff Raff and Magenta are the Femms; Rocky even weeps over Frank's corpse like Morgan does over Saul's.

If *The Old Dark House* is a bitter satire, *Rocky Horror* is a joyous bacchanale. Yet Whale's films are seen as works of art, while *Rocky* is often called trash, only good because it's so bad. In contrast to other cult classics like *The Room* and *Troll 2,* however, *Rocky* seems fully aware of its intentions.

From the opening credits, as red lips sing about erotic

midnight movies, the film turns genre expectations on their head. *Rocky Horror* doesn't strive to make heroes of its heterosexual leads. The union of Brad and Janet inspires little enthusiasm—they're stilted, awkward, and joyless, ripe for an awakening. Richard O'Brien's script is full of jabs at their naïve worldviews. When their car breaks down and Brad offers to find a phone, Janet says fearfully, "The owner of that phone might be a beautiful woman"—a delicious touch of irony.

As they approach Frank-N-Furter's castle, Brad and Janet sing, "There's a light over at the Frankenstein place . . ." They hope for salvation, not knowing that they've been doomed to transform. The guests of *The Old Dark House* reaffirm their identities, but Brad and Janet will never be the same. They enter Frank's castle in granny panties and a sweater-vest, and leave in heels and lingerie. They can never go back to their comfortably chaste engagement.

There's nothing scary about this transformation, though. Despite its name, *Rocky Horror* contains no real shock or dread. It's no wonder the film captures our queer imaginations. The whole cast is hot. The sex is plentiful, mostly consensual, and has no mortal consequences of its own. Frank-N-Furter's line, "There's no crime in giving yourself over to pleasure," awakens something essential in us.

In the end, Frank is cut down for his transgressions. His peers destroy him for trying to live his fantasy, justifying their actions with antigay vitriol: "Your lifestyle's too extreme." "Society must be protected."

Frank isn't a guiltless victim, though. His flamboyant persona is an old dark house of its own, a grand, shambling structure erected around his yearning soul. He embodies many toxic gay stereotypes: He is vain, jealous, and manipulative, putting his own pleasure and satisfaction before everything else. He forces his vision of freedom upon others, contradicting his own mantra. Columbia cries at him, "You're like a sponge—you take, take, take and drain others of their love and emotion."

Yet, as he explains in his final song, all he wants is a home.

He performs the number to an imagined audience, then dies scared and alone. He learns the hard way that you can't manufacture a community.

As a queer person, I also struggle with these contradictions, the twin desires to find acceptance within a community and also to rebel against it. In *The Velvet Rage,* psychologist Alan Downs describes a similar feeling. He outlines three developmental stages for gay men: Stage One, Overwhelmed by Shame; Stage Two, Compensating for Shame; and Stage Three, Cultivating Authenticity.

All queer people, Downs posits, grow up with an innate sense of having been rejected. He writes, "If you hold the fundamental assumption of shame that you are critically and mortally flawed, how would you cope with this? One way, as we have seen in stage one, is to avoid confronting the shame"—perhaps like the characters in *The Old Dark House,* hidden away from the judgmental world. Frank's solution, meanwhile, is to "compensate for shame by striving for validation from others."[7] His elaborate musical numbers, diabolical schemes, and quippy histrionics are nothing but appeals for love.

Rocky Horror is a cautionary tale, a warning not to get lost in our own fantasies, no matter how out of place we feel in the world. A reminder that, joyful and exciting as it might be, the old dark house is still a prison. That the "eccentric" always dies in the end.

At the same time, the film remains a liberating force. When I first entered Frank's castle, I was awakened. Watching his tragedy is a rite of passage for so many of us. We move through his haunted corridors and find our true selves on the other side.

So what is the cost of this awakening? In claiming our place in the old dark house, what do we lose in the world outside? Is the house a haven, or a tomb?

After finding myself in the old dark house, I struggle to reenter the realm of "normalcy." My affinity for monsters causes me pain. My family loves but does not understand me. I drift between cities and communities, embracing loneliness instead of people who might accept me as I am.

In this way I identify with the Franks and Femms of the world. I want to shun normalcy and everything associated with it. I want to hide in a haunted house of my own making. Rather than overcompensate like Downs' second-stage gay, I want to erupt into otherworldliness, and leave reality behind for good.

Yet this desire is a fantasy in itself. The old dark house must burn down, and the Transylvanians must blast off to their home planet. The storm passes, and one must step out of the house and into the sunlight.

In Stage Three of *The Velvet Rage,* Downs explains that the path to happiness lies in authentic self-acceptance. But what good is self-acceptance in a world of rejection? How do the residents of the old dark house reenter society, when society refuses to welcome them? "How does one function in the world without the familiar ways of being?"[8]

These questions haunt me more and more. Throughout the 2020s, queer American communities have suffered increasingly violent attacks. With hundreds of antiqueer laws passed, books by and about queer people deemed harmful and censored, queer and trans people harassed, assaulted, and murdered, it's hard to feel safe in the world. The promise of the old dark house, a place where we can define our own reality, is more enticing than ever.

At the same time, it seems vital that we insist upon our existence. In the past decade, the old dark house has been lit up, made visible to the world, no longer hidden but brazenly present. We belong here, and we cannot hide at a critical moment. Our openness may invite attack, but it will also invite acceptance. It's just a matter of how much we can withstand before acceptance comes.

Where is the balance of safety and validity, presence and protection? We won't find the answer in a haunted house, or any midnight horror-film screening. But these spaces are still necessary for our cultural health and growth. *Rocky Horror* is the first film I saw that celebrated the queer bizarre, even made it seem enviable. Despite his tragic ending, Frank-N-Furter's joy and celebration persist through our own.

There is always a place for us in the old dark house, even if someday we must move on, into a world that belongs to us as much as anyone. Until then, we can dance the Time Warp and find kinship with monsters.

Notes

1. Harry Benshoff, *Monsters in the Closet: Homosexuality and the Horror Film* (Manchester University Press, 1997), 43.
2. Benshoff, *Monsters in the Closet*, 45.
3. Benshoff, *Monsters in the Closet*, 45.
4. Paul Jensen, "James Whale," *Film Comment* 7, no. 1 (1971): 52–57, http://www.jstor.org/stable/43752787.
5. Jensen, "James Whale."
6. Benshoff, *Monsters in the Closet*, 220–21.
7. Alan Downs, *The Velvet Rage: Overcoming the Pain of Growing Up Gay in a Straight Man's World* (Da Capo Press, 2006), 75.
8. Downs, *The Velvet Rage*, 109.

To Find the Truth I've Even Lied: Self-Deception and Liberation in *The Rocky Horror Picture Show*

Magdalene Visaggio

IT WAS, of all people, my conservative Christian father who introduced me to *The Rocky Horror Picture Show.*

Perhaps that's shocking; it wasn't to me. I come from a family rooted in that era's rock music; it's how my parents met, at a Long Island scene party in the late seventies. My mom was a groupie for Twisted Sister before they hit it big, and my dad played the Hammond organ for Burning Rose, sort of an E Street Band–style working-class rock act headed up by a guy with the incredible name of Billy Falcon. Music was the language we spoke at home, and so much of our lives revolved around the radio. So there was nothing suspicious to me about my dad wanting to share the wicked sounds of the Time Warp. But he didn't know, and couldn't know, what he was passing on to me. I didn't, either. Not yet.

My dad's been on my mind a lot lately. He passed away following a long illness just about a month ago as of this writing, and the last thing he said to me was unbelievably cruel: that he wished he'd pushed back harder when I transitioned, and that he'd been a coward for putting our relationship before his religion. The irony is that, while I was and would have been trans either way, he who most vehemently refused the truth of my nature was the very person who gave me the keys to the safest queer kingdom I had ever known.

In his mind's eye, *Rocky Horror* was probably just something that combined the science fiction movies he'd loved as a kid with rock music, the great passion of his life, which made it a rare opportunity for the two of us to bond. In that same mind's eye, the sexual content was probably casual enough to be laughed off, taboo enough to be ridiculous; and anyway, all the immoral behavior is ultimately punished.

Like every object of human culture, *RHPS* is multivalent: It's a sex comedy, it's a horror movie, it's an intoxicating invitation to wanton abandon, it's a searing critique of the excesses of the sexual revolution—anything at all, really, to the right observer. To wit: When I was younger and way more, how do I say this politely, *fucking stupid*, I bought into that last one. How else was I, a serious young Catholic intellectual, to understand that ending: Frank abandoned and murdered, Brad and Janet left crawling in the dirt and singing about the meaninglessness of their existence? What else *could* it be saying? It seemed so clear to that wide-eyed college kid so insistent on moralizing everything, as if every other interpretation could be shuttered away.

But I have twenty years on that kid I used to be, and things look very different from here. The same stupid ape brain now just as confidently sees something else, something stranger and more powerful than the scolding (and frankly queerphobic) version of the film that once I believed in: It's about the truth. Or, more precisely, the lies we tell ourselves to avoid it.

The truth, after all, is a funny thing. It gets slippery, a subject of our senses and reason, left broken and unfinished by the limits of what our eyes can see and our brains can apprehend. Everything I see, everything I feel, every single experience I have is mediated through my sensory organs—skin, eyes, ears—and then apprehended by this ape brain of mine (and yours, incidentally), one optimized first and foremost to forage for nuts and berries, and second, to make sense of the faces of other land apes.

But if the only tool we have to examine ourselves—our wants, our intentions—is the very thing doing the wanting and intending, that overclocked ape brain mentioned above, what are we bound to if not the immutable logic of subjectivity? We only have access to what we have access to, which is, ultimately, only our own minds. It should perhaps come as no surprise that we humans are exceedingly skilled at deceiving ourselves.

Rocky Horror is a cavalcade of lies. It begins at the church and doesn't end until Frank floats face down in the pool after putting on a show for nobody but the denizens of his own fevered imagination. However we want to define what a lie actually *is*, it gets difficult to keep count of the falsehoods flying left and right. It's easier to point to the few characters free of them—really just Eddie and Rocky. Everyone else has something to hide and something to prove, even if only from or to themselves. We talk a lot about *performativity* in queer circles, especially performative gender roles, mostly as a route to physical or emotional safety through conforming to socially expected behavior. But we are our own observers first and foremost, both subjects and objects of our internal discourses. We perform for nobody as much as ourselves, and the lies we tell ourselves are tailor-made for an audience-self eager to believe them.

Frank's lies are easy to parse, and their consequences the most obvious. He avoids answering questions directly as much as possible, preferring to deflect into his self-mythology. He sees himself correctly as a brilliant scientist, but his vision only extends so far as that, and the brash persona he maintains masks a genuine and deep-seated fear of the very people he both abuses and depends upon. He has constructed a castle in his mind, and however reified it has become, it is still ultimately a product of his own mind: that he is invulnerable, surrounded by devoted servants, free to do as he pleases, as long as he pleases, without consequence. To Frank, all of his bluster is absolutely true because it *must* be; the alternative, that his life is not a constant parade of triumph upon triumph, cannot and therefore will not be tolerated. Even at the end, as he sings his final song for ghosts no one sees but him, he positions himself as piti-able but ultimately victorious by changing the terms of victory. Where before he wanted Charles Atlas, now all he wants is to go home and escape the sadness he felt in his original leaving. Thus, he transforms defeat into a bittersweet finale, but only so long as nobody intrudes. Even when he has already been overthrown, his myth proves too potent for the truth to crack through until the laser gun is pointed right at him. His song is only for himself, a fitting capstone to a life of the self-deluded mind. But we do the film and ourselves alike a disservice if we let Frank's garish, air-sucking centrality prevent us from looking beyond him.

Brad and Janet, of course, begin the story as little more than stock characters—a couple of "regular kids," a reification of white suburban American gender roles. Brad is tall, square-jawed, intelligent, and dominant, while Janet is pliant, submissive, fearful, fretful, weak. Even their names conjure this: *Majors* evokes the military, the Six Million Dollar Man, conflict and strength, and *Weiss* simply means white or blond. At the wedding in the film's opening scene, Janet catches the bouquet, and then Brad proposes. It's easy. It's simple. It's *quaint*. And it is the movie's first lie, because Brad and Janet are neither of them the uncomplicated caricatures they first appear to be as they perform the essential act of heteronorma-tivity. Janet makes the right sounds—she marvels at the ring, she sighs wistfully at the idea of being a "Mrs. Ralph Hapschatt" and subsuming her identity into Brad's—but the best Brad can muster is that he loves how hard she tried to catch the flowers, and that love can be mediocre. If it all feels a little pro forma, that's because it is, a note that director Jim Sharman underlines by having the couple literally dancing through (and ignoring) a graveyard and a funeral. There is no celebration for their love, only a pain they refuse to acknowledge. You know as well as I that before the sun rises over the next day, both will be irrevo-cably changed. Both will have had to face the truth.

I draw your attention to Janet's part in "Dammit Janet," where the cause for her celebration isn't the engagement itself, but the ring and the ease with which she can fold herself into Brad's life. "Now we're engaged and I'm so glad / that you met

Mom and you know Dad" is hardly a ringing cry of love, but the shallowness of the feelings both she and Brad express for one another is the point. These are only words they are expected to say, and therefore aren't meaningful communication of mind to mind. It's an act, not meaningfully different than what the actors themselves were doing on set: reciting their lines and hitting their marks.

And so Brad and Janet venture forth into the night, ostensibly to celebrate their engagement, driving into heavy storm clouds and a dead end, symbols of doom as potent as they are obvious. They will end up stranded in the darkness, or would have if not for "a light over at the Frankenstein place." The light of truth, the light of discovery, and ultimately the light of the morning after. Darkness is where lies live; they cannot bear the brunt of day.

But in the meantime, the lie is all they have, and they follow it as long as they can. Brad keeps up the strongman act—and it is indisputably an act. He makes a show of resistance, but makes no actual efforts to resist. Janet's merest suggestion that they do *something* to get out of this situation is met by a vague plan to "play the aces when the time is right" while Brad lets himself and his fiancée be stripped to their delicates. He stands there, seemingly helplessly, faltering in his manly duty to protect Janet. Janet, of course, has the fallback of being a "helpless woman," a framing the movie places over her again and again to justify her passivity. But Brad? Brad has no such excuse, and his pretend strategizing only serves to highlight the truth that he will put up *no* meaningful resistance. Because, deep down, he *wants this*. He simply has no permission structure to allow it. Janet, however, doesn't need one; it is expected a woman will submit, and so she does. She has imbibed an ideology of virginity where her wants, ultimately, don't really matter.

Thus are Brad's and Janet's lies systematically dismantled; both ushered to separate quarters, where both fall for the flimsiest of excuses to indulge themselves. Frank's deception boils down to a wig and a voice, and is so ineffective as to collapse almost immediately as many times as it's tried. It turns out that the truth was far more effective at tempting them than the lie ever could have been; had it been Brad arriving in Janet's room, for example, there is no reason to believe they would have had sex. It's not clear it's something they even terribly wanted from each other. Brad would not have pressed Janet on the matter. Janet would have made no effort to persuade. But for people theoretically so in love with and committed to each other, engaged for literally hours, the fall comes swift and easy. Both partake of forbidden fruit, able to tell themselves the comforting lie that they were fooled—and besides, their partner will never know.

This encounter unlocks the door for Janet permanently; there is no going back once she has "tasted blood," because now she "wants more." Where once sexual desire embarrassed or shamed her—"it only leads to trouble and . . . seat-wetting"—she is now fully awakened to her body and its desires. It's easy to frame this primarily as the experience of sexual liberation, which is certainly the framing the film provides, but there is something else happening here: Her *self*-conception is crumbling, the lie she told herself about who she really, deeply *is*. I need to do some intertextual work here and draw your eye to the nonsequel sequel *Shock Treatment*, which again uses Brad and Janet as stand-ins for a particular kind of American experience. In that movie, we see Janet's parents, especially a misogynistic and homophobic father who proudly recounts the ways a man is supposed to be a dominant and even destructive force. A man, her father sings, "should be the mister / and the master of his sister . . ." These are well-worn patriarchal tropes so common as to be unremarkable, but they get their power from their seemingly infinite renewal and lay profound psychic waste to the minds they inhabit. Janet's mother, in contrast, is given no songs to express her own wants, existing entirely in the orbit of her husband.

Young women internalize this entrapment, treat it as given, a brute fact about the world. Young trans women do, too.

Insofar as both Janets in *Rocky Horror* and *Shock Treatment* are abstractions of American womanhood, the latter shines a light on the former by saying plainly what *RHPS* only briefly touches upon: Janet's self-deception is precisely that limitation on her freedom, taught to her by others but maintained by the chains of her own mind.

Brad's story, however, takes a decidedly different turn. He looks perturbed after his sexual encounter with Frank, unsettled by having let himself be taken in such a way, and the swift arrival of Dr. Scott (or Dr. *Von* Scott, a sly allusion to a hidden Nazi past) gives him a way to immediately resume his position. While he may not be Janet's source of comfort anymore—she flies to Rocky after the revelation that they'd all eaten Eddie— he can still serve as Dr. Scott's partner in science, a safe role that replicates and preserves his masculinity. But it's still a farce; Brad doesn't seem in control as he wildly wheels his old teacher from room to room, and once again, the only time he even attempts to resist what is done to him is when he is powerless to do so. "My God! It's like we've been glued to the spot!" he shouts, raising his fists for the first and ultimately only time, in a demonstration of his futility. Janet is changing in light of the truth; Brad doubles down harder on his self-delusion. Why?

I think there is a compelling argument to be made for Brad's transsexuality, but regardless of where he might land on the alignment chart, it is plain that he is not a heterosexual man, and is therefore treading on decidedly different terrain than Janet. Janet's self-revelation is that, well, sex is good and she is allowed to like it, allowed to want it, and this does not fundamentally demean or diminish her. This is, even in the context of the era, a moment of obvious positive growth and self-actualization, what Simone de Beauvoir would call *transcendence*, as in the freedom to exist *beyond* the constraints of one's own body and circumstances. De Beauvoir, in *The Second Sex*, conceptualizes this lack of freedom (which she calls *immanence*) as the essential condition of womanhood as such, the primary means by which it is contrasted with manhood. So for

Janet, experiencing sexual liberation is her first meaningful taste of transcendence.

Brad's situation is more complex, or at least has fewer obvious routes toward resolution. The profound taboo of male-coded homosexuality (and by extension transsexuality, which was not readily distinguished from the former in 1974) is just as rooted in the same theoretical and material conditions as Janet's degradation, i.e., a reality that treats femininity as essentially frivolous, unserious, and lesser. Janet, in embracing sexual agency, is "stepping into" a traditionally masculine and thus empowering space. By contrast, Brad's sexual coupling with Frank symbolically makes him feminine. What's worse is that he enjoyed it. He wanted it. He wanted it the whole time. And that means he *isn't* what he conceives himself to be.

Which brings us, at long last, to the Floor Show, the centerpiece of the film's moral universe. It is there, on the stage-within-a-stage, where Brad and Janet (alongside Columbia and Rocky) are afforded the theatrical and emotional distance to finally *tell the truth*. It is in the performance where lies fail under the spotlight's savage glare and are exposed.

I haven't touched much on Columbia, who is caught in her own self-deception; she spends the bulk of the film as Frank's loyal lackey, but witnessing Frank's brutal murder of Eddie, the almost-love of her life, makes clear to her that she has spent too much time in service to a selfish, homicidal *user* who "takes, takes, takes and drains others of their love and emotion." On stage, she is the first to say that she has "rose-tinted" her world to keep her "safe from [her] trouble and pain"; in her case, burying her anger and sorrow at Eddie's disappearance to maintain the life she knew. It's hard to miss her eyeing Frank hungrily during "Sweet Transvestite," and as she herself admits, "it was great when it all began." Rocky, too, has a great moment of truth—that he is innocent, unsure of what is happening, and that he was created only to be a sexual object.

But while Columbia and Rocky lament the ways Frank has hurt them, Brad's and Janet's verses are a striking departure.

Janet's is a paean to Frank's opening her eyes: "I feel released / bad times deceased / my confidence has increased / reality is here." Her deception has been stripped away, and she sees only a boundless future in which she has power over her own body and desires. "The game has been disbanded / my mind has been expanded / it's a gas that Frankie's landed"—she calls Frank's arrival in her life "a gas," a delight, and for her, it is. Despite his crimes, his violence, *she* has been changed for the better, and she now lives in the truth rather than the external, socially imposed lie that created her womanhood in the Beauvoirian sense. Janet is now an actualized subject of her own life rather than the vehicle for someone else's.

There is an incredibly specific kind of relief that accompanies that sort of experience; even as you know that not every problem is solved, *you* aren't the problem anymore. Janet's hair-flip joy is so genuine in its intimacy, its honesty—it's like a light has shined on her for the first time. Her discovery is simple: She is allowed to exist as an entire human being and not merely inhabit the parts of life prescribed for her. Once conservative and demure, she wears her overtly sexual costume as if stepping into her own body for the first time.

But not Brad. Where Columbia, Rocky, and Janet each strut and dance their way across the stage with bravado, Brad ventures forth uncertainly, his steps wobbling from his stiletto heels. "Rose Tint My World" is primarily in the key of D major—upbeat, danceable, triumphant. But Brad steps out and the fun glam-rock feel of the song evaporates into the key of F# minor—a lamentation that points to the future. Where the others make bold declarations of clear-headed truth, he starts: "It's beyond me . . ." Even in this moment, he struggles to articulate the truth and begs his absent mother to take these feelings away from him if he promises never to indulge again. But he can't deny them, cannot pretend he doesn't like the way he looks, the way he feels —sexy, free—not even for a moment. "What's come over me?" he demands of himself before "Here it comes again!" To this viewer, Brad's verse seems much more complex than an expression of bisexuality; the man who has spent the entire film trying his best to Be A Man is now dressed in sequins and fishnets like a showgirl, and he loves it. While drag and homosexual culture were and remain deeply intertwined, Brad isn't evoking some playful subversion of gender but rather is caught in the earthquake of discovering he *likes looking like this*.

It's worth once again mentioning *Shock Treatment*, which in early drafts centered the collapse of Brad and Janet's marriage, with Brad embracing his homosexuality and moving out. That immediately complicates any conceptualization of Brad as anything but explicitly and primarily androphilic; both characters describe their relationship as "bitchin' in the kitchen" and "cryin' in the bedroom all night"—except we learn later that the tears and sleepless nights are *Brad's*, as he is weighed down by an obsessive idea he cannot detach from. The finished film places Brad in contrast with a more overtly masculine version of himself in the form of a long-lost identical twin named Farley who taunts him: "You lost your baby when you lost your balls." The taunt serves to demonstrate how Brad is framed as *insufficiently* masculine; putting that in dialogue with "Rose Tint My World" is quite revealing, because Farley is *right*: Brad lost Janet when he stopped being a man. There is no way forward for their engagement in the wake of the Floor Show. They cannot ever go back to the way it used to be, to the people they used to be. The illusions have fallen apart; all that's left is the cold, dawning light which shines on them as they crawl in the wreckage their lies have left behind.

Because that's what lies always leave.

I transitioned at thirty-one, and my dad obviously didn't take it well. He'd always told himself he had nothing to worry about, that this would pass. My whole family knew what I was and always had; I was a pretty queer little kid. When I was really little, I loved to borrow my sister's clothes and dance around for everyone's delight. I was caught cross-dressing in middle school, and I would often swipe my mom's and sister's makeup.

As sneaky as I thought I was being, it was less a secret than a thing we didn't discuss, and my mom had no illusions about where it was headed. But my dad? He kept that possibility shut out of his mind for as long as he could. He took up any counter-argument that presented itself: when I went to seminary after college, and when I got married the first time, he called up my mother specifically to say "See? See? I told you he'd be fine. I told you everything would work out."

We are very skilled at deceiving ourselves, but my father's parade of self-imposed illusions is difficult to best; an absent father who told himself he raised his children, a neglectful husband convinced his wife left him for no reason, a man who claimed to hear the voice and know the will of God, which was somehow, coincidentally, always what he wanted. In his mind, he bore little responsibility for his misfortunes, but was beset by obstacles on all sides—a disloyal wife here, rebellious children there—and it only intensified toward the end of his life. He had done no wrong, failed nobody—except me, because he couldn't stop me from being trans. That was the perspective his brain brought to the situation. That was the only tool he had to examine the world and himself. And so the world he lived in was one of his own invention, one bearing little relationship to what we might call reality.

It's hard for me to disentangle my feelings about him from my experience of the film, so tied together are they in my heart and memory. He gave me the safest place I could be queer, a primping, preening, screaming farce called *The Rocky Horror Picture Show*, and then held that queerness against me for the last decade of his life. The same man who sang "Sweet Transvestite" with me told me he didn't know if he could ever bear to see me again and went to his grave convinced I was his punishment for the sins of his youth. There would never be a moment where he, like Brad, stumbled forth uncertain, overwhelmed by a truth he could not deny—not when he could keep his eyes firmly closed.

Again, the irrefutable logic of subjectivity rears its discolored, gangrenous head and demands of me that I account for the world he lived in, because it was the world he built for me to inhabit, too. I won't pretend to be immune from the subjective. Nobody is. My trans reading of Brad's story arc ultimately exists in my mind; probably everyone projects themselves onto the screen to some degree. I see so much of myself in Brad: my shame, my fear, my resolute refusal. I look at him and see the paper-thin shell of a man, a costume he would do anything to take off were it not for the fear of what might happen if he ever did. I was already anxious that my father didn't want to be in my life; why would I do anything to force the issue? So I didn't transition. Over and over again, I didn't transition. And knowing—*knowing*—he would reject me for it was a massive part of why.

So I, too, had to build my own lies. My dad wanted me to be a son, so I would be one. My dad was religious, so I would be, too. It was almost fun, building this demented half-born version of myself out of scraps of him, trying to emulate him to capture a moment of his attention, a little bit of pride, half an ounce of respect; and to whatever degree it worked, it was worth it to me. But at a certain point, the lie stopped doing what it was supposed to. It hadn't drawn him any closer to me, but I'd sold my birthright for a mess of pottage. It ultimately didn't *matter* whether I could be the son he wanted—and I had to acknowledge my own lie, the one that said he would ever be a real father. He wouldn't. He didn't. He couldn't.

And then he died.

So was it worth it? Was the lie worth a damn? Was it worth all the pretending, the hedging, the hoping, the prayer? The phone calls, the anger, the absence? All to satisfy one man's distant judgment, or his conviction that he alone could know the meaning of my life? Every mewling moment of pain, each morning of bitter conviction that, *no, this is the life you were made for, this is the life your father wanted for you*—all evaporated in the face of the simple truth: that I am a woman, and he was no father.

That sometimes, people choose to live in lies.

If there is any single "moral" to be taken from *Rocky Horror*, it's that lies are fragile, and there is no amount of subjectivity or self-deluding that can keep reality at bay forever. It will come crashing down around you, one way or another. It doesn't matter if you're ready for it. It doesn't matter if you're comfortable. Subjectivity has an irrefutable logic, yes, but the truth—the truth will always assert itself. You either stand to meet it or let it crush you once and for all.

The Sound of Home in Daydream

Rocky Halpern

THE RECEPTIONIST AT my doctor's office starts every call by saying, "Is this Rocky, like *The Rocky Horror Picture Show*?" And I laugh, and she laughs, because she knows something about me that I also know about her. Not unlike a midnight screening of *Rocky Horror*, my doctor's office is a haven for queer and trans people. The receptionist can probably see a different name somewhere in my chart. She knows it's not important. She doesn't need to ask if that's my real name, just like I don't need to ask for her pronouns. From nine words and the lilt of her honey contralto voice, an intimate and sacred connection is forged. There is safety and sweetness in the act of being clocked by someone from your home planet.

Upon hearing my name, other queer and trans people can't help but bring up *The Rocky Horror Picture Show*. It's a way of saying *I've noticed you're kind of freaky and queer—I am too*. Straight people often ask me if I'm named after the boxer movie: a ridiculous thing to ask of a fat, glitter-coated transsexual with a clown tattoo.

For many of us, Dr. Frank-N-Furter is our first exposure to something a little gender-weird. Tim Curry in fishnets, with red lipstick spread across a devilish feature-creature grin, does something for girly boys, boyish girls, and everyone in between. When I was a dysphoric teenager drawn to femininity but struggling to find a way to make it feel right on my body,

Dr. Frank-N-Furter's sultry crooning was a portal allowing me a glimpse of Transylvania.

"Don't dream it, be it."

An itch, an inkling of what might be possible, what might be coming.

I tell the doll receptionist on the phone that yes, it's exactly like *The Rocky Horror Picture Show*, but the truth is more complicated than that. I didn't name myself after Dr. Frank-N-Furter's golden-assed creation. My first chosen name came from a different blond musical theater starlet: Roxie Hart.

I was ten the first time I saw the movie *Chicago*. It was full of scandal, secrets, delusions of grandeur, glitz, and sex, and it lit my prepubescent brain on fire. *Chicago* joined the ranks of my other childhood musical theater obsessions—*Wicked, Phantom of the Opera, Moulin Rouge*—soundtracks I played on an endless loop. Musicals about outcasts, villains, tragic figures, creatures of the underground living outside of society: They touched a part of me that I hadn't yet contextualized as queer but that felt connected to a secret world brewing inside of me. They sounded like home.

Musical theater became even more important as I approached puberty and it felt like my world was beginning to crumble. I was a month shy of twelve when my family left New York and moved across the country to California. I was leaving behind the first girl I ever had a crush on and my proximity to Broadway. The secret world I felt brewing inside of me was beginning to break through to the outside. I didn't have the language of *queer* or *trans* or *dysphoria* yet. All I knew was that I felt different. I wanted to be a version of myself that I could perform with the same fervor with which I sang *The Wizard and I* at my school talent show, a cappella and covered in green paint.

I thought about how Roxie Hart shaped her reality to be exactly how she wanted it. She wasn't bad, she wasn't a killer, she didn't gun down a man and make up a pregnancy. No lie was too great, no story too outrageous to try out on her adoring public. I didn't have an adoring public, but I did have a captive audience in the form of my new sixth grade class. This was a chance to reinvent myself.

Just like Roxie Hart capitalizing on her murder charges to gain the fame she'd always longed for, the start of something new turned my fear and despair into a chance to be different than I was before. I was scared to leave my life in New York behind, but the dream of who I might get to be at a new school was exhilarating.

I insisted my name was Roxi, and so that's what it became. *Don't dream it, be it.*

I discovered *The Rocky Horror Picture Show* the year after I reenvisioned myself as Roxi. It was the freakiest thing I'd ever seen, and everything I aspired to be—perfect in all its nonsensical, horny, weird, queer glory. It helped me put language to what I felt brewing inside of me. It also helped me feel less alone during a time when I was the only openly gay thirteen-year-old at my conservative Orange County middle school. I couldn't and wouldn't hide who I was, and if that made me a freak, *Rocky Horror* was an excellent reminder that it was okay.

There was some part of me I couldn't name yet. Being called Roxi felt right enough, and being out as gay felt close to being true, but something was missing. Like Dr. Frank-N-Furter, I was chiseling away at the masterpiece that would become Rocky. I was headed toward something, but I couldn't see the full vision yet.

Act 1 as Roxi, I chose. Act 2 as Rocky chose me, when I found my fellow freaks. Rocky was a gift given to me by the queers I surrounded myself with in college. A butchering of Roxi that took hold during *Rocky Horror Picture Show* viewings with my chosen gaggle of drunk queers. Being in community with other freaks brought me closer to home. I liked the way being called Rocky felt so much that I realized Roxi was an in-between space. Like Riff Raff and Magenta on earth, I hadn't made my way home yet. Knowing other queers and feeling understood allowed me to become Rocky, to try out new pronouns and explore why, once again, I found myself longing for the act of reinvention. Reimagining the name I dreamed up for myself in childhood turned into the realization of a new dream altogether.

It's a delight to watch *The Rocky Horror Picture Show* as an adult in a relationship with another trans person, to feel secure within myself as Rocky alongside someone else who made the journey back to her home planet. During our most recent viewing, my girlfriend and I discussed that while Dr. Frank-N-Furter is the obvious choice for projecting early queer feelings onto, there's some other interesting stuff going on as well. Our titular character, Rocky, encapsulates the profoundly trans experience of being a newborn in an adult body and being horny and weird about it. Magenta and Columbia watching Janet and Rocky during "Touch-a Touch-a Touch-a Touch Me" is charged with truth-or-dare-kiss, slumber-party energy. The musical is a treasure trove of queer and trans experiences.

While talking about how much *The Rocky Horror Picture Show* meant to both my girlfriend and me during our pre-transition eras, it's hard to ignore the giant, red-lipped elephant in the room. While our love of *Rocky Horror* remains, it seems that love flows only in one direction, as its creator has dispensed some deeply troubling ideals about trans people, in particular trans women.

"You can't be a woman. You can be an idea of a woman. But you can't ever become a natural woman."[1] These are Richard O'Brien's words from an interview with *Metro* magazine, when asked for his opinion on the views of some very vocal trans-exclusionary radical feminists who argue that trans women are men. O'Brien, who uses he/him pronouns and identifies with being "70 percent male and 30 percent female,"[2] also describes himself as transgender and has been on estrogen for over twenty years. It's a confusing and hurtful position for him to take. Plus, few things in this world are natural, so what does that even mean? We're always learning how to be, how to fix ourselves up in the way that feels most like home. I wasn't born a bisexual, genderqueer dykefag adorned in glitter and pink hearts with a patchy beard, though it's easy to forget that when I wear it so well. My journey here began with being exposed to *Rocky Horror*, with getting to be in community with other queer and trans humans. O'Brien betrays and misunderstands his own people and fan base when he kowtows to the type of bigots who will never see him as human anyway. There is no point in trying to appeal to the Act 1 Brads and Janets of the world who cannot grasp the full, gorgeous scope of our humanity. They can either join us, or fuck off.

O'Brien has made other statements about transness and trans women throughout the years, and it feels like he's working through some serious self-loathing, though it's hard to be overly empathetic to O'Brien's personal struggles with gender when he's working it out on the backs of trans women. Still, I feel sad for him, this person who could dream up a fabulous and delightful musical romp about transsexual aliens from outer space but is still bound by the made-up prisons we've created on Earth.

The most brilliant thing about being trans is what we can dream, how we can create something out of nothing. I don't know how to be a natural man or woman because no such thing exists. There is nothing natural about what the gender binary demands. Whether or not Richard O'Brien believes trans people are natural doesn't change that trans people use *The Rocky Horror Picture Show* to clock and flag and find our way home to each other. It doesn't change the excitement I felt the first time I was called Rocky, or how good it feels that I get to pay homage to a musical theater legend through my name, how powerful it feels that my name itself has transitioned.

"I'm Going Home" is Dr. Frank-N-Furter's melancholic farewell, a final plea of understanding. She's not bad, just misunderstood. With eyes closed and arms stretched out, she is reaching for something. Then, her eyes are open and she's grinning and crying. It's a moment that captures the feeling of finding the way home, of moving into the truth of who you're meant to be, even if the cost is great. She knows what's coming, but through smeared makeup and tears, there is a glint of hope and a dream of what could be. To me, all transsexuals are that dream.

Notes

1. Nick Duffy, "Rocky Horror Star Richard O'Brien: Trans Women Can't Be Women," *Pink News*, March 8, 2016, https://www.thepinknews.com/2016/03/08/rocky-horror-star-richard-obrien-trans-women-cant-be-women/.
2. Jo Fidgen, "Richard O'Brien: 'I'm 70% Man,'" *BBC*, March 18, 2013, https://www.bbc.com/news/magazine-21788238.

My Words to Dr. Frank-N-Furter

Grace Lavery

A POST-STONEWALL, pre-DOMA musical, whose visual and textual idiolects derive from mid-century sci-fi B movies, in which a normcore straight couple is seduced into the pleasure and degradation of sadomasochistic sex, while remaining ambivalent about having done so, until an apocalyptic event reveals them, and every other human being, as nonagential objects of a cosmic death drive: This would seem to be a unique object. Except that there are two of them, and while *Little Shop of Horrors* has been the subject of many trans feminist critical appraisals, most elegantly by Morgan Page and Casey Plett, *The Rocky Horror Picture Show* has retained, it would have to be admitted, an appreciative audience not conspicuously constituted along equivalently minoritized lines. The difference itself is surprising: Of the two shows, it is *Rocky Horror* that walks the walk, depicting a gay bed trick, including frank and unhedged words extolling the virtues of masturbation and the female orgasm, and unabashedly focusing its erotic attention on a transvestite male lead. This transvestite, moreover, occupies the role of Victor Frankenstein in the plot: a literary forebear often thrown at, and no less frequently brandished by, any trans woman who disturbs the attention of a cis gay readership. (Susan Stryker's "My Words to Victor Frankenstein Above the Village of Chamounix" articulates that subjection directly, and in so doing inaugurated trans studies as a field of

scholarly endeavor.) *Little Shop*, on the other hand, sequesters
its kink in two locations where it can be moralized into noth-
ingness: in the heel Dentist ("who wants their teeth done by
the Marquis de Sade?") and, via a Black racialization, in the
marauding plant Audrey II, whose vegetal hardiness ends up
destroying the world, but whose affect and voice (supplied by
Ron Taylor in the Off-Broadway original, and the Four Tops'
Levi Stubbs in the 1986 film) evoke Blaxploitation soundtracks,
a slightly anachronistic counterpart to the show's narrators,
whose names (Crystal, Ronette, and Chiffon) place their vocal
styles within the genre of Phil Spector–produced Black girl
groups. And while the plant-triggered apocalyptic ending of
Little Shop regrounds the show in the B-movie genre and
recoils from the troubled erotic interiorities of the show's two
leads, and thereby reassures its audience that this world is
not, after all, their own, the apocalyptic end of *Rocky Horror*
amounts to a scalar distortion within which even the thermo-
nuclear anxieties of a 1950s B movie seem small—a universal
heat death, "lost in time, lost in space, and in meaning," as the
god-narrator leaves the room, turning the light off on a cheap,
spinning globe. A related scalar distortion occurs at the end of
Milos Forman's 1979 cinematic adaptation of the 1968 hippie
musical *Hair*, where all our hairy naked flower children, who
have spent the show letting all their individual eccentricities
hang out, are shaved and packed, within a couple of minutes,
into army uniforms, into tight lines of formation, into armored
carriers, into minimalistically adorned graves, and then into
the Mall in Washington, DC, where they change at last from a
chorus into a movement—though a movement in what direction
remains uncertain.

In his beautiful study of Broadway musicals, D. A. Miller
wonders what is lost when the supposed aesthetic merit of
gay self-expression is institutionalized into a genre with
mass appeal, and where (moreover) the straights are knock-
ing at the door, and, armed with seemingly limitless money,
a low-intensity homophobia, and an almost complete inability

to detect irony, the 1980s mega-musical made itself known in the bombast and blast of *Phantom* and *Cats*, *A Chorus Line* and *Fame*, *Les Mis* and *Miss Saigon*. These shows, authored by Andrew Lloyd Webber, Alain Boublil and Claude-Michel Schönberg, and Marvin Hamlisch, reinforced without irony the melodramatic generic tropes that, a generation earlier, were read by sophisticated audiences as evidence that it was not Bobby, but his friends, who were missing something when they chimed at the start of Act 2 of *Company* (1970) that "Bobby ought to have a woman." For Miller, that was really when the rot set in: "Being Alive," in his telling, resounds with the cruelty of an ex-gay conversion narrative. But there is no doubt that, for him, the out-and-proud bravado of the *Rocky Horror/Little Shop* moment makes the worst of it, with the camping rehearsal of *The Day the Earth Stood Still* and its ilk relegating not merely the ostensible subject matter but the queeny denizens of Broadway themselves, whose gestures and mode de vie are (in his view) imitated only lovelessly and exploitatively, in the service of a booming sector of the culture industry. "First you're another sloe-eyed vamp / then someone's mother / then you're camp," as Sondheim has one of his own resentful theatrical ghosts spit out, almost atonally and almost asyntactically, in *Follies*. The exuberance, it would feel churlish to admit, had more to do with money ("kept rolling in") than with gay liberalism, which, if it had seemed on the march in the era of *Rocky Horror*, faced, by the debut of *Little Shop*, the dual mortal threats of a pandemic and a bloodthirsty anti-sodomy movement, represented by Ronald Reagan in the US and Margaret Thatcher in the UK, which didn't bother to hide its murderous delight in the mass death of a generation of homosexuals.

In its ability to stage the coming crises for the inhabitants of the Frankenstein house, then, *Rocky Horror* is shockingly prescient—all the more so because of its apparent ambivalence concerning the viability of the life it brings into being. That is to say, on the one hand, the life of the character Rocky, the show's microcosmic avatar—a basic pleasure model (so to speak) created in much the same way as Frankenstein's monster, but with a narrower purpose—which is ended when Riff Raff (played in early runs and in the movie by the show's composer and lyricist himself, Richard O'Brien) murders him, the sweet(ish) transvestite Frank-N-Furter, and Columbia, one of the lovely ladies hanging around. But more broadly, the show finally registers fairly terminal doubts about the possibility of converting Brad and Janet into the perverts that, we had been encouraged to think, they wanted to be. This is not a coming out story, for good and for ill. At the end, Brad and Janet are left to rebuild, somehow, the reductively ludicrous heterosexual life they had set out upon before the transvestite and his cohort got their mitts all over the lovers. The vigor of the show's bait-and-switch plotting startles everyone: This was not, it turned out, a show about the seduction of two closet cases into the life delicious, but an allegory about the futility of desire in the face of apocalypse, the tendency of all relationships to fracture and all allies to betray one another, and the essential loathsomeness of the human species.

Such ambivalence cannot but be registered, partially, as structurally phobic, activating as it does the familiar device of scapegoating the homosexual, as queer, for the irresistible quality of desire that, in fact, makes pigs and insects of us all. But it cannot just be that, either. There is something genuinely bizarre about the world that *Rocky Horror* convenes for its audiences. How, in the end, are we supposed to parse the following, overfamiliar disclosure:

> I'm just a sweet transvestite
> from transsexual
> Transylvania

The show's vocal score gives Frank's line as "sweet transvestite," lowercase, and then the choric harmonies (separated into "women" and "men," rather than by vocal part) repeat it with initial capitals: "Sweet Transvestite." We would be inclined, I suspect, to infer that the chorus was therefore naming the song, rather than amplifying or contesting Frank's self-description, were the next word out of Frank's mouth not "Transylvania," a proper noun (warranting thereby the initial capital) serving, somehow, as the final form by which "transvestite" and "transsexual" might be harmonically copositioned. Useful, if so, since the mutual disgust levied between the two constituencies named by those terms remains somewhat legendary some decades after the fashioning of the term "transgender," which was initially formulated to dignify the transsexual with the charisma presumed by the transvestite. Indeed, surely Frank is a transvestite, and not a transsexual—he doesn't claim to be, merely to be from transsexual (Transylvania). As the tricolon of the lyric resounds bombastically, what had seemed like it might have been synchronic thereby reveals itself as shockingly sequential, not to say hierarchical: transvestite, underneath and before which is the transsexual, underneath and before which is Transylvania. The trope's final movement occurs in the show's terminal sequence, at which point "Transsexual" is resignified as, perhaps, a planet, rather than a class of person— the location from which Riff Raff and his crew have departed, to which Ithaca a future return is a promised, and in that sense deferred, event.

The role of Frank-N-Furter is generally played in mainstream productions by shock-cast (but what is the shock?) straight cis men who, if they take the role in order to admit to the pleasures of wearing frilly knickers once in a while, do so precisely as a homeopathic prophylaxis deployed to deter any further inquiry and perhaps even, in that surreal and oxymoronic formula, to demonstrate that they are *comfortable in their masculinity*. Tim Curry, who originated the role, has spent the last fifty years denying he is gay; the first out gay man to play the role in a major production was David Bedella for the fortieth anniversary revival in 2016; in the same year, a delegate from the planet Transsexual, Laverne Cox, was finally invited to assume the role for an adaptation on the Fox television network.

More usually, Frank-N-Furter has been played by an actor on whom straightness seems to fit almost uncannily well: Anthony Head (who, later, would play Giles on *Buffy*); Tim McInerney (a British character actor still probably best known for his roles on the 1980s historical sitcom *Blackadder*); and Julian McMahon, whose major role is that of the thirsty fuccboi Christian Troy in the early Ryan Murphy joint *Nip/Tuck*.

Could a transsexual exist in such a world as that depicted onstage for *The Rocky Horror Show*, except as a midpoint between the ancient Hungarian hinterlands and the swaggering, satin-clad cad? It isn't clear, and Richard O'Brien's statements about his own relation to transsexuality over the years leave one without much of a sense about how he wants the show to be historicized along with the grand narratives of gay liberal perseverance and trans liberal collapse. O'Brien has been married to three women and disclosed in 2013 that he had taken synthetic estrogen for the preceding decade,[1] following an interview in 2009 in which he described his iconic bald head as the result of the "feminizing" act of shaving.[2] O'Brien's baldness might be upstream, indeed, of an another fictional trans-something: Denis O'Hare's mesmerizing Elizabeth Taylor in *American Horror Story: Hotel*. He has also described himself, in 2020, as "transgender" in another interview—or, rather, he almost has: "Being transgender is a nightmare for many people. I'm lucky I'm in showbiz where I can be this eccentric person. If I were a primary school teacher maybe that wouldn't be the case." A piquant example: Indeed, trans educators are among the most viciously pursued targets of the current purge that leads to, for example, a far-right president adopting language directly from the UK's supposedly left-leading TERF movement in an edict entitled "Defending Women from Gender Ideology Extremism and Restoring Biological Truth to the Federal Government." Is it clear, though, that O'Brien considers that purge unjustified, or is he merely relieved that he's exempt from it, safe in the seclusion of showbiz eccentricity? He goes on:

We've seen what's been happening with J. K. Rowling. I think anybody who decides to take the huge step with a sex change deserves encouragement and a thumbs-up. As long as they're happy and fulfilled, I applaud them to my very last day. But you can't ever become a natural woman. I think that's probably where Rowling is coming from. That's as far as I'm going to go because people get upset if I have an opinion that doesn't line up with theirs. They think I'm being mean-spirited and I don't want that at all.[3]

If it isn't clear what might lie behind these not especially tactful evasions, it is at least clear that O'Brien sees himself aligned more directly with J. K. Rowling—a famous person misunderstood and vilified for failing to parrot the trendy cant—than with the primary school teacher he deployed as a punchline a few minutes earlier. The mainstreaming of a queer aesthetic qua aesthetic has been paid for with the negation of queer ways of living and of knowing—the final destination of the straightification of Broadway. The studied anachronism of *Rocky Horror*, then, endures into a present scene where the meaning of phrases like "I Can Make You a Man" seem, if no less titillating and suggestive, suddenly possessed of a strange mixture of irrelevance and moral exigency. That the show ends with O'Brien shooting the sweet transvestite to death does not succeed in securing top billing for "the handyman" Riff Raff; rather it signifies the irrelevance of the show's celestially mobile victors, Riff Raff and Magenta, to the stories of those they gun down on their way off planet. Perhaps also, then, they have proved their irrelevance to us insects, who remain below, bleeding and immobilized, in the world which the stars pass over.

Notes

1. Jo Fidgen, "Richard O'Brien: 'I'm 70% Man,'" BBC, March 18, 2013, https://www.bbc.com/news/magazine-21788238.
2. "Richard O'Brien: 'Society should not dictate gender,'" *Pink News*, August 18, 2009, https://web.archive.org/web/20120227150829/http:/gay.pinknews.co.uk/2009/08/18/richard-obrien-society-should-not-dictate-gender/.
3. Richard O'Brien, "Rocky Horror's Richard O'Brien: 'I should be dead. I've had an excessive lifestyle,'" interview by Ryan Gilbey, *The Guardian*, November 5, 2020, https://www.theguardian.com/stage/2020/nov/05/richard-obrien-interview-rocky-horror-trans-crack-stroke-70s.

Double Feature

Tanya Marquardt

> *It works on so many levels, doesn't it? It works as a trashy, fun, camp piece of theatre, but, like all fairy tales, we don't know why they've had the longevity that they have . . . and though we accept them on a surface level, subliminally there's a darker tale in there, and I think* Rocky *works a little on that.*
> —Richard O'Brien, creator of
> *The Rocky Horror Picture Show*[1]

THE FIRST TIME I saw Tim Curry, aka Dr. Frank-N-Furter, his white platforms glowing against the darkness of a descending elevator, it reminded me of the first time I wore leather to a kink party. Sixteen years old, 1996, a hundred and twenty pounds, six feet tall, at this club called the Hungry Eye. Later I would go to the Twilight Zone and then Celebrities. You didn't get carded then, and you could still smoke inside the clubs. My best friend, named Tanya G., put thick, clown-red lipstick on my lips, sealed them with gooey, sparkle shellac. That night I was pulled into a bathroom stall by a different Tanya—so many Tanyas—and she kissed me, soft but desirous, a hungry mouth-to-mouth resuscitation, lipstick on lipstick, thick as steel girders.

At the clubs, I watched my friends hit each other a little, sometimes a lot, watched them fuck each other, in public mostly, but sometimes in private, their clothing strewn all over the floor of Tanya G.'s apartment: multicolor polyester sashes and *Fifth Element* orange wigs, extra-large mesh bodysuits and size-fourteen heels. Her apartment was hidden down a back alley off Davie Street, the main drag for gay men in Vancouver, British Columbia. It was filled with chain mail in emptied-out ice-cream buckets, and homemade leather masks, and Tanya G.'s hand-tailored men's thrift-store trousers. And always, after a long night out, everyone's clothes off but mine, a hand would reach out from their puppy pile, stretching out to me—*Wanna join?*

I would sit on my hands for quite a few years before extending one back across the void.

I can identify with every character in *Rocky Horror,* but I start out as Janet Weiss. Susan Sarandon nailed this part. She calls Janet "kind of sweet on the outside, but a bitch underneath,"[2] a foil to Sarandon's other iconic contribution to queer cinema as Sarah Roberts, the boyishly femme future vampire in the 1983 film *The Hunger.* Made eight years post-*Rocky,* Sarandon plays opposite David Bowie and Catherine Deneuve, who land the '80s goth aesthetics of the fictional and ancient vampires Mr. and Mrs. Blaylock. If one were to overlay Janet Weiss under Sarah Roberts—a kind of double feature—echoes of Weiss's performative femininity would be challenged and reinvigorated in Roberts ("Are you making a pass at me, Mrs. Blaylock?"). Pencil skirts and tight buttoned collars transposed on top of short-cropped orange curls, gray slacks, and white cotton T-shirts, the soft butch version of Sigourney Weaver in the 1986 film *Aliens,* a space-soldier with a white undershirt and shaved head—a triple underlay/overlay—like my transness, a god-mess of cinematic reference, literature, lived experience, gesture, gender fuckery, rebellion, criminality, and desire. And the miracle of being seen as queer by other queers. We're movies for each other. Fairy tales. Hoof foot, wolf heart, sharp teeth. I'm Frankenstein's Creature, the Big Bad Wolf, Magyar-Hungarian furrowed brow barely hiding my vampiric Transylvanian incisors. But we're getting ahead of ourselves, no?

The movie starts at the wedding of Brad and Janet's friends. *Who are they?* we think. *Old college friends? Heterosexuals marrying?* It doesn't matter. Brad is shaking in his loafers, complimenting Janet on the "skillful way" she caught the bride's bouquet, the trope of tropes in romantic comedies, a sign of impending marriage, the escalator of monogamy calling to the future promise of social acceptance and respectability.

Everyone's doing it, Brad . . .

Janet practically mauls him when he finally offers her an engagement ring a few stanzas into the song "Dammit Janet," and you can feel the manic panic of their enforced gender roles weighing on them, walking up the aisle in lockstep while belting out Richard O'Brien's orchestral '50s doo-wop stylings, a mix of science-fiction Foley, the tin-can exuberance of cabaret-meets-camp-meets-circus, with a horror film's screechy undertones. The church is sun-kissed but next to a graveyard, the wedding party driving off in a flurry of pop cans dragged from the back of what looks like a gigantic Plymouth Suburban, the classic American family car. As the wedding guests disperse, we see that the church is staffed by barely disguised "Transsexuals," O'Brien's appropriation of the beloved but antiquated term, used in the movie to refer to a specific alien race, one from the nebulous and transgender galaxy of Transylvania. Riff Raff, played by O'Brien and rarely seen without his sibling and lover, Magenta, appears with her in the human coupling ceremony dressed as the pitchforked farmer from Grant Wood's painting "American Gothic," while Magenta is his tight-bunned wife. Later, Janet and Brad are given a photograph from the wedding and see Dr. Frank-N-Furter standing in the group shot, posing stoically in layperson's clothing: slacks, crisp white shirt, slicked and parted hair, a scratch in the record.

Heterosexuality always felt like the pink scratchy dress I was forced to wear to Sunday mass. My mother took me to church in a Roman Catholic stained-glass monolith not unlike the Frankenstein place in *Rocky Horror,* represented on film by

Maidenhead's Oakley Court mansion, a double for the Villa
Diodati, Lord Byron's Geneva mansion where Mary Shelley
famously penned *Frankenstein* while stuck in a rainstorm with
her husband, Percy Shelley; his lover (and Mary's stepsister)
Claire; Lord Byron; and Lord Byron's drug-wielding doctor-lover
John Polidori, who later wrote *The Vampyre,* meant as a foil
for the rejection by Byron and fodder for Bram Stoker's 1897
bisexual epic *Dracula.* Oh, how the queers delight.

My first church was in the Saskatchewan prairies, but there
were others, found every time our family moved westward, my
mom filing us into a pew while my heretic stepfather sold vacu-
ums door-to-door and did cocaine. We stopped going after my
parents' merciful divorce, and Mom and my two brothers found
our way to the Salish Sea, all the way west, to Vancouver.

I loved church. I loved the intensity of the liturgy, the way
Latin could be mic-dropped into Old English at any moment, a
place where men dressed in black robes verbally, ritualistically
confirmed something I felt—that there were other realms, that
beasts existed alongside the angels, that Satan used to be an
angel of God, that one could encounter these beings through
the consumption of blood and flesh made manifest through the
consecration of water and wine, a consumption of substance
for ecstatic purposes, ones meant for my salvation. As an
addict, I have often confused redemption with consumption: of
booze and cigarettes and self-destructive sex. Being a Scorpio,
death and sex are forever entwined for me. And I'm Magyar.
Hungarian. Along with the Romanians in Transylvania, we
helped originate the modern vampire, with furrowed brow and
a brooding taste for blood. There's some truth to the stereotypes.
Vlad "the Impaler," ruler of Wallachia or Romanian country,
is a national hero, thought by some to be the inspiration for
Bram Stoker's *Dracula.* Vlad expertly impaled his victims so
they would remain alive for days, writhing in pain outside his
castle, a warning to nobles and peasants alike. Vlad waged war
against the Ottomans, and Hungarians fought alongside him
after establishing their own country, Magyarország.

Magyars are known for being overly nostalgic, sentimental lovers of poetry and suicide. "Gloomy Sunday," a song whose English version was recorded in Billie Holiday's deep, quivering tenor, was originally written and sung by Rezső Seress in 1933— the interwar years. It was not a great time to be a Hungarian, and an even worse time to be a Hungarian Jew, which Seress was. Titled "Szomorú vasárnap" and gingerly referred to as "The Hungarian Suicide Song," the lyrics recount the horrors of war, the death of a lover, and the desire to kill oneself as a result, which Seress did in 1968, first jumping out a window, then finishing the job by choking himself to death with a wire while being treated in the hospital for injuries from the first attempt. The song has a mythos around it, not unlike a Black Sabbath tune, the mythos being that if you listen to "Gloomy Sunday," you too will kill yourself. Mix all this up and you get a pretty sexy vampire, or at least one with a lot of feelings. As Antonio Banderas said to Brad Pitt in the 1992 film adaptation of Anne Rice's *Interview with the Vampire*, "You feel too much. So much, you make me feel."

Years later, after I got sober, I returned to the church with an addict's fervor. I went four times a week, sometimes five. I walked the Stations of the Cross while weeping redemptive tears in front of cold slabs of marble made to look like Mary holding the dead thirty-three-year-old Jesus, the age of his Saturn return. Tough break. The sermons, whether in Latin or English or both, had a structure that my wild, chaotic, dogged-drunk heart was in desperate need of. I grew my hair long. I bought flower-print dresses and got a wooden cross. I found a Roman Catholic Church off the Jay Street subway stop in Brooklyn, one that was pro-abortion, with gays on the board. I started dating David, a Jewish man who loved me enough to come to Christmas mass, something he had never done before. We listened to Benjamin Britton sung by a children's choir and watched *Love Actually*. "I must love you a lot, because that's the worst movie I have ever seen," he said, and we laughed. I was happy.

I started a garden on his back deck and started taking folic acid. When my Canadian visa expired, we moved in together and went to City Hall and got married. My friend Emily painted my nails a soft pink, and we used two different kinds of curling irons for my ass-length, dirty-blond hair. I was a wife. I would be a mother. My mother was so happy. David and I immediately looked around for property, someplace upstate where we could have peace and raise a child.

When I talked to one of the parishioners of my church about how I could formally become a member, I asked, "Can trans people be members of your church?"

"I don't see why not," he said, "the church is changing. Maybe a little too slowly, but it's changing."

"Yeah," I said, relieved. "I don't know why I asked that. It's just important to me that everyone is accepted at the church I go to."

As I said it, I held my wooden cross in my pocket and felt held by God.

When it came tumbling down—this Janet Weiss persona—I was so fucked. It was like a brick house being blown down, a wolf swallowing Little Red Riding Hood, the wolf as Little Red Riding Hood, and then—just the wolf.

There is a moment—one I've only heard about, a rumor—when a lion is about to eat its prey, a zebra maybe, or a gazelle. And it puts a kind of spell on its victim, maybe through eye contact or pheromones or spit, and then the gazelle-zebra-creature seems to want to be consumed, will lie down and willingly give itself over. And though I am no victim and no vampire, I see this as a kind of analogy for coming out— as queer maybe, but certainly as trans. To be trans requires such a vehement turning away from what a body is "supposed" to be, from what its perceived function might be. To become what I am sometimes feels like it might require the breaking of bones, that I may have to break myself into the billion parts that make me up, then put myself back together, a reassembly

with whatever is lying around, becoming my own Dr. Frankenstein, whose description of his Creature coming to life feels
like my own, my "dull yellow eyes" as they open for the first
time, "the glimmer of the half-extinguished light" against my
gasping breath, a convulsive motion jump-starting my heart,
blood, brains.

Frank-N-Furter's entrance by elevator etched itself into my
memory the first time I watched *The Rocky Horror Picture
Show* the whole way through, well into my own transition. Post-
church, post-second-coming-out, I watched his shellacked lips
curl, the descent of the elevator hidden under the thumping
beat of everyone's throbbing hearts, syncopated in desire. The
body never lies.

That moment—the creaky, ungreased door flung aside—
unleashed Tim Curry's Frank-N-Furter on the world (*Oh
Tim, Oh Tim, Oh Tim*), his vampiric brow and wolf teeth and
Frankenstein-mad eyes. Curry is lip-syncing to his own voice;
it's not live theater, and you can watch him mouthing the words
to "Sweet Transvestite" in the "making of" video.[3] Everything's
a double feature—the Transylvanian partygoers dressed not in
parishioners' clothing but in the garments of their people: neon
wigs and leather tops and cross-dressing suits and misshapen
sunglasses and and and—

Frank-N-Furter throws back the curtain, which is his
vampire cape. Underneath, he's in full black lace lingerie,
garters with little red ribbons, no tucking, no removal of body
hair, platform pumps that look mountainous, sparkled lips
and pearl-white teeth crooning a confession: "I'm just a sweet
Transvestite / from Transsexual / Transylvania." *No Shame.
No Shame. No Shame.* I gasped the first time I saw Curry whip
that cape aside. Then I cried. *That's me,* I thought, *Fuck, that's
me.* Then Janet Weiss fainted. Which totally made sense to me
at the time.

I get it, I nodded, *I get it.*

When I was figuring out the extent of my queerness—I am
profoundly homosexual and at one point was profoundly
self-closeted—somewhere between church and club, I had daily
panic attacks. On the way to work one day, a beyond-handsome
queer emerged through the opening doors of the L train at the
Metropolitan subway stop. His eye grazed me, long eyelashes
like a young colt, scuffed Doc Martens, slightly tinted cherry lip
gloss (I could smell it), a tight, cropped button-up, black with
neon slashes, like knife cuts, peeking through his unbuttoned
but perfectly preened trench. A wave of panic flooded through
me, so severe that I clutched my heart, melodramatic, a swooning woman in a noir film. I didn't faint, but I came pretty damn
close. In the middle of the night, I would wake with a gasp, on
the verge of hyperventilation, anxious breath pumping, speed-
ing up, beginning to take over. I would have to go stick my
head in the toilet, not to vomit but to let the cool water in the
porcelain bowl soothe the heat coming off my dreams, settling
my lungs, bringing me back to some semblance of what I was:
a body. A body in distress, but a body nonetheless.

I felt I was going mad. I felt like Janet Weiss after she sleeps
with Frank-N-Furter, feeling she's done something oh oh so
bad but oh oh so good, and she can never go back, only left
with her "if onlys." If only I hadn't stopped going to church
after the latest round of sexual abuse scandals. If only I hadn't
danced in that queer ballet, *Sleeping Beauty & the Beast*.[4] If
only I hadn't listened to all those dancers announcing their
pronouns during rehearsal check-ins. If only I didn't want to
wear David's clothes. If only I wasn't what I am, what I have
always been.

I don't know what makes the man, or the woman, or the
human, nature or nurture or culture or what, but when I was
in my twenties, I played Antigone in a gender-bending version
of the Sophocles play.[5] I actually thought I was cis; it was the
early aughts and gender theory hadn't found me yet; I thought
I was just a hired performer on a gig. As part of the show,
we researched the lives of Brian and David Reimer, twin boys

born in 1965. Six months after they were born, David's geni-
talia were badly burned during a surgery to correct phimosis.
Dr. John Money, an Australian psychologist and sexual identity researcher, heard about the twins and reached out to the
parents, poor Manitoba Mennonite farm folk—to assure them it
would be healthier to raise David as a girl and Brian as a boy,
because gender wasn't innate but socially imposed. He felt he
had a rare opportunity to enact a forbidden experiment on the
twins, to test his theory of nurture over nature. To make sure
the two were developing and to prove his hypothesis, Money
brought the twins to his lab once a year, where he conducted
abusive compare-and-contrast experiments on them, and when
puberty hit, injected David with a panoply of hormones to hear-
ken an enforced female body. The results were disastrous. Brian
overdosed in 2002, and David, after transitioning to his chosen
gender and struggling with the effects of Money's forbidden
experiment, committed suicide in 2004. Steven, the director of
Antigone, used this story as a jumping-off point for his version
of the ancient Greek play, one that underscored what happens
when the state enforces social roles, familiar or gendered. I
played Antigone as if I were a boy on the inside while present-
ing as a girl. Ismene, my sister, was played by my friend Bill,
who was asked to portray the part as AMAB but as if he didn't
know it, unwittingly forced to present as a girl. Bill dressed
ultra-femme, a sort of Marilyn Monroe type, and I was more of
a Patty Hearst/Patty Smith punk-revolutionary type, shirtless
in a leather jacket. For the show's poster, Steven asked the
photographer to wrap us in sheets, draped selectively across
our bodies to confuse whose body was whose, with me embracing Bill from behind. Just before the photographer snapped
the picture, Steven said, "Tanya, you're a boy. Look out to the
camera like you're seeing through your boy's eyes."

What a fool I was. How hard I fought myself. A year after I
finally came out to David—"I'm not a woman and I need to fuck
a lot of women"—after we battled through couples counseling
and read all the polyamory literature—I kissed a femme in

Central Park after our date at a Mapplethorpe exhibit, and my panic attacks subsided, my breathing as easeful as putting on a pair of Doc Martens. The hyperventilation, the clutching at my chest—that was my old life dying, the last spasms before the vampire awakens to "see the world through his vampire eyes," as Tom Cruise says to the newly minted Brad Pitt in *Interview with the Vampire.* Although I prefer to think of myself as my own creator, the way Frank-N-Furter owns his ability to create new life in *Rocky Horror:* "The spark that is the breath of life . . . yes . . . I have that knowledge."

Frank-N-Furter is the antagonist you love to hate and love to love, an embodiment of taboo in all its forms, fucking, fighting, feeding, fleeing. He wants what he wants, when he wants it. His alien ways mean he sees humans as toys, things to get off on, experiment on, look down on. When his toys have emotions—and worse still, boundaries—we begin to see Frank-N-Furter's ulti-mate flaw. He can't bear rejection, and when met with a "no," his reactions range from petulant to psychotic, sexually assaultive to sociopathic. This means he's got no problem with killing. When Eddie shows up—a criminal biker played by a surprisingly young Meat Loaf, smashing his motorcycle through a wall to reunite with his lover, the bedazzled, redheaded Columbia—Frank-N-Furter, in an exquisite reference to the mother in Hitchcock's *Psycho*, grabs a pickaxe, struts over to Eddie, and as the camera cuts to Frank-N-Furter's wild-maned silhouette, hacks Eddie to pieces. After Frank-N-Furter catches Janet postcoital with "his" Rocky, Dr. Everett Scott, who is Eddie's uncle *and* Brad and Janet's old teacher, shows up. All are invited to a clothing-op-tional dinner. The climax of the meal comes when the tablecloth is pulled back to reveal the young criminal's dead body encased in a glass tomb fashioned as a tabletop. The screams are true horror-film-tastic. Columbia is devastated; she "very nearly loved" Eddie after all, a desire mirrored in Janet's hunger for Rocky. This doubling of desire ultimately reveals what's under Frank-N-Furter's fear of rejection. "Rocky's behaving the same way Eddie did," Frank-N-Furter moans in the following scene.

He was Eddie's lover before being abandoned for Columbia, and wanted to be Rocky's lover before being abandoned for Janet. This is a double rejection for Frank-N-Furter: the pain of being left for cis women twice, abandoned by cis men for couplings that, on the surface, look more conventionally heterosexual. Frank-N-Furter doesn't know how to process that pain because he has no language for that particular form of rejection. Frank-N-Furter's murderous rage at catching Janet with Rocky is beautifully articulated by trans activist and scholar Susan Stryker in "My Words to Victor Frankenstein": "Like the monster, the longer I live in these conditions, the more rage I harbor. Rage colors me as it presses in through the pores of my skin, soaking in until it becomes the blood that courses through my beating heart. It is a rage bred by the necessity of existing in external circumstances against my survival."[6]

Having grown up pressed under the thumb of compulsory cishet society, I know what it takes to break from that, and I am now a proud and self-actualized slut, attracted on some level to every consenting humanoid variation from eighteen to eighty. I'm also sensually aroused by literally everything: the sun, the tree across the street from my writing desk, knives, bathtub faucets, table legs, mackerel sashimi, the feeling of salt water gliding over the surface of my skin, fresh-cut leather scraps, the smell of library books, my notebook, the pen I'm using to write this right now. It all turns me on. But I understand. Not everyone has the option to break from compulsory cisheteronormativity, and some don't want to; some even enjoy it. Others have a much narrower palette when it comes to their sexual desires, at least the ones they'll let the public see. I've been a lot of people's secret romantic friend/lover, which has given me the pleasure of midnight kisses and the deep hurt at being hidden from the light. I identify with Frank-N-Furter because, whether you think of him as persona or caricature or camp, he's an excessive version of a whatever-the-fuck-I-am. And it hurts when the thing you desire doesn't see you and no longer desires you back, especially if you're a whatever-the-fuck-I-am.

Though I've long stopped sneaking out of college parties to go home with straight girls, the rejection of my transness by cisgender lovers can elicit a flavor of fury that borders on blind rage. More often than not, the rejection has been present as an undertone from the start, a subconscious drumbeat gradually crescendoing: acknowledging my pronouns in public but wanting to relegate me to one gender in the bedroom, experimenting with me around sexual positions or a couple of performative gestures—whose hands on top, who gets to be the chivalrous one and pull out the chair at the restaurant—like a visitor on a bus tour through the place that I actually live.

I've had to process tumults of emotion postbreakup with long-winded journal entries, midnight walks, Bette Midler movies. Trans friendship seems to be the ultimate salve, that and trying again and again to learn self-love. I take time with new people, and David and I have worked incredibly hard to break away from where we were on our wedding day to a more shimmering version of where we are now, something that shifts from Oscar Wilde faggotry, to bois giving each other hand jobs while watching basketball, to soft, tender make-outs and slumber party spooning, to all manner of human gestures of care, mostly mysterious, often wordless, skin to skin and heart to heart. In this way, I am blessed.

There are ways to break from tradition, there are also ways to play the return. But it's tough. As Frank-N-Furter says after turning Janet, Brad, Rocky, Columbia, and Dr. Scott into naked statues and then back into their human forms, clad in black, lacy lingerie: "It's not easy having a good time . . . Even smiling makes my face ache."

"And, when shall we return to Transylvania?" Magenta calls out.

My teacher Linda says that it's hard to come back to a person, a place, or a thing, especially after a long time away, but to write from the heart, to act from a place of truth, to create, artists must learn to do something she calls "playing the return."

Maybe you've been on a long journey, and whether it was an

inner journey or an outer one, maybe it was arduous. Maybe you battled a monster, or were put under a spell, turned into a mythical beast or a handsome prince, or touched the fires of hell, and you were forever altered. Maybe someone or many someones helped you on your path, or maybe you had the dumb luck to be returned to your life. Well then, it may feel hard, or even impossible, to reintegrate into the ways you were living, because everyone and everything will feel static, while you have changed. And sometimes this change will be too much for those around you, and you might be asked to be what you were, before your house was blown down, before all the parts of you were haphazardly sewn back up. But we can't, none of us can go back, and so it's like there are two of you—the one who *was*, and the one who *is*. Longing loosely joins the two and creates a feeling of want, but until you can reconcile the two parts, until you play the return, you can never move forward. The feeling of want, of being two things or in two places at once, I feel that a lot. Born in Saskatchewan and now in New York, I'm a prairie boi surrounded on all sides by glass and brick and steel. My eyes desire the horizon, but I'm cut off from the skyline; I get hints of it, a faint glimpse between buildings. And every morning when I wake up, I have a wolf in me, my former addict self, when I was an active user. I have to placate this wild animal, who desires nothing but to eat the world, make it burn, watch the ash rise from the embers. I must speak nicely to this beast, "a little more than kin, and less than kind." I must use soft, healing words. I must sit in silence, or as much of it as I can; the silence of a New York morning is deafening. I must breathe measured breath to douse the rage I have no name for, that I have a multitude of origin stories for. And if I do this every day, the breathing makes my fangs recede, the sun comes out, and I am me: Tanya, or the Magyar name I've been trying out, Tamás. It means twin.

I returned to Budapest in June 2023, after four years away. I went back to learn a Magyar folk dance called the legényes, or "Lad's Dance." Traditionally taught to men, the legényes is a communal dance, and if you go to Budapest, you can see it performed in National Theatres, though it was never meant to be performed there. These dances were done in communities— town squares, parties, at bars, just for one another—exuberant, passionate, a boisterous display of prowess and cologned masculinity. There are many examples on YouTube, which I highly recommend. They are hotter than hot, filled with much leg slapping, performed by mustached men in tight black slacks, asses round from jumping so much, loose linen shirts shimmying as the hands slap and snap to the rhythm of violins, hats adorned with feathers, leather boots riding up the leg to just below the knee.

I wanted to learn the dance because it looked like the kind of masculine I wanted to feel. As I began to move into nonbinary space and wondered at what masculinity was for me, what I was going for, I realized that I wasn't going for the magazine cover, didn't want to look like Brad Pitt, not even his perfectly preened vampire self. No, I was going for something else, something under the surface, something more than wearing muscle tees and putting my foot up on step stools, or sitting wide-legged on park benches. So I searched, one Instagram DM at a time, until I found Balázs, Julcsi, and Gergő, queer dancers in Budapest who could teach me the legényes. I arranged an artist residency and went to learn the dance.

My ancestors Josef Vörös and Mary Kovach immigrated to Saskatchewan in 1907. They were peasants; they couldn't read or write. Because Magyar folk dance is an expression of peasant culture, the dances are one of the few things I have of them. When I dance, I feel echoes of them in me, sometimes see pictures of them in my mind's eye, feel their ground under my feet.

One day, after rehearsal, Gergő's mother took me on a tour to the Hősök Tere or "Hero's Square," which features statues of seven men on horseback, commemorating the hét Magyar. In the ninth century, the hét Magyar, or the Seven Magyars, met on horseback to elect the first Magyar king, King Arpád.

The seven clansmen swore allegiance, sliced open their arms, and bled into a chalice. Once it was full, all drank. A blood pact.

As Gergő's mother walked me around the square, she talked about the ways that these old stories, myths of how Hungary came to be, were reinterpreted by nationalists, who use Magyar folk dance as a way to promote their right-wing ideologies. I thought, *How can I be both proud of the dance and separate it from this nationalistic bullshit?*

Two weeks later, I traveled to Hahót, where Josef and Mary were born, and I saw the graves of my ancestors. Gergő translated as we talked to the villagers at the local bar, who made jokes by talking shit about my family. All of us stayed in a cabin near Lake Balaton. Gergő started a fire, and Julcsi and Balász taught me how to make lecsó with a bogrács, sprinkling marjoram and paprika over peppers and tomatoes into a heavy pot and swinging it over the fire by its tough aluminum handle, the smell of the food wafting up over the trees.

And later I thought, *What does any of this have to do with the legényes? And what does any of this have to do with me being queer?* The queer lot of us walking into town to buy bread—we must have looked so out of place, sides of heads shaved, just one side, and single earrings. (Why do queers want to just do the one side? The single earring? Maybe we want to look how we feel—a little lopsided?)

For me, queerness isn't just who you fuck, or what gender you are, or even what your politics are. It's a doubling of self, time, influences, confluences. And that doubling doubles, and that doubling doubles, and that doubling doubles, until I feel like a doppelganger of a doppelganger, a part of the universe, a supernova, a planetary system, a hologram. I'm no longer looking at the thing I desire, I am the thing I desire.

And so, I extend my hand out to you my friend, across the void, to arrive at the shores of whatever the fuck we are, to create ourselves, to love the land, and, as Frank-N-Furter says: "Don't dream it. Be it."

Notes

1. Richard O'Brien, "An Evening with Richard O'Brien, Part 1," interview by Mark Sainsbury, posted June 27, 2010, by Fiona Jackson, YouTube, https://www.youtube.com/watch?v=omeUM1UoAk8.

2. Susan Sarandon, "Susan Sarandon Breaks Down Her Career, from 'Thelma & Louise' to 'Rocky Horror Picture Show,'" posted September 19, 2022, by Vanity Fair, YouTube, https://youtu.be/WaxEVWMwQSo?si=pTWW8gRUwEWni29r.

3. "1975: Rocky Horror Picture Show: Behind the Scenes," originally broadcast July 26, 1975, on BBC, posted March 4, 2022, by BBC Archive, YouTube, https://www.youtube.com/watch?v=5yZcJwfJCKU.

4. *Sleeping Beauty & the Beast*, prod. Ballez, dir. Katy Pyle, chor. Katy Pyle with Jules Skloot and the Company, music by DJ Samson and Queer Urban Orchestra, La MaMa Moves! Dance Festival, New York, NY, April 29–May 8, 2016.

5. *Antigone Undone*, prod. Leaky Heaven Circus, dir. Steven Hill, devised with performers Lesley Ewen, Billy Marchenski, and Tanya Marquardt, dramaturgy by Michele Valiquette and Heidi Taylor, Russian Hall, Vancouver, Canada, May 13–24, 2009.

6. Susan Stryker, "My Words to Victor Frankenstein above the Village of Chamounix: Performing Transgender Rage," *GLQ* 1 (1994): 244.

Three Ways

Dave Madden

1.

In the beginning, sex was just a signal. On cable TV, a closing doorway winnowed to a shard of damp lamplight, or a camera panned windowward—a genteel suggestion, though whatever those bodies were now doing off camera no grown-up would come clean about. I'd discovered masturbating, a new trick I could pull, and I took the classes my parents signed off on, the principal telling us boys in the cafetorium all about sperms and ovums, but sex remained only a word on the blackboard. Anybody's lips while talking or chewing? Not Sex. But a person's lips could become sex when framed in a certain light.

Like, say, on the cover of a videotape brought home by two thirteen-year-olds one slow night in Herndon, Virginia. An education in sex—what it was, what it was not, what it could be—began that night, though it would take years to stick.

In the lab, on the slab, Rocky is framed in gauze: Not Sex. Except the gauze is tight, snug, the wrappings braided down his forelegs like the binding of a bodice, but I barely noticed anybody's legs. What was another leg? Or a face? And what are the muscles revealed once Magenta and Columbia scissor the arm gauze off? They're a spectacle, a rare bird, but they aren't yet the signal I was looking for. Rocky revealed has the face of a dolt and the hair of a boy doll, corn silk hacked into reputable shape, vacant blue eyes befitting a made thing. He never speaks, but once he sings, he sings about his imminent death, like a mayfly, his torso thoracic as he twirls, the gals unspooling the last of the binding. Then he is bared, a sculpted creature, like the Attic statues that line the lab. He is bronzed in golden underwear, and still: Not Sex. Even with his initial spelled at the hip in rhinestones, Rocky's as R-rated as Olympic divers, or pro wrestlers on afternoon cable. But soon, Rocky turned, and there it was: the hint of shadow right at the small of his small back, a suggestion of what I wanted to see but knew I wouldn't be shown.

Controlled exposure of skin—of white skin, of calibrated tans, of the blond, white, all-American English boy who I'd been taught deserved such exposure—that, for me at age thirteen, is all sex was: TV's endless stripteases. Sitting on the brown carpet in the family room, covered toe to neck in black, myself a scrawny accident no one got to see, I watched Rocky both discover and display his body, everyone onscreen gazing at him, and I knew I wanted in on it, this glorious, impossible object, this key to life's most mysterious door. I was not hard, just soft nerves and racing heart, worried my friend could see where I was looking, and what I was looking for: another reminder of sex's secret, itself getting unraveled as we friends dared to speak of blow jobs and fingering. We both impressed and fooled one another. "Screwing a chick is when you put your dick in her and rotate your body around, like a screw."

Oh, Rocky! Rocky Horror in the lab signals that sex is coming; of course he was my favorite.

Rocky, then Eddie, then Frank. My teamsters.

2.

In a dream, you walk through your home—the home you live your waking life inside, or a home your dream has fashioned for you—turn a dusty corner, open a suspect door, and there it is: a spare room you didn't know about. Or a whole wing of rooms, ready to be filled. In later years, that's what sex became: an extra wing, the affirmation that somewhere within me lay an allure I didn't know I had. Everywhere I could, I looked at men, but men never looked back. Men looked at women. I knew this, knew I, too, had to start looking at women, but I kept forgetting to, kept failing to keep up appearances. When, at times, the men looked back, their looks got me in trouble—enough that I hid, got small, my voice turned down so as not to arouse attention.

In any group, the quiet voice waits its turn. *There's going to be a lull. Really, any minute now.* Eddie literally bursts onto the scene without so much as a pause, his arrival announced by a siren, an urgent blinking light, Columbia screaming his name. He is a wild, undead thing, an icy, sideburned blast from the past, wearing denim and leather, with a motorbike and a saxophone—all the paraphernalia of the dangerous boy your parents are quick to hate.

Eddie wears HATE on his left hand. His danger is that he needs nobody; he doesn't even need to be looked at. Eddie is all eyes; the gash across his forehead forms a bleeding unibrow to frame them, and at one moment, singing to Columbia, his eyebrows pop with a subtle shrug, suggesting both how passionately he can fall for a girl just from the taste of her, and how little it really matters, how this sort of thing happens to him every time he crosses the street.

The flash of that look—as dense with feeling as an orgasm—floods Columbia with a sea of promises, and she tugs at his clothes to get just another second of it. I was right there with her, every time I rented the video. What brought me back, again and again, to *The Denton Affair*, this baffling case of mingle-mangled bedmates? Hard to overestimate the allure of something not just different, but enduring; that the movie still had midnight screenings meant I wasn't alone in feeling so strange it took a movie like this to make me look normal. Besides, camp fantasias suit the poor boy for whom reality is such a drag. I was no longer the clueless kid I once was, but neither, I felt, was I sexy. What was sexy now was the gaze returned, the other man to see through my disguises, my makeup, and find not a fag but a fellow. The bigger the man to do this to me (or for me?), the bigger I could imagine myself.

Eddie is big but his body is nothing to look at. His body is something to fuck with. Shoot up junk with. It's a barrel, a boulder, a bulk that blocks everybody's path, and its job is to bring other bodies closer. All he has to do is pull one finger himward and Columbia comes running. He expects her to. Just the sight of him makes everyone in the room scream and run, but soon he has them all dancing in unison, singing a song about fucking teen girls. Do they know they'll soon sing songs of him? "I very nearly loved him," Columbia says, and I wondered what it was that held her back.

When you see sexy bodies everywhere but in a mirror, you don't feel that sex is yours. Sex is for other people, like jiujitsu or Finnish. All I wanted was to be looked at by a big man telling me how fun sex was. What more could love be?

LOVE is on Eddie's right hand. His jerking-off hand? Eddie the ex–delivery boy embodies such dark secrets. The fantasy of Rocky is that you can just be made sexy, like in sci-fi. The fantasy of Eddie is that you can be made sexy by a sexy man's desire. But the truth of Eddie is that your first attempts, your shortcomings, your monstrousnesses will return and haunt you. They'll show up the moment you think you're free of them, requiring you to dig out the pickaxe. Add it to Eddie's allure: He's alive for three minutes and twenty seconds, but they can't stop talking about him. *What a guy.* He's the loudest man in the room, even long after they eat him.

3.

Frank sings a lot of songs. He sings about his confusing body, about Rocky's perfect body, about Janet's wanting body. He sings about absolute pleasure and absolute ruin, and about blinding himself to the horrors of the world he's made. I once saw such blinding as naïve, and Frank a cruel, selfish mess. Now I see Frank as an oracle.

Like his ex, Frank feels less a desire to be looked at than an assurance that it's always already happening, and like his creation, he first appears covered up, primed for an unveiling. Naturally, Frank's is as sudden as a slap in the face. All at once we're given his hard parts and his soft parts. A corset over pectorals. Torn fishnet stockings with the leg hairs showing through. Pearls like jawbreakers. Lips like ruby slippers. None of this, not even his strut, is framing his body. Frank's body is the frame.

My slap in the face felt like this: There was always something very hetero in my homosexuality. Like a telescope, I pointed to what was alien. Hairy men. Athletes. Straight athletes. "I thought you'd be into guys more like you," my sister said after I came out, and I said I already had me. Why would I want another one of me? Not feeling like even half of a half of a man, I thought only the manliest man could make me feel whole. These boneheaded terms. When Frank says he can make you a man, he means it literally, out of not-quite-whole cloth. The manliest man for Frank is nothing but a toy. Columbia's right: He chews people up and spits them back out again, because why wait to be noticed by some dumb lunk when it's far more fun to make yourself unignorable?

What happened for me to turn sex from petition to election was that I finally had a lot of it. Few of the men I fucked were Eddies—or all of them could be, if I looked at them right. Two or three were stunning Rockys, but most of the men were like me: unsure, ignorable, daring ourselves into doing in secret what we trusted could make us feel like the hero of some story. On my knees in a public toilet, reaching under the stall to tug on a man I knew only by his footwear, I could feel a lot of things. Aroused by this warm and serious dick in my palm. Admitted into some genial fraternity. Ashamed to be doing this again, inches from where most men shit. Like getting good grades, I felt this might affirm a thing or two about who I might become, which is the trap of Eddie-style validation sex: Getting your body looked at doesn't teach you how to use it, much less why to.

I looked at Rocky and Eddie, but I loved Frank, and for many years love precluded sex. Love was for my friends and family. Sex required lust. Dr. Frank, an alien, was too human to be hot for. Foibled and fishnetted. A confusion, not a signal. The confusion is ours. Frank's never strung out by the way he looks. It's not confidence or dominance, those alpha/beta obsessions, it's complete disregard for the terms of the argument. "I'm not much of a man by the light of day, but by night I'm one hell of a lover," he says, pointing out the manliest thing a man can be.

It's not a fucker.

The promise of Frank is that we don't have to dream about what we might someday become—a Rocky object, an Eddie objective—what we are is already enough license to become it. That this requires a certain trans-formation—the naïve turned to stone, fitted out in Frank drag, and tranced into a swimming-pool orgy—clues us in to what sex might ultimately be: an alien encounter. A chance to let other men rub off on you (or not), rather than waiting for other men to fill you up. Or other women. Or unconventional conventionalists.

Which brings us to the handyman, the hero, the rival scientist—what did they promise this gay boy in training? Being a Brad, I felt nothing for another Brad, and Dr. Scott's age and wheelchair made him unfairly desexed: the only man this movie doesn't let fuck. Riff Raff fucks, but he fucks his sister (a boner killer to any gay boy watching). Why do they live to see the morning while none of my teamsters do? In all this talk of promises, here's a troubling other: The crime of being superhero sexy will lead to your ruin. It's an assurance we nerds provide each other, a story we tell to get out of our otherwise empty beds each morning.

Frank, of course, would laugh at this idea. After all, he's killed by an ugly person, and isn't that the real crime? Everybody in the picture show gets to sing a song, but Frank can sing and laugh, often at the same time. He even laughs during sex. He laughs at sex, with sex, for sex. It's a joke I'm over here trying to be in on.

To Absent Friends: AIDS and the *Rocky Horror* Community

Akira Albar-Kluck

THE FIRST TIME I attended a live screening of *The Rocky Horror Picture Show* with a shadow cast, losing my so-called virginity, I was fourteen years old and on vacation in Orlando. It was November 2016, and Donald Trump had just won the election. I cried my eyes out. I was filled with an overwhelming sense of dread and grief over what our country would face. My mother felt bad, so when we saw that *The Rocky Horror Picture Show* was playing at Universal City Walk Cinemark, she finally said yes to taking me. I was already an avid fan of *The Rocky Horror Picture Show* film and its surrounding community and culture. I had read *The Perks of Being a Wallflower* and seen the film adaptation. Seeing Patrick's character get to express himself and his queer identity in a time and place where that was very limited spoke to me deeply. I thought it seemed like the most interesting way to experience theater and engage with other people. I listened to "Sweet Transvestite" on repeat before I had to give a speech in front of the whole school for student council. It gave me the confidence I needed to speak in front of my peers, who had consistently bullied me for my queer identity.

I next saw the film in a theater with a shadow cast in 2022 when I was a junior in college. The morning after, I was in a graveyard for a field trip and I received news that a friend from high school had died by suicide. I threw myself into my local *Rocky Horror* scene, becoming a regular attendee, doing an ethnography of the subculture for my undergraduate thesis, and working on the tech crew for a shadow cast for a summer. My dear grandmother and several family friends passed away during my time in the *Rocky Horror* subculture, and I was always comforted by the feelings of community and catharsis it gave me.

In 2023, Sal Piro, an icon and, in many ways, one of the founders of *The Rocky Horror Picture Show* subculture, passed away. Piro's *New York Times* obituary included many moving reflections on his role in establishing the community, including from the producer of *The Rocky Horror Picture Show*, Lou Adler: "'He said to me, we're both reaching ages where something might happen to either one of us,' said Mr. Adler, who is 89. If that happens, he said Mr. Piro asked him, 'Who is going to watch over *Rocky*?'"[1] As my perspective on life was shifting due to my grief, I began to understand just how important it is to make the most out of communities and connections. I believe it is up to us to watch over *Rocky*—it is the job of the new generation to both honor previous generations and forge a new path for *Rocky Horror* and shadow casting.

I started to think about how I could do my part, as an academic and an artist. My undergraduate thesis was specifically studying the contemporary *Rocky Horror* shadow-casting culture, and I also had a class on feminism and healing. I decided to channel my grief into community art and give back to the community that has given me so much. I thought a lot about Frank's toast—"To absent friends"—and seeing the line used at the memorial show for Sal Piro put on by Red Bank, New Jersey's Friday Nite Specials shadow cast, stuck with me.

The line calls to mind an issue that I had yet to see mentioned in the *Rocky Horror* community: the AIDS crisis. It struck me that there were no panels of the NAMES Project or AIDS Memorial Quilt with references to *Rocky Horror* on them. Here was a queer subculture that was extremely popular in the 1980s, and there was no widespread understanding of how the AIDS crisis had impacted the community. Typically, when a member of the

Rocky Horror community dies now, a memorial show will be held, in which the deceased's shadow cast will say a few words about them and their life. The show will have some callbacks themed around the deceased, and during the film's toast, "To absent friends," audience members will share a drink to honor them. I could not find archival or documentary evidence about how people who had passed in the early years of the AIDS crisis were mourned. Due to the ephemeral nature of the *Rocky Horror* subculture, people come and go and names are lost. We have no way of knowing just how many people our community lost, but we cannot let them be forgotten. I thought of all the people who would never get a memorial show, whose lives were cut too short by a government apathetic at best and malicious at worst. They never got the chance to grow old and become legends in our community.

I became increasingly intrigued and distraught by their stories, especially as a wave of homophobia and transphobia swept the United States, with violent attacks by individuals in the form of hate crimes and by the state in the form of legal repression. Every Pride, we revel in making it another year, and rightfully so. However, our joy should not overshadow the fact we did not all make it. Let us remember all of those who have gone before us, as their spirits live in every performance.

NAMES Project AIDS Memorial Quilt

The NAMES Project AIDS Memorial Quilt was created by longtime gay rights activist Cleve Jones. He had been a friend of Harvey Milk, the first openly gay California politician and member of the San Francisco Board of Supervisors, who was assassinated in 1984 along with San Francisco Mayor George Moscone. A year later, leading up to the memorial march on the anniversary of Milk's and Moscone's assassinations, AIDS was ravaging San Francisco, and Jones felt like nobody cared. He told his friend that if people could see just how many people had died, they might understand and respond. They got poster boards and Magic Markers and told members of the San Francisco LGBT community to write the names of their loved ones who had died. The night of the march, Jones taped the names to the wall of the San Francisco Federal Building. When he stood back and looked at it, he realized it looked like a quilt.[2]

The NAMES Project AIDS Memorial Quilt, which grew out of that, is one of the most personal memorials ever created. Each panel is a three-by-six-foot rectangle, roughly the size of a coffin. Many, but not all, of the panels were made by a loved one of the individual who died. Many people made panels for strangers, performing a labor of love so the person in question would not be forgotten. Some people with AIDS made panels for themselves when they thought they were going to die. No two panels are alike: They vary in color, material, crafting techniques used, and what is depicted. Some are humorous; some are angry; some are sexual. Some even criticize the individual they memorialize, such as the panel for Roy Cohn, an infamous conservative lawyer and prosecutor who was known for often harming the queer community. He served as chief counsel to Joseph McCarthy during the Red Scare and the Lavender Scare while having sex with men and refusing to identify as gay. Each panel speaks to the person it is dedicated to, and who they were as an individual. One project staff member said, "It is a celebration of a person's life. Not a comment on death. Hell, we know he's dead. But she was a scream when she was alive."[3]

The quilt has provided tangible ways for people to grieve. Making a panel is a way for loved ones to remember that person and lay them to rest. It can be a cathartic experience to make something so personal, as well as to become part of a collective of many people who have experienced the same loss. The quilt itself serves as a graveyard of sorts. AIDS was so stigmatized, and so little was known about it in the early years, that many funeral-home directors wouldn't embalm the body of someone who had died. Many families of people who died of AIDS did not claim their bodies, whether it was because they could not afford to hire a private funeral director or because they were not on good terms. Many New Yorkers who died of AIDS were buried in an isolated area on Hart Island,[4] an unknown number of whom were buried in a mass grave.[5] Many people at the time (and many more today) considered the practice distasteful. The quilt allows people to visit their panel and reflect, as one would in a cemetery. Families and loved ones will often leave flowers, stuffed animals, or other objects on the panels. In some cases, the quilt is literally the final resting place for someone, as a few panels have pockets with the individual's ashes.[6]

The quilt reflects the complicated relationship between death and life in the communities it represents. Focusing on the deaths of these individuals might have turned them into just part of a statistic, taking away their individuality, just as the sickness took away their lives. Each panel of the quilt makes the viewer contemplate that person's life, and understand the tragedy of that loss. No longer just a name on a list or a number, people see each panel and understand that this was someone who had a vivid inner life cut short by government indifference and hate, that someone out there loved this person, and now they are gone forever.

The quilt was born out of the desire to both remember what had already happened and to motivate people to do something. One cannot look at the quilt laid out on the National Mall and not be struck by the totality of the tragedy. Volunteers there have pamphlets about how to get involved with AIDS activism. There were significant monetary and cultural impacts of the NAMES Project AIDS Memorial Quilt. The inaugural tour of the quilt in 1988 raised $500,000 for hundreds of different AIDS service organizations.[7] The project brought lots of visibility and awareness to an issue the government was giving minimal attention and resources to.

The importance of finding and naming the dead cannot be understated. Memory is keeping someone's spirit alive; it is protecting them from further harm. In their essay on the lack of obituaries for the war dead in conflicts of American aggression, Judith Butler defines those without obituaries as "the unburied, or the unburiable"[8] and declares "If a life is ungrievable, it is not quite a life."[9] There is a long cross-cultural tradition of being forgotten as a curse. In ancient Egypt, to erase the memory of a pharaoh was to erase their spirit.[10] The way to honor someone in Judaism is to say "Yehi zichra baruch," or in English, "May their memory be a blessing." There is another phrase, however, for when someone dies violently, particularly due to domestic violence: "May their memory be a revolution."[11] In activist circles, memory can serve as a creative force.

I knew I wanted to name and remember the individuals in the *Rocky Horror* community who were taken far too early by AIDS, and I wanted them to be more than names, faces, or statistics. I wanted to remember them as they were, as beloved members of their communities. I also wanted to participate in the broader queer tradition of the obituary that names the victim's killer, AIDS. According to academic Dagmawi Woubshet, queer obituary has "political and ethical imperatives: to break the interdiction on queer/AIDS loss, to state the truth as a matter of public record, and, ultimately, to openly bury those subjects deemed unburiable."[12] Queer obituary rebukes the idea that victims of AIDS were somehow guilty or inhuman, and reminds readers that the person was loved and that they will be missed.

How *Rocky* Reacted to AIDS

Throughout the 1990s, several casts organized benefit shows for AIDS charities and research, and many still do today. A prominent example of an AIDS benefit from a *Rocky Horror* shadow cast is the eighteenth anniversary "Age of Consent" convention hosted by Midnight Insanity of Long Beach, California, in 1993.[13] In 1995, Completely Crazy of Chicago recorded a cast album and sold it to raise money for AIDS.[14] However, what was arguably the *Rocky Horror* community's most important response to AIDS was that the community kept going. It still provided joy and levity on the weekends in very dark times. It kept people's spirits high and allowed people to explore their gender and sexuality outside of the boundaries of heteronormative society. It kept people in contact with one another, and it allowed people who were facing isolation and alienation to continue to make connections. For people who regularly attend shows, whether they are shadow-casters or regulars in the audience, a sense of community is fostered on those nights with the people they choose to make their community and kin. "A crowd of strangers come together in an urban theater at midnight, ready to participate in a communal ritual: to express their collective outsider status together as a group. It makes them feel better. In fact, it makes them feel great."[15] Many of those in the *Rocky Horror* community develop close connections, often considering each other to be a family. Queer people often experience rejection or misunderstandings with our families of origin; engaging with other like-minded people in spaces like *Rocky Horror* screenings allows for kinship bonds to be formed and can provide a sense of solace.

Only by acknowledging the harm that AIDS did to our community, and remembering those we lost to it, can we begin to heal. I decided to make a panel for the quilt to put the *Rocky Horror* community in solidarity and unity with the thousands of other groups and individuals who have memorialized loved ones with their own panels. People who created the *Rocky Horror* culture and traditions we know today, like Sal Piro, were gay and have participated in the broader queer community since at least 1978, when Sal and Dori Hartley performed numbers from the show at the Christopher Street Liberation Day Parade.[16] I wanted *Rocky Horror* to be part of this other queer tradition as well.

Rocky Horror Panel

I created the design of the panel very carefully. It features the words "To Absent Friends" in the *Rocky Horror* font, in red letters on a black background. I cut out each letter from red velvet felt and glued it on. I chose not to list any names, as it would be impossible to find everyone who had died, and I thought it would be disrespectful to leave anyone out.

My next project was to find the loved ones our community lost to submit to the NAMES Project, the current name for the AIDS Quilt. This was not easy, as the nature of *Rocky Horror* as both a youth and queer subculture means it is mostly temporary, and many people do not stick around very long. Most people active in the 1980s and 1990s have since left the community. In addition, many people in the community take "*Rocky* names." I took an ethnographic approach to finding the names, contacting elders in the community and asking them about their loved ones who had died of AIDS. I also researched other memorials and social media posts, and cross-referenced them with obituaries from the period.

Here are their names:

Rufus Collins played a Transylvanian in *The Rocky Horror Picture Show* and one of Neeley's camera crew in the sequel, *Shock Treatment*. He was a brilliant stage actor and was a member of the Living Theater Collective in his youth. He eventually settled in Amsterdam where he directed *The Kingdom,* an opera about the Haitian Revolution featuring forty amateur opera singers of color.[17]

Pierre La Roche was a consultant on *The Rocky Horror Picture Show* as a makeup artist. He was known for designing David Bowie's iconic Aladdin Sane makeup.[18]

Paul Jabara took over the role of Frank-N-Furter after Tim Curry left the Los Angeles stage play to do the movie. Paul was also an icon of disco, cowriting the Weather Girls' "It's Raining Men."[19]

Steven Davies was a beloved member of the Boston *Rocky Horror* shadow cast and gay scene. His performing name was Peter Berlin. At the end of the film, he would say, "Thank you for coming. I came twice."[20] Steven and a friend once went to visit Peter Hinwood (who played Rocky) at his home in England. Hinwood slammed the door in their faces.

"Queen" George Hamilton was a member of the Tiffany Troupe in West Hollywood in the late 1970s and through the 1980s. He regularly played Rocky. He was very warm and inviting and made all the newcomers feel welcome. He was known as the go-to man to get anything you needed, including "Disco Biscuits."[21]

Jim Bennet was the ticket salesman at the Tiffany Theater, and he was a beloved friend to many members of the Tiffany Troupe.[22]

Indecent Exposure of the Bay Area, from the 1980s to 1990s, lost Darlene, Jason, Nevada, and Kevin. At Kevin's funeral, they played the Roxy version of "I'm Going Home."[23] The song is often played at the memorials of *Rocky* community members.

It will be impossible to find and name every person who was involved in *Rocky Horror* subcultures who died due to the AIDS crisis. As I cross-checked obituaries and asked loved ones, I continuously had to remind myself that the work is essential, but will by nature never be complete. The work was incredibly fulfilling, especially as I worked through my personal grief. It gave me another outlet to grieve and remember through this community I held so dear. In so many ways, these were members of my community, and to remember them feels like giving them a space they deserved.

Notes

1. Richard Sandomir, "Sal Piro, 'Rocky Horror Picture Show' Superfan, Dies at 72," *New York Times*, February 19, 2023, https://www.nytimes.com/2023/02/19/movies/sal-piro-rocky-horror-picture-show-superfan-dies-at-72.html.
2. Cleve Jones, *When We Rise* (Hachette Books, 2016).
3. Marita Sturken, "Conversations with the Dead: Bearing Witness in the AIDS Memorial Quilt," in *Tangled Memories: The Vietnam War, the AIDS Epidemic, and the Politics of Remembering* (University of California Press, 1997), 188.
4. Adriana Usero Elyse Samuels, "'New York City's Family Tomb': The Sad History of Hart Island," *Washington Post*, April 29, 2020, https://www.washingtonpost.com/history/2020/04/27/hart-island-mass-grave-coronavirus-burials/.
5. Corey Kilgannon, "Dead of AIDS and Forgotten in Potter's Field," *New York Times*, July 3, 2018, https://www.nytimes.com/2018/07/03/nyregion/hart-island-aids-new-york.html.
6. Sturken, "Conversations with the Dead," 198.
7. "The History of the Quilt," National AIDS Memorial, accessed January 24, 2025, https://www.aidsmemorial.org/quilt-history.
8. Judith Butler, "Violence Mourning Politics," in *Precarious Life: The Powers of Mourning and Violence* (Verso, 2020), 34.
9. Butler, "Violence Mourning Politics," 34.
10. Mary Kay McBrayer, "Hatshepsut: Egypt's Forgotten Female Pharaoh, Re-Examined," *The Archive*, September 20, 2022, https://explorethearchive.com/queen-hatshepsut.
11. Rachel Stomel, "The Revolutionary Jewish Way to Memorialize George Floyd," *Kveller*, April 21, 2021, https://www.kveller.com/the-revolutionary-jewish-way-to-memorialize-george-floyd/.
12. Dagmawi Woubshet, "Archiving the Dead AIDS Obituaries and Final Innings," in *The Calendar of Loss: Race, Sexuality, and Mourning in the Early Era of AIDS* (Johns Hopkins University Press, 2015), 57–84.
13. Troy Martin, "18th Anniversary 'Age of Consent,'"

RockyWiki, accessed December 18, 2023, http://www.
rockyhorrorwiki.org/wiki2/index.php?title=18th_
Anniversary_%22Age_of_Consent%22.

14. Collin Souter, "We'll Meet Again: Watching Rocky Horror
in the 2020s," *Roger Ebert*, October 10, 2022, https://www.
rogerebert.com/features/well-meet-again-watching-rocky-
horror-in-the-2020s.

15. Liz Locke, "'Don't Dream It, Be It,'" in *Reading Rocky
Horror: The Rocky Horror Picture Show and Popular
Culture*, ed. Jeffrey Andrew Weinstock (Palgrave
Macmillan, 2008), 150.

16. Robin Lidner, ed., "Transylvanian Flashes," *The
Transylvanian*, July 1978, https://imgur.com/a/AwcwAIt.

17. Georgia Collins, "Obituary," *Contemporary Theatre Review*
6, no. 1 (1997), https://doi.org/10.1080/10486809708568404.

18. Jacqui Palumbo, "Remember When David Bowie Made This
Lightning-Bolt Look About Way More Than Makeup?,"
April 20, 2020, *CNN*, https://www.cnn.com/style/article/
remember-when-david-bowie-aladdin-sane-lightening-bolt/
index.html#.

19. "Paul Jabara," Paul Jabara Estate, accessed November 7,
2023, http://www.pauljabara.com.

20. Tom (former member of the Boston shadow casting
community), email message to author, December 2023.

21. Lisa (former member of the Tiffany Troupe), in discussion
with the author, December 2023.

22. Lisa (former member of the Tiffany Troupe), in discussion
with the author, December 2023.

23. Becky (former member of the Indecent Exposure from the
Bay Area and current leader of Michigan Rocky Horror
Preservation Society), in discussion with the author,
December 2023.

A Light in the Darkness: Coming Home

Juniper Fitzgerald

1.

The Rocky Horror Picture Show is about Home. Mostly.

2.

I run my hand up a sheer stocking, held up with a garter made of knotted shoelaces and underwear elastic. I am thirteen and she is fourteen: magical thinking, magical belief structures, magic as necessary for different worlds, worlds where running my hand up a sheer stocking held up with a garter made of shoelaces and underwear elastic is not criminal. Not deserving of eternity in Hell.

I believe my friend—not girlfriend, not lover in spaces of suburbia, but something similar—can read minds, hiding behind vending machines, hiding under blankets during sleepovers, sneaking extra Gushers, Cheetos, until we puke.

We pantomime sexiness clad in makeshift lingerie.

3.

I am a sex worker, just a few years later. Lingerie is my armor. I charge men for what is usually expected of me for free, talismans of my high-femme devotion to other women waving in the wind of masculine desire.

I am, perhaps, not high femme.

It has always been so fucking hard to see myself.

In the dressing rooms of peep shows on Arizona reservations, in the back rooms of bikini clubs in Nebraska, in backstage Vegas revues, I paint my nipples in layers of latex, I crisscross my crotch with cotton thongs, and I pull on sheer thigh-highs with glitter woven into the seams.

I sell my underwear to the highest bidders. Sometimes, I describe the ways I will destroy men, over the phone, for ninety-nine cents a minute.

My belly aches with the pangs of alcohol in the bed of an overnight client. He paid two grand for two nights, he orgasms and is content. He loves me.

I am laminated in the lingerie I procured for our time together, insides turned to outsides.

4.

It is desperately cold outside. It is difficult for us to pull out the "Defense of Marriage" signs from the frozen ground in our suburb, which was built atop an old landfill. The sign has two men in bowties holding hands, with a giant red *X* across their bodies. It is the 1990s in the Midwest, and most people here argue that queerness is akin to pedophilia and bestiality, although we don't have the word "queer" yet.

Marriage equality, or rather "gay marriage," is the only way we conceptualize liberation.

If we let men marry other men, then it's just a slippery slope until people marry their dogs.

And two women?

Two chicks are hot.

I hold hands with my bestie, my Home, my Allie Awesome.

When we're not stealing queerphobic lawn signs out of our neighbors' yards, we are writing plays and poems and smoking cigarettes inside Omaha's only safe space for young gays and theys—Stage Right, a coffee shop next to our local theater, an old Vaudevillian performance space renovated and rebranded as "family entertainment" in the 1970s.

My mother's

Home

in the 1990s is something of a microcosm to me, a minia-ture of what to expect from society writ large. Over macaroni and cheese from Boston Market, I tell my mother that I do not believe in God. Over TCBY parfaits, I tell her that I am writing a play about being gay in the Midwest. Over half-priced brie and crackers, I tell her that I am a sex worker. These things, these paradoxes of Home—the ache of normalcy cleverly hidden under sweet and savory things, heavy things, rich things, things revealed only in the ostensible eccentricities of an outsider. *The temporality of the place is operatic, childlike, the fatalism that of a culture dominated by wilderness.*[1]

She tells me

I will burn in Hell.

My gaze is predacious.

I smell

I am dirty. *A pig cannot smell itself,* she says.

I am not to return.

        Ever.

Finality.

    A solitude absolute.

Home

like a black hole.

5.

I tell my mother I am pregnant, and she says,
  Are you prepared to be a single mother? despite my having
a partner.
  In *my* house
  that I purchased with the fruits of my sex-work labor
      my daughter makes space for herself. She asks:
  Whuzzzzzat? in her bouquet of baby babble.
  She says, *C'mon Mama! C'mon Mama!* when she worble-
wabbles her first steps and wants me to follow.
  A boy at school said he'd cut me with snizzors, Mama.
  A boy at school threw a rock at my head, Mama.
  The popular girls say I'm cringe, *Mom.*
  Mom, what is masturbation?
  Mom, please ask before you hug me.
  Can an orgasm get you pregnant, Mom?
  You embarrass me sometimes, Mom.
I tell my daughter many things:
  The names of her body parts.
  That curiosity is natural.
  That I love her unconditionally.
  Do you know what "unconditional" means? I ask.
  Yes, yes, she says. *You tell me all the time.* She rolls her eyes.
  I am floored with the complexity of love, that my loving her
is so ubiquitous to be something of a nuisance.

6.

"*Whatever happened to Fay Wray?*
  That delicate, satin-draped frame?
  As it clung to her thigh, how I started to cry,
  'cause I wanted to be dressed just the same," sings
Frank-N-Furter.

Willa Cather—the namesake of my daughter, my
    Home
longed to be dressed the same as her male contemporaries.
I named my daughter after a dream in which my babe relayed
her name to me among infinite gradations of Blue. And because:

> [Cather's] relationship to gender is refracted through this
> [Nebraska] wild prairie grass: itinerant and unwieldly,
> forming unlikely alliances with other living histories.
> . . . This suggests that historical transgender styles don't
> disappear entirely, even as new categories emerge.[2]

Cather, queer in ways that very organically avoided definition, both ephemeral and fundamental in its refusal to be
categorized, intimately tied to the changing body of the prairie.

7.

When I am young, *The Rocky Horror Picture Show* is about
making a
    Home
for queerness. A tool for surviving life on the prairie.

When I am older, it is about parenthood and creation and
death: *ecology*. It is about reclaiming the prairie in all her queerness, all her change, all her unwieldy transness.

Karl August Möbius coined the term *ecology*, which comes
from the Greek word for house.

Samantha Hunt says that making a child is to make a little
death. In the house of self, no doubt.

This is the shameful secret, dense and heavy, that every
parent holds close to their bursting vests, a singularity of
secrecy, a haunting in the
    Home
of one, the knowledge that all houses fall. That all children
die. This is true for all creatures in our vast ecological habitat,
and it sits sour and hard in my heart.

I never used to understand the ending of *Rocky Horror*. They all die? What was the point of that? Now, when I watch it with my ten-year-old, I find it even more authentic than when I desperately needed the film as a queer youth surviving the banality of Midwest Nice. Yes, yes, the problematic parts and yes, yes, O'Brien is transphobic trash. And yes, yes, the creature and all his symbolic queerness, just like Mary Shelley's, is contained in the end.

But.

Those things notwithstanding, in order to *be it*, not *just dream it*, one must die a little bit, surrender. I think of this when my mother writes to say she does not wish to have a relationship with me. Again. When I awake from nightmares that I am back, stuck, trapped in my mother's

Home

I am de-Medusaed just long enough to find myself wading in a pool of terrible ambiguity, dreaming of

Home. A new one. One of my own creation, a painting even, with strokes from the timid fingers of my offspring.

8.

One of my reoccurring nightmares is that I'm working in a hospital that is also a TED Talk, and I am appropriately dressed in the uniform of The White Liberal and my daughter is appropriately playing in the mezzanine, because I am not a helicopter parent.

Then she is killed at the hands of a disgruntled group of teens with AK-47s; she is gone before I have the chance to think, to feel, to plan my experience. She is gone before the logical mind can process the emotional one, and I wake, always, screaming in my

Home.

Please don't kill her, I plead in my dream and in the tiny spaces of my room.

We kill everyone in the mezzanine, always, they say, as if I am on their side, their confidant, like they know that I am the originator of my daughter's death.

9.

I am in my twenties and in love with the man who will become my child's father. I buy beautiful little crystals of meth in the bathroom of a dive bar; we share the drug with strangers; we make a witchy little circle, holding hands, and eat the gorgeous nuggets because we do not have the tools to smoke them. A middle-class problem, to be sure.

I am in my teens and my friends and I start the first Gay-Straight Alliance in Nebraska, and subsequently receive death threats. Little notes tucked into our rusting lockers like nesting love letters.

One of us completes suicide. Westboro Baptist Church protests his funeral with signs that say,

"GOD HATES FAGS"

and the rest of us wear angel wings strapped to our backs.

Brad was an angel.

He killed himself in his

Home.

We spread cocaine in perfect lines across the table of Village Inn.

10.

The man who will become my daughter's father paints a picture
of the end of the world, a kind of precipice off which we all fall,
dangling in the shadows of its infinite cliff.
    Willa Cather wrote:

> I wanted to walk straight on through the red grass and
> over the edge of the world, which could not be very far
> away. The light air about me told me that the world ended
> here: Only the ground and sun and sky were left, and if one
> went a little farther there would be only sun and sky, and
> one would float off into them, like the tawny hawks which
> sailed over our heads making slow shadows on the grass.[3]

The man who will become my daughter's father has a painting and it is a sign that he, this man who makes Child with
me, is
                      Home
            at least for a while.

11.

I watch *The Rocky Horror Picture Show* with my ten-year-old
daughter.
        What do you think?
                W: I dunno . . . seems like this is just a love story
                . . . Women get treated like products, and objects
                . . . I liked it, though. Seven out of ten. And it's
                a little rapey. Also, a little bit sexist because
                Frank-N-Furter kills Meat Loaf out of jealousy.
        So, what did you *like* about it? I plead.
                W: Considering the time period, it's queer and
                    funny, I guess.
    Why do I feel compelled to explain away the rapey and misog-
ynistic and transphobic parts? Because that's what we do when
we are forced to choose between Homes that hurt.

I've seen, oh, blue skies through the pain
Through the tears in my eyes
And I realize
I'm going
Home.

12.

I have nightmares that I am back in my mother's
  Home.
Waking up to the slow, almost-silent fall of swollen snow-
flakes outside, the temperature inside is just as frigid. A
north-facing window is a constellation of rime and hoarfrost,
frozen spiderwebs unraveling into precariously cold crevasses.

My daughter and I share an early twentieth-century bunga-
low adorned in skeletons and other talismans of death, kitschy
reminders of the inevitable.

A juneberry is harvested for pie.

A catalpa makes perfume of the spring air.

A lilac cowers in the shade of the catalpa's boisterous leaves,
still demanding to be seen, observed, loved.

Pansies, once frozen and wilting, spring back to life, grateful,
reaching for the sun.

Squash eventually rots, their seeds plunging into earth in
anticipation of spring.

My daughter crawls into bed with me every night; she has
what I call
The Midnight Sads
            wherein thoughts of my mortality as her mother,
as her
            Home
                  creep into her waking conscious-
ness, however flawed and irrational in the exhausted mind
            and she is forced to imagine
            Home
                  without
                        Mother.

13.

Pepper LaBeija, Crystal LaBeija, Angie Xtravaganza, Willie Ninja, Octavia Saint-Laurent, Paris Dupree, Kevin UltraOmni, Raphael Excellence, and others. . . . Mother as
     Home.
     Mama Lee pushes my tits up in a bikini that she designed and sewed. She smokes a cigarette in between hits of asthma medication; she tells me I'm too fat to work in Las Vegas as a stripper. This makes everyone laugh, me included.
     I've never worked around so many women; so many women inhabiting so many colorful bodies. I always work holidays, especially Christmas Eve. I love getting a sweet little baggie of cocaine on Christmas Eve, spending the sacred day in my
     Home,
     a strip club called The 20s in Omaha, Nebraska, where I tell the manager, Rick, that if I die, I want my funeral procession to convene here. With neon thongs swelling to the beat of survival.
          Mama at the Las Vegas strip club is a Pacific Islander and tugs on my back fat,
               Too fat! Too fat! she says. Mama Lee called it.
          I see myself in the reflection onstage where my hands brush the drop ceiling caked in mold and think—we often speak in platitudes, a simulacrum of language, referencing, endlessly referencing, turtles all the way down.
     Jenny and I caress each other in the back room of the strip club, our garters and seven-inch platforms tossed carelessly to the matted, rouge-colored carpet. Jenny and I steal homophobic yard signs from the yards of God-fearing Christians in the 1990s. Jenny and I are Young Democrats in college together; we are "good" feminists. Jenny and I pantomime cunnilingus onstage for monied men on Christmas Eve after snorting coke off the vanity in the dressing room. Jenny and I get so high, *so high*, after a night of work that I believe I've turned into a fox. And she pets me cautiously the way anyone would do with a rabid beast.

14.

The Rocky Horror Picture Show is about coming
Home (mostly)
to the self, even if it kills you.

15.

Queer theorist Lee Edelman describes the "death drive" of
queerness as necessarily antithetical to what he calls the Futuristic Child—a nebulous and collective fear of harming some
metaphorical child in some metaphorical future at the expense
of real children with real material needs.[4] A fear that fuels the
fire of fascism, to be sure. All the "save the children" and all
the "queers are pedophiles" are just placeholders for the ache
of normalcy cleverly hidden under sweet and savory things,
heavy things, rich things, things revealed only in the ostensible
eccentricities of an outsider. An outsider like me. A queer like
me. A sex worker like me. A mother like me.

   To be an outsider is to reject the Futuristic Child for the sake
of the present, for the sake of real, material realities unconfined
by platitudes or propaganda. Willa Cather does this through
nostalgia, wherein her writing is "morbid and melancholic, a
stubborn refusal of . . . heterosexual relations" and through her
"energetic resistance to life."[5] Frank-N-Furter does this through
the death and rebirth cycle, embodying what Cather meant
when she said, "The world is little, people are little, human life
is little. There is only one big thing—desire."

   The death of my mother's
        Home
   the death of Land-as-Mother, the death of Land-as-Woman,
and the death of Land-as-Raped-and-Pillaged. The death of
wordless shallowness, of Language Games, prosaicisms, the
death of heteronormative intimacies that bleed over onto me,
now Mother

to a ten-year-old girl in a crop top, a girl who wants to walk
around

Home

in her bra

she says

*Mom, I should not have to cover my body for the
sake of men.*

But then, she doesn't want me to follow her into the dressing
room of Target. Locks her door when changing at Home, does
not want me to do my makeup in the same little bathroom of
our House when she showers. I am convinced it is because she
believes what society writ large says about me—that I am a
predator, a monster, that she must be saved *from me.*

It has always been so fucking hard to see myself.

But then The Midnight Sads. And the snuggles. And the "tell
me a story about Thumbelina, Mama," the

Mama

instead of Mom

the way Thumbelina is a bat in my rendition instead of
a little girl, the size of a dime, pollinating . . .

and I close my eyes, holding the little death I created inside
my own body, wrapped in the plankton of sleep, inhabiting my
largeness—and hers—my monstrosity, my prairie-coneflower
hands with Child in

Home

as

Mother

queer

sex worker

as a

Creature of the night.

Notes

1. Joan Didion, *South and West: From a Notebook* (Penguin Random House, 2017).
2. K. Allison Hammer, "Epic Stone Butch: Transmasculinity in the Work of Willa Cather," *Transgender Studies Quarterly* 7, no. 1 (February 2020): 78.
3. Willa Cather, *My Ántonia* (Houghton Mifflin, 1918).
4. Lee Edelman, *No Future: Queer Theory and the Death Drive* (Duke University Press, 2004).
5. Christopher Nealon, "Affect-Genealogy: Feeling and Affiliation in Willa Cather," *American Literature* 69, no. 1 (March 1997): 7.

Sweet Transgression

Sarah Gailey

ALL MY PASTS live inside me, just like all your pasts live inside you. One of my pasts is a nightmare of respectability as ambition. I spent a long time being an I'm-just-like-you queer, a we-aren't-so-different queer, a halfway-in-the-closet queer who was certain that politeness was the key to acceptance. This meant cardigans and pencil skirts and lipstick that never quite looked right on my face. This meant saying nothing when people assumed I was straight and cis. This meant attending a church that was "welcoming but not affirming," knowing that people like me were neither affirmed nor welcomed, and suggesting over and over that we should change the policy without ever saying *because I am part of the community it targets.*

All I wanted, for so long, was to do everything right. I knew in my heart that if I could accomplish that goal, I would be rewarded with safety, stability, and community.

It's not that I didn't want to transgress—of course I did. I'm made of appetites, and I wanted to indulge those as much as any other animal might. The problem was that I thought I could choose whether or not I was, myself, considered a transgression made flesh. I thought I could deny my status—in the eyes of many—as an embodied wrongness, as someone who was breathing and bleeding and heart-beating in a way that denied some fundamental truth of the world. I thought that, through careful posture and deliberate performance, I could control the way people reacted to me.

This was especially true of those people who claim that they have the right to define what is and is not worthy of respect. People in my life—members of my family, close colleagues, romantic partners—would tell me, as recently as a couple of years ago, that they were fine with queer people who weren't overly visible. The person I was a decade ago heard that and thought: *Yes. I can meet that brief. I can be less visible, and then I will be fine. They'll let me know if I transgress, and I'll know how to act in order to be okay.*

This was a trap. The person I am now knows it. I wish I could clasp that decade-ago me by the back of the neck and say *no, no, no, don't fall for it!* But that is impossible, and so I will say it here, instead.

Don't fall for it.

Here's why: When we define what is acceptable, we are also defining what is unacceptable; in a society where unacceptability is necessarily accompanied by punishment, we are defining what is and is not safe. Those who try to define respectability do so to define the terms of human safety. "As long as I can't see you, you're fine" is another way to say "If I *can* see you, I will ensure that you are *not* fine." "As long as I'm not aware of it, it can exist" is code for "If I become aware of it, I will stamp it out." If we fall for this trap, we agree that queer people who are not successfully invisible must, under these terms, be eliminated.

Thus, defining the terms of respectability is a method used by dominant subgroups to unilaterally define the terms of safety. If visible queerness is inherently a transgressive mode, then queerness must be secret in order to be safe; this means that queer people cannot safely make any demands for themselves, because to make a demand is to break the required mode of invisibility. This is the trap that, for so long, prevented me from speaking up for myself and my queer family: To do so, under the terms I had accepted, would have been to embrace our destruction.

The thing I didn't see back then—the thing I see now, with furious clarity—is that the terms I accepted for so long are bullshit. This contract promises safety only under the condition of unilateral interpersonal approval. For our existence to continue, those who hold the power in this agreement must feel, in some unbreachable chamber of their secret hearts, that we are not too much. That we are not too loud, too happy, too satisfied. They must feel that we are not transgressing. What we feel toward them, what we desire from them, how we love or hate or need or miss them—none of that matters. Our interior lives, our hopes and fears, our souls—immaterial. All that matters, in this agreement, is that the other side stays comfortable.

In this agreement, the stakes are profoundly unequal. They stand to lose comfort; we stand to lose our continued existence. All the power flows toward them, and all the consequences flow toward us. Why would we ever sign this contract?

Why did I ever sign it?

Looking back, I can understand my instinctive response to comply with those terms. I was told that the rules were invisibility or elimination, so naturally, I chose invisibility. Who wouldn't? But over time, a question became louder and louder in my mind: Why are the rules being set by people who hate me? Why would I allow my existence to be governed by people who want nothing from me, who want nothing *for* me, beyond my invisibility?

Who the fuck are they to tell me to hide?

That question uncovered a secondary problem, which is that "Who the fuck are they?" is not a question with a simple answer. Sometimes, *they* are cops with guns, who can kill me and get a pension for doing it. Sometimes, *they* are the judges and politicians who decide what bathroom I'm allowed to piss in. Sometimes, *they* are members of my close community, who I love and admire and want to hold in high regard, who I am sure will love me back if I can just find a way to do and be everything they say is right.

And sometimes—hardest of all—*they* are other queers. Queers who are so desperate to feel safe that they will turn on other queer people in order to enforce the rules they think they know how to follow. In their desperation, they buy in to the idea of humanity as conditional, and they participate in the practice of revoking that humanity as punishment for the crime of transgression. They are so compliant, and so certain of the safety that compliance can buy, that they don't even realize they are transgressors, too. That they will never be able to escape the crime of transgression, no matter how well they behave and no matter how invisible they become.

The fact is, in the eyes of those who wrote that poison contract, all of us—every queer, everywhere, at every moment—are the human embodiments of transgression. No amount of compliance can change that.

We cannot hide our way out of being hated.

I should have rewatched *The Rocky Horror Picture Show* sooner. I grew up watching it and loving it for its absurdity, for the music and the camp, for the clumsy and perfect humor of it. But watching it now, I see them clearly—my beloved, infuriating, petrified, compliant queers: Brad and Janet, cardigan'd and quiet and correct. I have been them (I have been you) and I know how bewildering it is to do everything right and still, somehow, wind up stranded and afraid.

The Rocky Horror Picture Show doesn't offer any instruction on how not to wind up stranded and afraid. It doesn't tell us how Brad and Janet could have avoided getting a flat tire, and it doesn't dwell overmuch on the fact that a better spare tire could have gotten them out of the woods. None of that is the point. The film understands—and asks us to understand in turn—that sometimes, bad things simply happen. The project of the film isn't moral instruction. Instead, it goes a different direction. It doesn't tell us how not to get lost. Instead, it shows us that just a jump to the left of *lost*, there is *free*.

Throughout our lives, we—especially queer *we*—are taught that there is danger in transgression. This isn't a lie. The threat is explicit. The danger is real. But it's not intrinsic. It's invented and imposed upon us by those who do not and have never loved us. People who don't want us to experience joy and safety create the danger, and then tell us to beware.

But *The Rocky Horror Picture Show* rejects the idea of respectability as intrinsically safe. It acknowledges the futility of trying to stay normal in order to avoid danger. Rather than representing safety, normalcy represents fetters and blinders that prevent Brad and Janet from understanding their circumstances and themselves. They are invited to cast off those limitations when they find themselves surrounded by, and invited into, transgression. This invitation begins with uninhibited dancing and outlandish dress, an experience familiar to anyone who has discovered a profound sense of freedom at a Pride Month celebration. It continues with the shifting rhythms of speech and music, and then the mad science of personal transformation, and finally, sexual liberation that unlocks unlimited, uninhibited, unconstrained physical pleasure.

Brad and Janet are confronted by transgression, seduced by it, and, for a time, freed by it. It's only when they embrace transgression that they're able to fully see the people they are and the situation they find themselves in.

As the film frees them, it shows us that, while transgression might not contain intrinsic danger, it does contain intrinsic joy. There is music, the film tells us, in transgression. There is dancing. There's sex, and motorcycles, and bright red lipstick and torn fishnets and swimming pool orgies. It is even possible, in embracing transgression, to make a whole new person. It's possible to *become* a whole new person. To experience pleasure beyond imagination, and anguish beyond comprehension.

And as we queers rewrite the social contract we are willing to sign, we must cling to the capacity for both. Pleasure and anguish are equally important to the fullness of our existence. We must not allow ourselves to define either one as a transgression.

Queer people have spent too long trying to contort ourselves into acceptable shapes for the comfort of those who tell us that they are the arbiters of our safety, and as a result, too many of us have forgotten how to feel real, wild, untamed joy. We know that we are meant to remain invisible, and so—out of necessity, for our safety—we tuck our celebrations and our performances away into spaces where we can remain hidden together. But we are never allowed to forget that, to those who hate us, our pleasure is considered a transgression all by itself. We all know that a night at a beloved queer bar might end in death. Whether that death comes as the result of police violence or a mass shooting, we are forced to acknowledge that our joy can never be hidden enough to escape punishment. For many of us, the result of that knowledge is a fear of uninhibited celebration. Many of us have, in the pursuit of safety, abandoned the idea of joy.

Queer people have also spent too long being told that our pain is inevitable, and as a result, too many of us have forgotten how to grieve. We have internalized the idea that our unedited emotional existence is too transgressive. To sob over the death of a queer child who was murdered by their classmates is to become overly visible; to scream at the violence endured by our queer family around the world is to seem naïve. "It's a hard life you've chosen," well-meaning loved ones have told me, and the implication is clear: *You've chosen this hardship, so don't pretend you didn't see it coming.* Queer people know that we are not allowed to be shocked or horrified, and so we compress our shock and horror until it is dense enough to become wry humor.

Our very emotions, then, are transgressions, too. But how is this a way to live? If we won't let ourselves *feel*, how are we supposed to survive?

The answer, of course, is by refusing the contract. Denying unacceptable terms, and instead, extending care and support and kindness to each other—and then, extending permission to each other. In *The Rocky Horror Picture Show*, Riff Raff opens the castle door and invites Brad and Janet into a strange, messy, frightening world of absolute freedom. We can do this for each other. We can invite each other out of the rain and give each other permission to dance, to fuck, to scream, to collapse, to yearn, to fight, to make messes. We can give each other permission to speak honestly and feel openly. We can make room for each other's vices and appetites.

We will survive by embracing the abundance that exists in the realm of transgression, and by sharing that abundance with each other. We will survive in a state of freedom and truth. We will survive together, even in the velvet darkness of blackest night.

We will transgress, and we will live.

This Town Is Neutered:
Queer Longing in the Far North

M. K. Thekkumkattil

MIDDLE SCHOOL: cybersexing in AIM chatrooms, a threesome in an abandoned house with my best friend and a boy I'd loved, girls giving blow jobs on the swings outside school dances. My oldest brother told me not to spell "come" like "cum." A boy put his fingers inside of me and it didn't feel like much at all. The principal told us the FBI was investigating the Geocities gossip site that recounted rich kid shenanigans.

When did I first hear about *The Rocky Horror Picture Show*? Was it at the library in the small liberal college town I grew up in, perhaps during a Teen Advisory Board meeting? Was it when I memorized bus routes so I never had to feel trapped in my family home, so I could escape to New York City or Philly? Was it in the quiet space between opening my brother's porn files and watching pirated movies?

I don't remember if I went to a live *Rocky Horror* show. I grew up in central New Jersey and I was always looking for a way out. I scanned the schedule for *Rocky Horror* showings in New Hope, Pennsylvania, scheming when I'd get to see it. I watched the movie on VHS countless times, despite not liking musicals. It was all around me, not in a material way—I didn't know the songs, I didn't dress up, and I didn't remember what anyone looked like or what it was about—but, in an ethereal way, knowing that somewhere, there were queer people; somewhere, there were people who existed so far outside of heteronormativity they'd built their own traditions; somewhere, a queer present connected to a queer legacy. Even if I didn't know how to get there, even if a friend's parents never drove us, even if the buses and trains didn't go to New Hope, even if it was just the movie that embedded itself in my consciousness, it was enough to know that queer people existed.

Twenty years later, I lived in Anchorage, Alaska. As regularly as the earth turned from summer to fall, fishing season transitioned into *Rocky* season.

For as long as anyone I asked could remember, one of our town's two gay bars had hosted a live production of *Rocky Horror* each year. The flurry of excitement was felt not only among the performers and their friends, but by everyone in town. Small talk with strangers in October shifted from salmon to *Rocky Rocky Rocky*: "Which show are you going to go to? Who's playing Frank-N-Furter? Who's directing? What was your favorite year?"

The first time I saw *Rocky Horror* in Anchorage was just before the pandemic. I'd moved back to town after my first queer breakup, yearning for home among queer and South Asian friends I'd met during my years living there on and off. I went to the show alone and sat in a second-row folding chair. I couldn't remember if I was a virgin or not, so I didn't raise my hand when they asked. I was surprised by the audience callbacks. I hadn't seen the movie in over a decade, during which I lived in major cities where no one cared about *Rocky Horror*. I'd completely forgotten what it was about and why I'd been obsessed with it as a child. I told friends afterward that I'd seen it countless times, but I still didn't get it.

The confusion didn't frighten me. Unlike the many years I had dated men, I felt like I was exactly where I needed to be. Being in this room of queers, I felt like I was among kin, even if I couldn't say why.

Many of us who have lived in bigger cities where there are more than two gay bars, where there are different bars for different letters in the LGBTQ acronym and a multitude of queer event options on a Friday night, treasure the simplicity of Anchorage's queer life. There are event spaces for special occasions, like the queer, Mexican-owned coffee shop, the vintage store that doubles as a community center, the women-owned independent bookstore, and the art gallery that hosts music shows and queer AA meetings. But at night, deciding where to go requires answering just one question: "Do I want food or not?" One of the gay bars has food, the other doesn't. The one with food hosts the annual *Rocky Horror* production and five-dollar drag shows every Friday and Saturday night of the year. Its predictability engenders a kind of soft sentimentality I never experienced in a bigger city. The bar feels as cozy and familiar as my living room.

As I became a regular at the gay bar where a lover performed drag, my friends and I would perch on the leather couches. We voyeured, watching baby queers search for their people; dykes tilting their bodies toward us because they knew who we were, even if we'd never met; exes avoiding eye contact; lovers bestowing kisses after leaving the stage; older couples unicorn hunting; gay boys feigning blow jobs on the dance floor; studs moving like molasses at the edges of the room. Everyone was flirting, or falling in love, or dancing, or wanting, all at the same time. As with *Rocky Horror*, whether you love or hate the gay bar, with its loud music, flashing lights, and queer excess, it is a community touchstone.

We gossiped about our mostly failed attempts to go on dates and have casual sex with people whose values, and sluttiness, aligned with ours. A truth emerged: *This town is neutered.*

Queers here didn't openly talk about sex. Neither of our gay bars had a back room, so public sex wasn't a thing unless you knew the ever-changing locations of the glory holes. Marilyn, my Tsimshian trans friend who grew up between Southeast Alaska and Anchorage, often heard friends and acquaintances claim queerness by bell hooks's definition: queer "not as being about who you're having sex with . . . but 'queer' as being about the self that is at odds with everything around it."[1] They knew they were not the arbiter of queerness, but they'd seen so many people claim political queerness for social capital while orienting their material lives within heterosexual structures. Marilyn questioned a queerness expressed only in words, and not actions.

When I met someone new and asked a friend, "Are they queer?" the question beneath the question was always, "How do they fuck?" Sex was central to my sexuality. I spent years naming my queerness before living it, but it wasn't until I fucked queerly that I understood that, for me, how I fucked was integral to how I lived.

This town is neutered: I couldn't remember who said it first, but it had been repeated in different friend circles. It was whispered, almost embarrassed—an explanation for why a community so rich in queers felt so scarce in debauchery.

Four years later, I went to *The Rocky Horror Picture Show* again. My lover played Riff Raff. As a regular drag performer, they sacrificed their usual income from drag tips to help recreate this tradition. On nights they weren't working, I fucked, tied, and spanked them, and they told me about their favorite roles to play and directors to work with. I joked that when I fucked them, I supported a pillar of the queer community. That year, I hadn't planned on going to see the show, but my friend Erinn, a white queer femme who had close ties to the drag scene, had an extra ticket and invited me along.

Since the last time I had seen the show, I'd found my way to kink. Through a D/s dynamic with my long-distance girlfriend-daddy Sarah, nights at dungeons with friends, and POC play parties, kink had become an important way I understood power, pleasure, and pain.

As I laughed, cheered, and clapped at the show, I marveled

at the kink dynamics I saw. Frank-N-Furter: a greedy bisexual trans switch, whose insatiability compelled him to create multiple lovers. Magenta and Riff Raff: service bottoms who thrived with strict rules governing their behavior, but whose lingering resentment led them to lash out against their dom. Columbia: a chaos brat who wanted to fuck around and find out, and was punished for her deviance. Rocky: the kind of lesbian I fucked when I first started queer dating, who concealed their flaws and incompatibilities because they wanted to make themselves so appealing I couldn't say no, more apparition than person. Eddie: whose eventual consumption revealed how we devour each other through desire.

After I saw my lover's tits in public and the narrator strutted down the aisle with their dick barely concealed by a top hat, I told Erinn, "I get it now. I needed kink to get it."

This town is neutered. What's important was not the actual production. It was *The Rocky Horror Picture Show*, and if you know *Rocky Horror*, you know what it was like. What felt important, though, was how *Rocky Horror* deneutered public space. In the hope that queerness could be contagious, queers exposed their tits, asses, and dicks. By pushing against the respectability of a gay culture that often tried to fit in, queerness could exist beyond normalcy, could burst out of decency into absolute pleasure. Queers could choose not to turn away from their lust.

The silences of this town, especially in queer community: that our bodies get wet and hard, that we transform when we put ourselves inside each other, that we want our holes filled, that we objectify each other, that we want to feel another's insides.

Rocky Horror's role in this town is to break these silences.

As I talked to my friends about *Rocky Horror* for this essay, I realized I've always thought the entire film was a scene. I wasn't sure where this interpretation came from. I couldn't remember how I was first introduced to *Rocky Horror*, so I wasn't sure if

I came to see it as a consensual scene because of a librarian trying to soften the rapeyness, a stranger's LiveJournal post, or a middle-school theory conjured between literal children.

I didn't understand *Rocky Horror* the first time I saw it in Anchorage, but my evolving relationship to kink changed my relationship to the film. After submitting to Sarah for four years, and after developing ongoing dynamics with submissives of my own, I could easily see myself in the role of Janet.

I imagined going to a dreaded heterosexual wedding with Sarah and asking her to negotiate a scene with my friends afterward. She'd pretend our car broke down and take me to a castle. All of our friends would act like aliens, dance in terrifying ways, rip off our clothes, and separate us. They'd make us believe we couldn't escape and we were being forced into a sex cult. In our most vulnerable moment, when we believed we were safe enough to sleep, they'd sneak into our rooms, pretend to be someone they weren't, and fuck us. I'd be terrified, disgusted, confused, and betrayed, but I'd also let myself have a kind of pleasure that can only exist when I get what scares me.

During *Rocky* season, the theory-queers among us discourse about the show. This happens every year: *Rocky Horror* gives us a way to talk about our desires, our transness, our lusts, our violations, by talking about something else.

In conversations about *Rocky Horror*, three friends in various parts of my life said they left the show disturbed by what they refer to as the "consent stuff," when Frank-N-Furter disguised himself as Brad to fuck Janet and as Janet to fuck Brad. They remarked on the dissonance between their internal reactions of horror, disgust, and fear, and the crowd's reactions of cheering and laughing, like it was all a good ol' time. The dissonance was so alarming that they decided they'd never go back.

One winter after *Rocky* season, Erinn hosted "Meat Mondays," a recurring horror movie night at their house. We reviewed trigger warnings beforehand and discussed how to deal with them: fast-forwarding, warning people before intense scenes so they could leave the room or cover their eyes, changing what movie we watched. We paused if needed, rewound scenes, and chatted about each movie afterward.

I hadn't watched horror films since childhood, and, through these movie nights, I got to know the genre through my friends' love for it. Nithya, an Eelam Tamil trans person, said they considered the best horror to be that which elicited extreme disgust or terror. They sought a confrontation so painful or disturbing that their body physically recoiled. They couldn't hide their depth of feeling through intellectualization when they were scared: They could feel without thought.

I thought about how my friends' intense revulsion was what made *Rocky Horror* effective as horror. The friends who were upset by the "consent stuff" hadn't been warned about what would happen. Unlike Meat Mondays at Erinn's, there was not an extensive discussion of potential triggers before *Rocky Horror* began; there was no pausing the show. Each moment of confrontation led to a subsequent intensification of violence or violation.

None of these friends brought up the trans predator stereotype inherent to the "trick" Frank-N-Furter pulled on Brad and Janet. They didn't mention the murder, cannibalism, or bisexuality listed on the show's description. They didn't mention the biphobia of listing bisexuality alongside murder and cannibalism, as if inherent to bisexuality was the kind of violence that required mutilation and consumption. They didn't mention the alien storyline, the transcendence of Frank-N-Furter's confrontation with death, or the gender fuckery. What elicited the most feeling for my friends were moments in which rape, desire, transness, and bisexuality collided.

Was it because murder, and even cannibalism, are more widely represented in media, while sex, whether good or bad, is rarely portrayed in our puritanical US culture? Or because these friends had their own experiences having been assaulted or violated, and got triggered at the normalization of sexual boundary pushing? Or was it that the sex was kept relatively hidden, portrayed through chiffon curtains and the gaze of Riff Raff's and Magenta's hidden cameras, allowing the viewer to transpose their own experiences onto the scene?

When I rewatched *The Rocky Horror Picture Show* with my friends' concerns in mind, I was struck by how closely the dialogue of the veiled sex scenes matched the dialogue of my favorite porn. The pornographic quality of the sex scenes allowed for an acknowledgement of illicit—queer—desires. I recognized the fear Brad and Janet expressed when they realized the person fucking them was Frank-N-Furter. I also recognized their refusal, their cries of "No" only moments before they orgasm. Despite my own experiences of sexual assault and rape, these scenes didn't remind me of the times I said no and was violated, but instead reminded me of the times I said no and wanted it.

Before I had sex with queers, I was in a monogamous relationship with a straight, cis, white man for nine years. With him, a dick was not enough sensation: I would place his hand on my throat and ask if he would fight me. Often, he said yes.

That was the good sex, the sex that thrilled me, the sex that made me feel strong and empowered even as I was overpowered. I asked for what I wanted and I got it: to scream "No" while he fucked me, to hurl my knees against his chest and try to push him off me, to wedge my hip against his to get his dick out of me. The harder I fought, the harder he fucked me. Always, I wanted him to win.

I was so afraid of queer desire. I knew I was queer throughout our relationship, but I could not imagine a queer life, which is to say, I could not imagine fucking queerly. I swiped on apps in secret, I gazed at girls while I was with my boyfriend at bars, I had fierce crushes who I fantasized about while my boyfriend fucked me in missionary.

I did not have an embodied sense of my queerness or transness. My body was afraid of my desire. In recreating fear through sexual performance, I could, briefly, confront my fear.

The world of *The Rocky Horror Picture Show* is so fantastical that it honestly portrays how so many of us queers have engaged with our desires. Before we were able to name it, our queerness showed up in our porn searches, our hidden lusts and thirsts. Our desires were often shrouded behind rape, incest, violation. Janet's and Brad's sexual experiences with Frank-N-Furter gave us a window into a kind of queerness that, for so many of us, didn't exist until we found our way to fucking queerly.

Anchorage isn't a place where sexual desire is named, seen, or represented in public often. *This town is neutered*, after all. Seasonally, *The Rocky Horror Picture Show* exposes queer and trans people, along with people who are not yet queer or trans, to what could happen if we succumb to our desires.

For those in bigger cities, where people don't rely on fantasy or horror to find other queers, *The Rocky Horror Picture Show* seems to have been phased out of the queer limelight. But for me, growing up in a small town and moving to the far north, the film and production puts me in conversation with a lineage of queers, people I didn't have to personally know in order to be touched by their work. *Rocky Horror*, and my relationship to *Rocky Horror* over the years, has extended my tendrils of self out to millions of queers who've loved and hated it. The film has allowed me to integrate a queer past into my conception of self while reimagining the self as always in cocreation with others. My bisexuality, transness, kinks, desires, and refusals have been practiced by generations of queers who made freaky, weird, low-budget art that continues to impact me and the people around me. I'm not alone in my want, and I never was.

Writing this essay has been its own kind of cocreation: It required reaching out to friends and lovers, digesting their experiences, translating my earlier longings, and transforming my understanding of my own experiences. Like my beloved queer kin who remade me in their image every time we fucked, loved, and challenged each other, *Rocky Horror* was integral to my queer formation.

Maybe *Rocky Horror* was a projection of my queer longing, or maybe *Rocky Horror* was a place I snuck out of the house in the middle of the night to get to, or maybe *Rocky Horror* was proof I wasn't alone, or maybe *Rocky Horror* was a way for me to grapple with my lust without having to touch it yet, or maybe *Rocky Horror* was an outdated, campy, trans predator stereotype, or maybe *Rocky Horror* was tits and dick out at the bar, or maybe *Rocky Horror* was a way to break the silence around sex, or maybe *Rocky Horror* was a way for us to love each other, transform each other, year after year.

Notes

1. bell hooks, "Are You Still a Slave? Liberating the Black Female Body," conversation with Marci Blackman, Shola Lynch, and Janet Mock, May 6, 2014, posted May 7, 2014, by The New School, YouTube, https://youtu.be/ rJk0hNROvzs.

One from the Vaults

Nino McQuown

HEATHER LOVED FAT BOYS. She loved me. She lay in the grass in the park underneath me and took pictures of my ass in my tight size-sixteens. She developed them and put them in an album with glitter between the pages, which her mother put in my hands after she died. There is only so much left of Heather, so it's incredibly precious. She thought I was really so hot, and this was not common when we were eleven, and fourteen, and seventeen. (Although later I would learn that it's a thing: Fat butch. Fat trans boy.) I waddle a little. I can pick you up and throw you around, like Eddie in *The Rocky Horror Picture Show*, except without the intense eyes and the heroin habit and the danger.

Heather and I were not dangerous. We were very good kids. Even if we did spend most days of our shared adolescence huddled on her top bunk reading pornographic letters to each other from her parents' magazines and watching their late-eighties skin flicks and sometimes going to the video shops in Times Square for more, more, more. Heather was so good. Arranged the color-coded folders for her classes in her binder. Was never late. Always had the assignment. Completely unlike me, who stayed up late listening to the Indigo Girls and drawing on my walls and feeling deeply so often that I failed first-period gym. Heather played on the school basketball team (the Lady Eagles), not very well, but it worked because she was incredibly tall. When I leaned into her body on the subway, my face fell into the side of her neck, just under the fringe of her shaggy, blond hair. When we fake-kissed for the crowds during spin-the-bottle sessions, she had to dip me like a girl.

We were both girls back then, but we were different kinds. She was a tomboy. I was unclassifiable, unwashed, and strange. I'd been a boy throughout my childhood, but since puberty it felt like my body had been hacked up and blended and poured out thick like a smoothie into this vessel the shape of a girl. I tried not to be seen by the real boys. I made myself a big body and I dressed it in big clothes. I read long books on the subway so that people would notice my mind. I was obsessed with David Bowie and *The Rocky Horror Picture Show*. Heather's parents worried about my influence. Heather's parents worried that we were in love. And we were, but not like that. We never really even kissed except for show.

What Heather loved was everything stupid: Disney movies, *Home Improvement*, and especially Meat Loaf, who in 1993 had come out with a sequel to his megahit *Bat Out of Hell* called *Back into Hell*, which she refused to turn off, even when I wrestled her for the remote to her Sony CD player until we both fell off of her bottom bunk. I can still sing you the lyrics to *Back into Hell*. And of course, thanks to YouTube, I can still watch the videos: Meat Loaf looking sad and disappointed with his big voice and his feathered hair in a trench coat the size of a wedding tent. Heather had his posters on her wall. She went to concerts. Had a hat that said "Meat Loaf" in red gothic script. He was another one of her fat boys. She loved me best but she loved us all.

In *The Rocky Horror Picture Show*, Meat Loaf plays Eddie, Frank's ex-lover, whom he's already tried to kill before the start of the film. Eddie gets only one scene, but he makes it count, busting out of the freezer, pale and resurrected, mounted on a vintage motorcycle, a gash bisecting his forehead from where Frank stole half his brain to make Rocky: a new, more perfect monster to fuck. Eddie's the old model, "one from the vaults," Frank calls him. But despite his obsolescence, he still manages to sing his song and get his girl and take his old lover's pickaxe to the brain all in one scene. And in spite of his ephemeral presence, by the end of the movie we know more about Eddie than we do about any other character in the cast. We hear his life story two times, hear him described by Columbia, Frank, and Dr. Scott. He's essential to the plot of *The Rocky Horror Picture Show*: It's Eddie who brings Dr. Scott to the castle, calling the FBI down on the Transylvanian menace and giving Riff Raff his excuse to take command.

Do I sound like I'm trying too hard to make Eddie important? In the credits, he's described as just "an ex–delivery boy." Heavy on the ex, I guess. Butchered, frozen, thawed when we meet him. I almost said meat. Eddie is meat. You can imagine him revving his hog at the front door of the mansion, can't you, on that fateful day when he met Frank? Thighs astride his purring bike like the protagonist in one of the pornos Heather dug up for us to watch on weekdays after school, tattooed knuckles gripping a pizza box. Frank opening the door in nothing but a lab coat, saying "Oh dear me, I've forgotten my wallet. Let me pay you inside." Eddie is so yesterday. So '50s, with his greaseless, unstyled, duck's-ass hair and his boots and his jeans and his hurt-bad, bad-boy feelings pouring out of those eyes. And that's pure Meat Loaf. In every Meat Loaf song Heather ever played me he's regretting something: bad motorcycle choices, objects in the rearview mirror, promising to love a girl forever only to find himself married and longing for the end of time. One of the many things that Meat Loaf brings to this role is those eyes: He looks at the world like he wants to devour it, but he knows it's going to eat him up before he can.

The first time we hear Eddie's story in the movie, he tells it himself. He's fresh out of the deep freeze, singing so thick and fast you can barely make sense of the words. If you can parse them, though, they're shockingly wholesome: A teenage boy and girl drive out to listen to the radio and fuck in the back seat of a car on a Saturday night. "I'd taste her baby-pink lipstick, and that's when I'd melt," Eddie croons, remembering the way that lust made him feel vulnerable. He sings, "She'd whisper in my ear tonight she really was mine," remembering how sex made him feel like he was in charge. In content, it's a classic Meat Loaf song, the character and the actor who plays him almost indistinguishable in their overlapping obsessions with the normie pleasures of cis boy teenage rebellion, of getting your feelings all worked up in the heady proximity of a girl. When I was a kid, I hated Eddie. Watching *The Rocky Horror Picture Show* over and over again, showing it to everyone I loved, I hated him. For his ingratitude in the glow of that cosmic light I longed for. For the way he turned Columbia—her short hair and shiny tux having made her the only reasonable candidate for a lesbian in the whole movie, to my young eyes—into yet another straight girl gone gaga over an unworthy boy.

In context, Eddie's loss goes existential. "Whatever happened to Saturday night? / When you dressed up sharp and you felt alright?" Eddie asks at the song's beginning, and it's as if Saturday nights are over forever now, as if you'll never feel all right again. "It don't seem the same since that cosmic light / came into my life," he sings. "I thought I was divine," he sings. The song is about longing for a past in which Eddie was the God of American culture. The cis straight boy. The one who makes things happen. The one in charge of his desire. His nostalgia's not for high school, exactly, so much as for a time before queerness, before being topped and thrown away. And I hated him for that more than anything. For the way he shows Frank as the villain he is. The way that even in the sick pink light of the lab, in the Frankenstein place, Eddie's death makes it undeniable: Transsexuals aren't safe to love.

I can't remember ever talking to Heather about transness when we were teenagers or young adults, but if I had, it would have sounded something like Richard O'Brien, the creator of *Rocky*

Horror, when he was talking to the *Daily Mail* in 2016. This was in response to some bullshit transphobia from Germaine Greer on the order of "just because you lop off your dick . . ." and Richard O'Brien agreed with her: "I think I agree with that," he said, "You can't be a woman. You can be an idea of a woman. You're in the middle and there's nothing wrong with that. I certainly wouldn't have the wedding tackle taken off."[1] When I was a teenager, I would have said the same thing. Absolutely not. No surgery. After all, one of the central lessons of *The Rocky Horror Picture Show* is that submitting to be made into a man by someone else means submitting to someone else's image of perfection. Eddie doesn't cut it, and neither would I. Even as a teenager I grieved this fact hard. I had a vision of myself as a kind of masculine that was thin and male and muscled and looked good in a top hat and tails (a huge top hat; this was the '90s). I accepted that I'd never have that. I accepted my unwanted girl-flesh, that surgery was mutilation, that hormones would make me a freak, and in that acceptance was a certainty that I could never be loved in my own body. It took me until I was thirty-seven to let myself go under the knife. And until then, to some extent, all the sex I had was protected sex, in the sense that there was a thick film of fantasy between me and every lover, every date. The word I had for this, from Leslie Feinberg, was "stone," but I longed to be Frankie. I wanted Susan Sarandon to sing about me that my "lust is so sincere."

Instead my lust was furtive and careful. I thought my desire was violence. I didn't want to hurt anyone. I didn't want to be like Dr. Frank-N-Furter. I didn't want to pickaxe anybody with my tiny little phallus. I didn't want to transduce anybody with my rage. Watching *Rocky Horror* when I was a teenager over and over again, in the basement and at midnight shows, surrounded by weird adults who wanted to fuck us, who screamed "slut" at the screen when Janet said her name, it was Frank I related to, and not Eddie. The one whose lust is evil. Who has to coerce people into sleeping with him, to trick them into revealing their latent desires. And I wanted Frankie to want me. Because I also saw him as a kind of God, entering Brad's and Janet's bedrooms like the biblical dove, bearing a destiny that blooms in the body, a change without a choice. I thought I needed that. I wanted to be forced, tricked, and coerced into becoming the self I feared I wasn't brave enough to transform into on my own. And I saw how it all turned out, too, and I was frightened not just for myself, but for everyone I wanted. In the movie, all of Frank's male lovers abandon him for women, following their more compelling and more natural desire. Frank rapes Rocky, murders and then eats Eddie. *It isn't easy, having a good time.*

It isn't easy, but it is possible to want two things simultaneously. To want to be a monster and to want to be safe. And it's possible to be two things at once. To be a monster and a little baby God.

When Heather and I are in high school, we take to wearing lacy underwear beneath our sweatshirts and wide-legged JNCO jeans. Partly this is mere convenience: There is a huge Victoria's Secret anchor store on Broadway a few blocks north of our high school, and it's got three-for-one deals on fancy lace underthings made, essentially, of plastic. We like them even though they give us yeast infections. Even though the underwires pop out in the wash and dig into our brand-new breasts. I don't think about this as gender exploration or performance. Again, this is the '90s and I haven't read Judith Butler yet. But I wear mine thinking something like, *Nobody knows that under all this I'm wearing just a strip of purple lace. Nobody can pin me down by looking at me.* And this is something that Heather gives to me too. I am, on the surface, a slick pile of unsexed teen. I feel like Eddie at the dinner party on most days, like a pile of meat under the table. I feel swallowed by the judgment of strangers, whose eyes sink into my 250-pound, fifteen-year-old body and brand me with *What a shame.* Who judge me coming and going and eating a hot dog on the street corner. I feel like parts of me are falling off the bone for the world to slurp up, and yet there is always too much more. But Heather sees me in a different way. She watches me eat a hot dog and she's mesmerized. Her hand flies up to cover her braces, laughing wetly through her long fingers. "What?" I ask, my lips holding back the Polish sausage and sauerkraut and onions that my big mouth neatly opened to admit.

"Nothing, nothing!" she says. "It's just, you'd be so good at sucking cock. What a shame!" And I think I laughed but maybe I got mad about it. It doesn't matter. Secretly I'm pleased.

Heather. From that moment on I have it. Deep in three-seat couches at parties where not much is happening and everyone is making out or more, and I—fat, queer, butch—am at the outskirts of attention, I have the certain knowledge in my heart that none of them, only my best friend who loves me, will ever know how effortlessly good I'd be at sucking cock. I don't have to prove it. I don't have to try it. We order Shirley Temples at the diner on the corner of 57th Street, and I tie two knots in the stem of a cherry with my tongue.

There has always been something queer about Meat Loaf's masculinity, something almost in drag about it, a clownishly intense fat boy decorating himself like a Christmas tree with the amulets and emblems of sex: labial frills on his perpetual prom-night shirts, long-tailed trench coats, spangles and leopard print and motorcycles. *The Rocky Horror Picture Show* made him famous in the mid-'70s, before *Bat Out of Hell* took him into the stratosphere. In early Meat Loaf the vibe is pure physical urgency—like in the duet he does with Cher on the title track for the 1981 album *Dead Ringer*. In the video, Cher and her girlfriends are hanging out in a shitty little neighborhood dive bar drinking beer and having huge hair when Meat Loaf and his loud, annoying softball team comes in. He's this tiny fat guy in shades more than half the size of his face but all he has to do is look at her like he knows what he wants, and the sexiest girl in the room says *Yes, absolutely, let's go*. As with other early Meat Loaf songs, there is no ambivalence whatsoever in this performance. Mr. Loaf is 1,000 percent convinced of his own desirability, his own goodness, hitting the high notes on a set of lyrics about how it doesn't matter if it's the real thing, it only matters if it turns you on.

In Meat Loaf's music videos from the '90s, though, at the height of his importance in Heather's and my lives, he is usually a monster. In the music video for "I Would Do Anything for Love (But I Won't Do That)," for example, he's a beast with a half-burned face and long, sharp, yellow fingernails that he curls and clenches with longing for a beautiful woman with windblown hair in the light of the moon. In the video for "Rock and Roll Dreams Come Through," he's a kind of djinn, with heavy makeup and a prosthetic chin. In his version of "It's All Coming Back to Me Now," he's a human, but he's in love with a ghost. Meat Loaf is always just outside the action in the '90s. Always untouchable and not quite real, always separated from the woman he loves. Back then, when I first encountered him, I assumed that this separation was about his discernible differences from other rock stars: the fact of his fatness and the excesses of his gender. This was, after all, how both fat people and queer people were always portrayed then, when we were portrayed at all: as longing and yearning and separate, animated by desires that our monstrous bodies made it impossible for the world to fulfill, hurling ourselves, instead, toward death.

In *The Rocky Horror Picture Show*, Eddie dies because he's a fat boy. Because Frank doesn't want him anymore. "He had a certain naïve charm," says Boss Frank, "but no muscle." And Rocky makes a bicep for his life. Watching *The Rocky Horror Picture Show* in the context of what I already knew about Meat Loaf, Eddie's ending fit. Ignominious and shrieking, he goes down like the gender traitor he is, no more masculine potency, no more girls professing to belong to him, an imperfect, soft man with half a brain and a pickaxe through even that. I hated Eddie, and I saw myself in him. Even in a house full of aliens, I thought, he's the monster nobody wants.

Heather liked sex. Liked having it, liked talking about it. It wasn't something that we did together, but it was something that we shared. We either saw one another or we talked on the phone almost every single day from when we were ten years old until she died at twenty-two. In our teenage years, this often meant recounting in detail all the flirting and the fucking she'd been doing, with her boyfriend, with other girls on the basketball team, and one summer with the grown-adult executive assistant at an office where she'd been interning. She wasn't suave, she wasn't cool, but it was easy for her. People felt freed by Heather's freedom, they felt whole in the light of her pure sincerity. Her desire was a rising tide on which you could float. She was like Frankie if he hadn't been a narcissist, but a good listener with excellent boundaries who liked animals and sports and politics.

With Heather, you didn't have to love each other, you didn't even have to want each other, you just had to want to make each other feel good. You remembered that your body was made for this. And we spent hours, whole nights, in my childhood that way, not Heather and me but Heather in one room and me in another and all our friends, boys and girls, everyone at the party, taking turns making out and turning each other on. Drunk on low-stakes delight and somebody's mom's vodka, safe, companionably kissing my friend Jack for practice in our other friend's bed in the dark. Breaking apart so he could say to me, "You know, you're really good at this." And I could say, "You're good at this too." Us building each other up. He wanted our friend Cindy, and he wanted Heather. And I wanted Cindy. And I wanted Heather too. Not a lot, not so much that it bothered me, but I would have said yes. And there was one time, her sixteenth birthday, in a limousine. Our friend Diego was kissing me. Everyone was kissing, and we were all extremely drunk, and Diego knelt down and started to work on my belt and I stopped him and he stopped, because that's how it was with my friends, and at the same time I locked eyes with Heather, and I leaned toward her and asked a question with my eyebrows, which she answered out loud. "No way, absolutely not," she said. And I shrugged, and went back to kissing Diego, who was calling me a tease. Even through the haze of alcohol, I knew it was about good boundaries, about our other kinds of intimacy, and not my monstrous body, which she loved.

"Being transgender is a kind of curse," says Richard O'Brien, the creator of *Rocky Horror*. He's talking to *The Guardian* in 2013.[2] And in 2009, to *The Times*, he said "all my life . . . I've been fighting never belonging, never being male or female, and it got to the stage where I couldn't deal with it any longer. To feel you don't belong . . . to feel insane . . . to feel perverted and disgusting . . . you go f***ing nuts."[3] And to the *Daily Mail* in 2016, talking about the success of *Rocky Horror*, he said the movie "made it okay for men to dress up as women, but it didn't make it okay for me."[4] He was in so much pain. And you can see it, in *Rocky Horror*, the way that the person who sings "Don't dream it, be it" is a narcissistic murdering rapist cannibal failure who has to be killed for the sake of the species. The way the one who says "Don't dream it, be it" is a mad surgeon who wants to make you a specific kind of man.

In the film, Richard O'Brien plays Riff Raff, Frank's servant and underling, which has always been interesting to me. Having written *Rocky Horror* and produced it, presumably O'Brien could have played any of the characters—and of all the characters to become, Riff Raff always seemed to me the least enticing. Transsexual, sure, but uptight, controlling, narrow, cruel, with dead eyes and thin blond hair like a zombie baby, a caved-in chest and a hunchback. By the time the credits roll he's revealed himself as a kind of interplanetary cop, condemning Frank and his mission as failures, murdering all his former friends and leaving the earthlings to bumble on in their self-righteousness and grievance in the mud and dry ice of the ending. Why would the creator of the show choose that character to embody? As a kid, I noticed then dismissed it: another layer of dissonance in that joyful moral mindfuck of a show. But as an adult, I think

I get it. I think of O'Brien telling *The Daily Mail* that he had "grown up believing there was something wrong with me and that I was somehow damaged and dirty."[5] Same, bro, same.

Technically, Riff Raff is the hero of *The Rocky Horror Picture Show*. With his antimatter laser he saves Brad and Janet and Doctor Scott from a future as sexy automata, forever kicking across the stage in a perpetual late-night floor show, doing the difficult work of trying to fuck in a pool. He kills Frank, he kills Rocky, he kills Columbia, all the monsters and the traitors, and he lets the humans crawl away. He takes the alien threat home to their own interstellar ghetto to do the Time Warp on moon-drenched beaches in a darkness that suits them fine. Dr. Scott says, "You're okay by me!" But Riff Raff hardly seems okay. Even his sister and lover Magenta is shocked by his orgy of violence. "You killed them!" she says, "I thought you liked them! They liked you!" and Riff Raff screams, "They didn't like me! They never liked me!" And it is about the damage and the dirtiness that never goes away no matter how much they say they like you. It is about queer unbelonging. It is about being a monster among monsters and not being wanted even there.

The cops win in *The Rocky Horror Picture Show*. Riff Raff's a space cop. Dr. Scott works for the FBI. Watching it now, in the midst of transitioning, after top surgery, after changing my name, still fat, still butch, that is what hits me. How Richard O'Brien chose to portray his own inner policeman, reinstituting law and order, taking himself off quietly after the murder of his own wild desires. "Give yourself over to absolute pleasure," croons Frank, and Riff Raff shoots him dead.

The second time we hear Eddie's life story, it's as told by his uncle, Dr. Scott, who seems to hate him. "From the day he was born, we knew he was trouble," Scott begins, over a dinner of Eddie himself. But there's something about Dr. Scott's version of his nephew that doesn't agree with me. Eddie causes his mother "nothing but shame," but Scott tells us himself that Eddie didn't begin his rampage of rock and roll, porn, heroin, and motorcycles until the day she died. Placed next to the image Eddie paints of himself, dressing up for Saturday night, getting high mostly on the smell of girls' perfume, it's hard to reconcile Scott's Eddie with his own. And then there's the teddy of the chorus: "When Eddie said he didn't like his teddy we knew he was a no-good kid." It's a deeply queer experience, this no-good thing that Dr. Scott sees in his nephew from the start. So many queer children's first experience of the wrongness of our desires happens through toys and action figures. We fall in love with Ken instead of Barbie, ask Santa for something no red-blooded American elf would give a boy. Not liking his teddy bear feels to me like Eddie refusing congress with the whole human race. Going off in a haze of mother-grief to love on motorbikes and aliens and violence, to shake off his God-given masculine divinity in order to bottom for an extraterrestrial transvestite and a deranged tap-dancing chorus girl. *What a guy.* I admire him now like I admired him then, under my veil of self-disgust. He didn't take the bait. He didn't stay a mere God among greasers. He had the guts to go off and get in over his head. And now Frank thinks of Eddie as both too fat and insufficient, his brain not enough for two boys. And Columbia imagines him as slipping through her fingers, as the one she very nearly loved and couldn't save. But this is of course exactly what happens after someone dies. We begin to tell stories about them that are really stories about ourselves.

After almost twenty years, when I dream about Heather she shows up my age, whatever it is at the time, and very often in the dreams we haven't talked in years. We aren't friends anymore. "I thought you were dead," I explain, filled with a grief almost as exquisite as the afternoon in her apartment when she showed me the clothes she'd bought to wear out dancing after she got better. New yellow leggings and lacey black underwear, real lace now. I had taken off work to hang out with her, because after she showed me her brain scans it was clear that there was only so much time left. "But you're not going to get better," I almost said, and then didn't because of her face. Which was the first and only time I ever lied to her, since not long after that she lost the ability to speak.

But before that, before that, we talked almost every day. Which was tough sometimes, because I found sex difficult, and Heather wanted to call me after school and narrate a blow-by-blow of her most recent important encounter, what exactly her boyfriend had whispered in her ear while he was fucking her. In a reverie, experiencing it all over again. And I remember, my body lit up like a dried-out Christmas tree, afraid of catching fire and killing everyone, saying "Dude, stop, you have to stop talking. You have to stop, please." And me finally getting through to her, and her saying, "Okay, but what's wrong?"

In the dreams I still have about Heather, she is still so much taller than me. I lean into her neck like I used to sometimes on the subway, since it was as high up on her as I could reach with my face. In the dream I can feel her feel nothing in response to my touch. "If I had known you were alive I would have called," I say, but in the dream she's over it by now.

In real life I came into the bedroom where she was lying in her diaper after she lost speech and lost mobility and sat next to her. She woke up and opened her eyes and tried to say something, and when I leaned in close to try and make it out, she stopped gabbling and grabbed the back of my head in her claw hand and pulled my face into the side of her neck and held me there, unresisting, for a long time while she gasped her shallow breaths.

In the dreams I used to have about Heather when she was dying, there was surgery. I'd be riding the city bus to her apartment with my face against the window and I'd be bargaining with God: *Take an arm, take my legs. I have an idea, we could both share my body. Put her soul in my body and we can both use it. Give her half my brain, we'll figure it out.*

But in real life, we were the Gods in this situation, and the surgeon had done everything he could.

When I'm thirty-seven and have just had top surgery, I begin to touch my chest for the first time. I didn't know that this would happen. But I am in love with the way I feel under my hands, even when it still hurts a bit. Even through the bandages, it is as if, for the first time ever, it is possible for me to be touched.

In the dream I am untouchable, a monster. It's a dream I still have sometimes. But in real life we can hold on to more than one truth simultaneously. I watch *The Rocky Horror Picture Show* yet again in bed with my wife while I'm healing, and I feel sad for Richard O'Brien and I feel grateful to him. For Frankie sliding down the elevator shaft, red lips like the torn-out heart of an enemy, for Eddie waiting behind his wall of ice. For deaths that can be undone by pressing play again. For reflecting the way I saw myself in all its complexity of sexiness and untouchableness and self-hate and agency and monstrousness and pleasure and anticipation. How someone can paste your image on their bedroom wall and you can still feel only very nearly loved. So many years, so many viewings later, the cats are asleep in the dips between our bodies, the windows open, bright sunlight on my living flesh, firing up the ghosts in my bed like neon in a fog.

"I'm not much of a man by the light of day but at night I'm one hell of a lover," says Frank, and because of Heather, I believed that. That in spite of everything, good sex was coming for me. It was the certainty I held in myself that she gave me, that I would give excellent head and didn't have to do anything about it. And it was true. Lovers of my life, I came prepared to your bodies. I studied. I did interviews. I crammed. Knowing that if I kept going, I'd come in the rain to the light in the Frankenstein place, and fat queer sex would come flowing into my life. I'd be welcome. I'd be a monster, and I'd be devoured, and I'd be the doctor and the master, and I'd learn to ask and hear yes and hear no. And I'd be Eddie, eyes open and arms out for a girl and I'd be wanted. And our whole childhood she was singing to me from that window, holding the light and singing in her terrible voice.

Notes

1. Nick Duffy, "Rocky Horror Star Richard O'Brien: Trans Women Can't Be Women," *Pink News*, March 8, 2016, https://www.thepinknews.com/2016/03/08/rocky-horror-star-richard-obrien-trans-women-cant-be-women/.
2. Caroline Rees, "Richard O'Brien: My Family Values," *The Guardian*, January 25, 2013, https://www.theguardian.com/lifeandstyle/2013/jan/25/richard-obrien-rocky-horror-show.
3. Dominic Wells, "Richard O'Brien: Rocky Horror? It Was All About My Mother," *The Times*, August 18, 2009, http://www.dominicwells.com/journalist/obrien/.
4. Louise Gannon, "My Rocky Horror Life! Richard O'Brien on Being '70% Female,' The Abyss of Breakdown—and the Show That Made Him Millions," *Daily Mail*, January 5, 2019, https://www.dailymail.co.uk/home/event/article-6553753/Richard-OBrien-discusses-Rocky-Horror-battles-gender-identity.html.
5. Gannon, "My Rocky Horror Life!"

About the Contributors

Akira Albar-Kluck is a public historian and community organizer from New Jersey, now based in Dublin, Ireland. Albar-Kluck studies AIDS activism and queer rights in both the United States and Ireland. As a genderqueer person who uses he and they pronouns, their scholarly focus comes from a personal place. Beyond their academic work, they are a linocut and fiber artist and are developing a roleplaying game for the incarcerated community.

Trey Burnette is a writer and photographer with an MFA from the University of California at Riverside. He studied comedy writing with The Groundlings and The Second City. He has a BA in psychology from the University of Southern California. His work has appeared in the *Washington Post*, *Los Angeles Times*, NBC News/NBC THINK, *Los Angeles Review of Books*, *Kelp Journal*, *Coachella Review*, *Hellbender Magazine*, *Tulsa Review*, and *The Sun* magazine.

Jane Claire Bradley (www.janeclairebradley.com) is an award-winning queer working-class writer, performer, and mental health practitioner based in Northern England. Jane writes fiction, essays, and performance poetry, usually about some combination of queerness, class, mental health, identity, and the uncanny. Jane is the author of a novel, two chapbooks, and a free fortnightly newsletter sharing stories, short films, and creative resources for writers, rebels, and multi-hyphen misfits.

Rosie Long Decter is a writer and musician. Her work has appeared in *Maisonneuve, Peach Mag, The New Quarterly, Xtra, Billboard, Herizons, Bright Wall / Dark Room, New Feeling*, and the 2022 anthology *Letters From Montreal* (Véhicule Press). She's released two albums with her band Bodywash, 2019's *Comforter* and 2023's *I Held The Shape While I Could*. She lives in Montreal with her girlfriend Sarah and their dog Leila.

Juniper Fitzgerald is the author of the first and only children's book to feature a sex working mama, *How Mamas Love Their Babies* (Feminist Press) as well as a memoir, *Enjoy Me Among My Ruins* (Feminist Press). She is a contributor to *We Too: Essays on Survival and Sex Work* (Feminist Press), and the forthcoming anthology *I Hate My Job: Thots on Labor, Sex Work, and Capitalism* (Working Girls Press). She lives in the Midwest with her remarkable and awe-inspiring daughter.

Flloyd has been involved in the NYC underground theater scene since 1984, performing at Wigstock Festival, featured in *Wigstock: the Movie*, and a member of the Blacklips Performance Cult. Flloyd's performance art includes several Tweed productions at Town Hall on Broadway; off-Broadway shows at La Mama, Kitchen, P.S. 122, Here, and Westbeth; and shows at galleries and museums including the Guggenheim, Exit Art, and The High Museum of Art (Atlanta). Flloyd wrote and directed stage productions including *Death, tooth: A Disco Butoh*, and *Trouble with Blacklips*; adapted *Nashville* and *Jem and the Holograms* for the stage and the Blacklips's play *Jack the Ripper* for film; and wrote, directed, and produced Gay Action News with Michael Wakefield. His work is on YouTube under nycFLLOYD.

Sarah Gailey is a Hugo Award–winning and bestselling author of speculative fiction, short stories, and essays. Their nonfiction has been published by dozens of venues internationally. Their fiction has been published in over seven different languages. Their most recent novel, *Just Like Home*, and most recent original comic book series with BOOM! Studios, *Know Your Station*, are available now. You can find links to their work at sarahgailey.com.

Aliya Bree Hall (she/her) is a lesbian author, freelance journalist, and founder of Sapphic Stories Book Club: Queer & Feminist Tales. She writes sapphic romance, and her short-form sapphic horror has been published in the *Bleak Midwinter Vol. I: The Darkest Night* and *Twisted Horrors* anthologies. Her creative nonfiction can be found in *The Rebis*'s *The Devil* anthology publishing in September 2025.

Rocky Halpern (they/he/she) is a Queens-based writer, social worker, clown admirer, and tenderhearted Pisces rising. Their work has appeared in *A Public Space, Glassworks, Uncharted,* and other various publications. Rocky is the 2019 recipient of the Bette Howland Nonfiction Award. Find Rocky on Instagram @rockyehal.

Genevieve Hammang is a tall, fat, queer lady who looks good in a short skirt. She graduated from UC Santa Cruz with a BA in linguistics and has since written a lot about dentistry, law, and hot people in fantasy garb. She was published in *Anime Feminist* a while back but hasn't had much time for writing outside of work since. She is currently pursuing a master's degree in library and information science at San Jose State University with the goal of fighting book bans.

Lindsay Katt is a queer nonbinary artist known for their broad range of multimedia artwork. Their music has been featured in shows such as *Castle, Alias, Switched at Birth,* and SyFy's *Being Human,* with music videos airing on MTV and Logo, and installations, performance art, films, and paintings exhibited throughout NYC and worldwide. Their recent work includes their critically acclaimed Academy Award–qualified film *The*

Avant-Gardener, which received 150+ awards from film festivals around the world, and their hand-illustrated picture book titled *Synonymous Isn't Scary: A Tale of Fabulous Creatures*, slated to be published in 2026.

Mel King is a trans and queer writer from Albany, NY. The writers with real lives far stranger than fiction are his kin. His work has appeared in *Catapult*, *Cortland Review*, and *North American Review*, among others. He has received support for his writing from Vermont Studio Center, Lambda Literary, the Yiddish Book Center, and the Truman Capote Foundation. He graduated from the fiction MFA program at Rutgers–Newark in 2016. King has spent his working life in the movement for LGBTQ+ liberation and has called Brooklyn home since 2006.

Benjamin Larned (he/they) is a creator of surreal fables. Their fiction is featured in *Vastarien*, the *NoSleep* podcast, *hex literary*, and *Seize the Press*, among others. Their short film *Payment* is streaming on ALTER. To learn more, visit curiousafflictions.com.

Grace Lavery is a writer and academic, author of the four books *Quaint, Exquisite* (Princeton University Press, 2018), *Please Miss* (Seal, 2022), *Pleasure and Efficacy* (Princeton University Press, 2023), and *Closures* (Duke University Press, 2024), and many essays on literature, cinema, and mass culture across a range of scholarly and public-facing venues.

Dave Madden is the author of *The Authentic Animal: Inside the Odd and Obsessive World of Taxidermy* and a story collection about queers in the Midwest. His essays have appeared in *The Guardian*, *Harper's*, *ZYZZYVA*, *Defector*, and elsewhere. He teaches in the MFA program at the University of San Francisco.

Carmen Maria Machado is the author of the bestselling memoir *In the Dream House* and the award-winning short story collection *Her Body and Other Parties*. She has been a finalist for the National Book Award and the winner of the Bard Fiction

Prize, the Lambda Literary Award for Lesbian Fiction, and the National Book Critics Circle's John Leonard Prize, among others. Her essays, fiction, and criticism have appeared in the *New Yorker*, the *New York Times*, *Granta*, *Vogue*, *This American Life*, *The Believer*, *Guernica*, and elsewhere. She holds an MFA from the Iowa Writers' Workshop and has been awarded fellowships and residencies from the Guggenheim Foundation, Yaddo, Hedgebrook, and the Millay Colony for the Arts.

Tanya Marquardt is a writer and performer in Lenapehoking/ Brooklyn. Their book *Stray: Memoir of a Runaway* was named a Best Queer and History Bio by *The Advocate*, and *Some Must Watch While Some Must Sleep*, their play about being a sleep talker, toured internationally and inspired an episode of NPR's *Invisibilia*. They are currently writing a memoir called *Creature*, about reconnecting with Magyar queer archives and folk dance, and will publish an essay about dancing in Budapest for the Playwright Canada Press anthology *Do Trans People Dream of Electric Sheep*. Their play *HOUSE*, a trans retelling of Henrik Ibsen's *A Doll's House*, is in development.

Nino McQuown is a trans poet, essayist, and performer. They live in Baltimore, MD, where they write, make puppet shows, build gardens, and host the podcast *Queers at the End of the World* (queerworlds.com). Their work on dirt, death, apocalypse, and chickens has been published in *Electric Lit*, *Catapult*, *Edge Effects*, *Barrelhouse*, *Hotel Amerika*, *Epiphany Lit*, the *Kenyon Review Online*, and elsewhere. See what they're up to @allsoils and at allsoils.net.

A. Ng Pavel (吳慧靈) is an interdisciplinary artist and writer from Chicago, IL. They are the founder of the Chicago Asian Writers Workshop, which offers free creative writing classes for Asian and BIPOC writers in the Midwest. Their work appears in *Chicago Review* and elsewhere. An MFA candidate in fiction at the University of Mississippi, they are currently at work on a novel and a collection of short stories.

Heather O. Petrocelli, PhD, is a film critic, writer, and researcher who employs transdisciplinary methods across film studies, queer theory, and public history, engaging with and rendering visible queer stories and experiences. This scholarly foundation—combined with a lifelong love of horror and a background in making, studying, programming, and marketing film—informs Petrocelli's debut book *Queer for Fear: Horror Film and the Queer Spectator* and the road show *Queer for Fear Live!*, which they cohost in cities around the world with drag icon Peaches Christ.

Victoria Provost is a New York–based writer, performer, theatre producer, and bookseller. Her plays *Starry Friendship*, *I'm Still Here*, and *The Frightening Door* have been produced in NYC and elsewhere. The focus of her art primarily lies in the intersection of trauma theory and long-form storytelling; her writing is informed by this and by her biracial and bisexual identities. She earned a BA in English from New York University and is a theatre MFA candidate at Columbia University. She is a tap dancer and has played Columbia with the New York City *Rocky Horror Picture Show* cast since 2017.

Birch Rosen (they/them) is a disabled transsexual poet, zinester, and essayist living in Seattle on the unceded land of Coast Salish peoples. They use personal writing to create space for more nuanced trans and nonbinary narratives. Their work has appeared in *Transmasculine Poetics* (Sundress Press), *Southern Review*, *Michigan Quarterly Review*, and elsewhere. Their zines include *T&A (Transitioning & Attractiveness)*, *Boobless*, and the *Trans Restroom Rants* series.

Roxy Ruedas is a queer, trans, and Filipino New Yorker who grew up loving theater and found *The Rocky Horror Picture Show* somewhere along the way. Roxy has a BA in both education and the study of women and gender from Smith College, and now works as an educator. In his free time, it enjoys writing tabletop RPGs and seeing various *Rocky Horror* shadow casts. This anthology marks Roxy's first publication, and it is honored to have been included in a project that has meant so much to him.

M. K. Thekkumkattil (they/them) is a trans, disabled, kinky writer and nurse whose liberation is bound up with Palestinian liberation. They write about care work, kink, and relationship with land, among other things. They have received a Rasmuson Foundation Individual Artist Award and fellowships from Queer Art Mentorship, Lambda Literary, VONA, and Writing by Writers. Their work can be found in *Black Warrior Review*, *smoke and mold*, *___figuration*, *Autostraddle*, *Fence*, *Year Round Queer*, and *In the Future There Are No Hospitals*. Find them on Instagram @thekkumkattilmk.

Holly Joy Wertman (she/her) is the director of a program that provides unrestricted cash assistance and peer community support to parents of infants living in homeless shelters in NYC. She earned her MA and BA in public health from Columbia University and UC Berkeley, respectively. Holly has spearheaded dignity-focused aid initiatives for gender minorities and LGBTQ communities in areas affected by homelessness and disasters globally. Her personal and professional writings have appeared in *SWWIM*, *LGBTQ Nation*, and the *Harvard Health and Human Rights Journal*.

Magdalene Visaggio is an Eisner-nominated writer known for sharp, stylish stories that blend punk rock attitude with heart. Her work includes *Kim & Kim*, *Quantum Teens Are Go*, *Eternity Girl*, and *Vagrant Queen*. She also collaborated with Zack Snyder on *Rebel Moon: House of the Bloodaxe*. She lives in New York City.

Acknowledgments

The creativity, enthusiasm, and effort of so many contributed to making this book a reality, and I feel deep gratitude to many more people than I could ever name here. So please consider this only a very partial list of my heartfelt thanks.

This anthology would not exist without Taneka Stotts, whose excitement, research, hard work, and many hours of conversation helped me dream up the shape of the book and begin to make that dream into something real. To Joe Vallese, for kindness and generosity, and whose book, *It Came from the Closet,* helped inspire this one. To Oriana Leckert, for endless support and bottomless enthusiasm for so many of my ideas and projects and schemes.

Sincere thanks to Jeanne Thornton, Rachel Page, Lauren Rosemary Hook, Nick Whitney, Jisu Kim, and the other people at Feminist Press who helped bring this book to life. Thank you to River Halen for copyediting and Jaci Menard for proofreading the anthology.

To the writers of this book, without whom this literally would not have been possible. I'm so grateful to you for sharing your stories, and yourselves, with the world.

To the Kickstarter backers, Rocky Horror shadow casts, and booksellers who are helping me bring this book to life through conversation, celebration, and community. And to everyone whose eyes have lit up when I told them about the weird book I was trying to create.

To the many people who have helped shape who I am: the folks at CTY, Smith College, every English teacher I've ever had, and every librarian I've ever had the pleasure of meeting.

My love to Elle Faraday, my wife and partner, for being my first reader and creative collaborator always. Thank you for building a life and a weird family with me.

And to the rest of my family, birth and chosen.

MARGOT ATWELL is a writer, editor, publisher, and creative community builder. She was once called "Book Biz Cassandra" by *Publishers Weekly*. She is the author of *Derby Life: A Crash Course in the Incredible Sport of Roller Derby* and coauthor of *The Insider's Guide to Book Publishing Success*, and she writes the *On the Books* newsletter about the intersection of creativity and money. Her writing has been published in Literary Hub, *The Creative Independent, Clarkesworld*, and elsewhere. She was the cofounder and publisher of the now-defunct Derbylife.com, and is the cofounder and publisher of micropress Gutpunch Press. She was a *Publishers Weekly* Star Watch honoree and received the Digital Book World Outstanding Achievement Award for her work creating The Next Page conference. She lives in Brooklyn, and you can find her online @MargotAtwell and www.margotatwell.com.

The Feminist Press publishes books that
ignite movements and social transformation.
Celebrating our legacy, we lift up insurgent
and marginalized voices from around the
world to build a more just future.

See our complete list of books at
feministpress.org

THE FEMINIST PRESS
AT THE CITY UNIVERSITY OF NEW YORK
FEMINISTPRESS.ORG